In My Father's Shadow

A Daughter Remembers
Orson Welles

In My Father's Shadow

A Daughter Remembers Orson Welles

CHRIS WELLES FEDER

ALGONQUIN BOOKS
OF CHAPEL HILL
2009

Published by
ALGONQUIN BOOKS OF CHAPEL HILL
Post Office Box 2225
Chapel Hill, North Carolina 27515-2225

a division of
WORKMAN PUBLISHING
225 Varick Street
New York, New York 10014

For permission to reprint photographs in this book, grateful
acknowledgment is made to the parties mentioned on page 283,
which constitutes an extension of the copyright page. All other
photographs are from the collection of the author.

Library of Congress Cataloging-in-Publication Data
Feder, Chris Welles.
  In my father's shadow : a daughter remembers Orson Welles /
Chris Welles Feder.—1st ed.
      p. cm.
  ISBN 978-1-56512-599-5
  1. Welles, Orson, 1915–1985.   2. Motion picture producers and
directors—United States—Biography.   3. Actors—United States—
Biography.   4. Feder, Chris Welles.   5. Daughters—United States—
Biography.   I. Title.
  PN1998.3.W45F43 2009
  791.4302'33092—dc22
  [B]   2009020353

                    10 9 8 7 6 5 4 3 2 1
                        First Edition

for my dearest Irwin,
the one and only

A great figure of myth like Don Quixote,
even like Falstaff, is a silhouette against the sky of all time.
These are people who have more life in them than
any human being ever had.

ORSON WELLES

CONTENTS

A NOTE TO THE READER

THE BOOK YOU ARE about to read is not another biography of Orson Welles. It owes nothing to scholarly research and everything to firsthand knowledge. It is an intimate memoir in which I give you the essence of Orson Welles, my father, as I knew him from my earliest childhood until the day he died.

This is the story of our times together and our times apart. It is also the story of the great impact my father had on me from an early age and how much I owe to him. To make it all come alive, I have told much of the narrative in dialogue. While I may not have remembered them word for word, all the conversations I have recreated here took place in real life. Nothing you are about to read has been invented.

In these pages, you will meet one of the most extraordinary men of our time — through the eyes of his daughter, Christopher.

CHRIS WELLES FEDER

PROLOGUE

OCTOBER 10, 1985. Orson Welles was found slumped over his typewriter. Sometime during the night, his heart had stopped. He had died not in Las Vegas, where he maintained a home for the third Mrs. Orson Welles, but in Los Angeles, where he had been living openly with his Croatian companion, Oja Kodar.

All that day, after I heard the news, nothing seemed real to me. I felt light-headed, as though I had walked into a soap bubble. How could my father have died when he was only seventy years old? It was true he had not been well for some time, but I had never expected to lose him so young, so soon. So suddenly.

Nor could I believe my father was dead when I had only to turn on the television and there he was, vibrantly alive. All day I sat in a daze of disbelief, watching the networks resurrect him. There was the middle-aged Orson Welles whose button nose twitched and whose great belly shook when he let loose with a thunderous laugh on the *Merv Griffin Show*. In another clip, he had changed from an amiable Santa Claus into a tall, flamboyant youth who looked vaguely like Oscar Wilde, a lock of dark hair falling in his eyes. It was unnerving to see him at every age in his masks and disguises, these versions of Orson Welles for public consumption, so different from the father I had known. Only the deep, resonant voice was unmistakably his. It was the voice of melting chocolate, rich and velvety, the voice that promised to always love his "darling girl."

It was late at night when I finally turned off the television. For hours I lay beside my gently snoring husband, my mind shut down, my heart closed, everything in me still refusing to measure my loss. At last I fell into a fitful sleep. Then something woke me in the pitch black room, my heart pounding. The illuminated hands of the bedside clock pointed to four in the morning.

It was the hour when nothing moved and New York City slept. I listened for the faint rumble of a car, but even the lone drunk who usually ranted up and down Fifth Avenue had been swallowed up in the silence. Soon it would be first light, and I shivered, for suddenly I knew I had been shielding myself all day, but I no longer could. The soap bubble burst, and I began to cry.

A FEW DAYS later my husband, Irwin, and I were flying to Los Angeles for the funeral being arranged by my stepmother, Paola, and my half sister Beatrice. Although Paola and my father had been living separately for almost two decades, she had nonetheless remained his legal wife. She and Beatrice were making all the decisions about the funeral, my father's cremation and his final resting place, not consulting either me or my half sister Rebecca, my father's child by Rita Hayworth. It was a sign of how disconnected we were.

I had already heard from Beatrice that the funeral was going to be "a very simple affair because Daddy left no money for funerals or anything else." Also, Paola was insisting the funeral would be open only to the immediate family and a few close friends. "Mommy swears she'll stay home in Las Vegas and won't come to the funeral if any Hollywood types are going to be there," Beatrice told me. That excluded Oja Kodar, whom I had been hoping to meet. How sad that battle lines had been drawn between "the family" and Oja, the woman my father had loved above all others.

At least, I hoped, the funeral would be an occasion to reconnect with my stepmother and two half sisters. Although Becky and I had remained in touch through the years, we had not seen each other since her student days at the University of Puget Sound. At that time she wanted to become a character actress, a career she did not pursue. Now she was in her early forties. As for Paola and Beatrice, we had last been together in Hong Kong when Paola was still a newlywed and Beatrice a mere child of three. Years had passed with no communication. Then, after Paola settled in Las Vegas in the 1970s in the home my father claimed as his legal residence, she and I had begun calling each other and exchanging gifts at Christmas.

The plane was beginning its gradual descent into Los Angeles when it struck me. "Do you realize," I exclaimed to Irwin who was fastening his seat belt, "for the first time in our lives, my two half sisters and I will be in the same room. Isn't that weird?" Irwin nodded sympathetically. "And you know what else is weird?"

"Try to stop thinking about how weird it all is." Irwin put his hand over mine. It felt so pleasantly warm and dry, his hand covering mine like a safe house in a thunderstorm. "Here, look at this," he said, handing me the newspaper he had been reading, "another obituary to add to your collection, and once again you're listed among his survivors as his son, Christopher."

That should keep the hounds of the press at bay.

("Daddy, why did you call me 'Christopher'?"

"I liked the sound of it—Christopher Welles. Your name has a marvelous ring to it, don't you think?"

"But I'm a girl, Daddy."

"So you are, and a very beautiful one, too."

"But Daddy, girls aren't called Christopher."

"That's right. You're the only girl in the world who is, and that makes you unique as well as beautiful."

"What does *unique* mean?"

"Different from everyone else."

"But Daddy, I don't want to be different. The kids at school tease me about having a boy's name."

"When you're older, they'll envy you. Wait and see, darling girl. The day will come when you'll love your name and thank your old father for having christened you while you were still in your mother's womb." He paused to relight and puff away on his cigar, his eyes twinkling at me through the cloud of horrible-smelling smoke. "Do you know what I did right after you were born?"

"No, what?"

"I sent out telegrams to everyone we know. CHRISTOPHER SHE IS HERE.")

All my life I had been repeating the story of the telegram—how in just four words, a marvel of economy, my father had said it all. Yet it occurred to me now, as our plane touched down on the runway, that I had never seen even one of those legendary telegrams announcing my birth.

MY OLD FRIENDS Bill and Penny Hutchinson put us up for the night. I had called them at the last minute to ask if we could stay with them, and they had agreed without hesitation. As Irwin reminded me before we fell asleep that night in their comfortable guest room, "You've had plenty of problems with your family, but you've been blessed with friends who've come through for you again and again."

The next morning we were picked up by Gary Graver, who had been my father's cameraman for the last fifteen years of his life. Slim, blond, almost handsome, sporting a California tan and dark glasses, Gary looked like one of the "Hollywood types" Paola had wanted to ban from the funeral, but he seemed pleasant enough. Beatrice had told me Paola was making an exception in letting Gary Graver attend because he had been "like a son to Daddy" and was "devastated" by his death.

As we wound our way through the lush suburb of Sherman Oaks, where Bill and Penny lived, I wondered what was wrong with me. My whole body felt numb, as though I were locked in a suit of armor and could move my limbs only with great difficulty. I saw myself sitting tense and dry-eyed through the funeral while the writer in me took careful notes. Perhaps I should have stayed home and let grief come to me in private.

We began to penetrate downtown Los Angeles. The comfortable split-level homes and tree-lined streets had given way to an endless strip mall of gas stations and fast-food joints. Revolving neon signs issued a nonstop invitation to gorge on tacos, burritos, burgers, or pancakes. The streets were littered with the leavings of junk food and empty beer cans. Few pedestrians braved the sun-baked roads, and only the poor stood stoically waiting at bus stops.

We had entered a slum where every other storefront was boarded up, and yet it was here that Gary pulled into a parking lot in a complex of ramshackle buildings. Irwin and I stared at each other in disbelief. "The funeral's going to be here?" I asked. Gary nodded, but for several moments I was too stunned to get out of the car. How was it possible that my father's remains had been brought to this destitute part of town? Why hadn't an appropriate funeral home been chosen in Brentwood or Beverly Hills — one worthy of a man like Orson Welles? Even if there were no money for a funeral, that was no excuse for holding it in such a dismal place.

Gary led us to a building that looked more like a hot-sheets motel than a funeral home. We entered, tentatively, and were given a room number, as though we were checking in, then waved toward a long corridor. On the way we passed a large, attractive room where another funeral was taking place, and I had to wonder why it had not been reserved for us. Continuing on, we reached a small room at the end of the corridor. Why had we been given this crummy room instead of a much larger one, as though Orson Welles were of no importance? It reminded me of another genius, Wolfgang Amadeus Mozart, who had been unceremoniously dumped in a pauper's grave.

My two half sisters and my stepmother stood huddled and weeping in the corridor. Beatrice, transformed into a statuesque blond, was wailing "Oh my

God!" and standing with a protective arm around her mother. Becky was taller than I remembered, but she still had a wealth of dark hair and carried herself with a quiet dignity that reminded me of her mother. Although tears were streaming down her face, she was not eliciting sympathy. I gave her a hug anyway. Then we were all hugging and kissing one another, barely able to speak. The door to the room stood open, but no one wanted to be the first to walk through it.

We were still hesitating when Roger "Skipper" Hill walked briskly toward us. He had flown in from Rockford, Illinois, to say goodbye to the man he had called his foster son and had loved more than anyone in his life, apart from the wife he had buried two years before, my Granny Hill. Everyone called him Skipper because he was born to pilot a boat, fly an airplane, and drive anything that moved. With his shock of white hair, his penetrating blue eyes and weathered face, he certainly looked the part. Now a man of ninety, he still walked with a roll in his step like a jaunty young salt on shore leave.

How ironic that Skipper was coming to my father's funeral instead of the other way around.

"Well?" Skipper eyed us as though we were a bunch of sissies. "What are we waiting for?" And with that he marched through the door of the dreaded room and sat down on one of the plastic-covered sofas.

I immediately followed and sat down next to him. Squeezing his hand, I was about to say something consoling when he whispered furiously, "This is awful! Awful! Orson never wanted to be cremated. He hated the whole idea of cremation. Thank God he doesn't know what they did to him!" We both stared at the plain pine box containing the ashes, which had been placed on a stand in the middle of the room. "God, how awful," Skipper was muttering, more to himself than me. Then he heaved a sigh, patting my hand. "Well, there's nothing to do about it now."

It was extremely upsetting to be so close to my father's ashes now that I knew his last wishes had not been respected. At first, I could not see anything in the room except the pine box, which looked grotesquely large to me. Until that moment I had assumed that the body of a man even of my father's gen-erous proportions would dwindle in the fires of cremation until nothing was left but handfuls of dust. There must be huge pieces of bone . . . I shuddered, looking around the room for the first time.

It had the look of a cheap motel room—the impersonal air of a place in constant use by people whose passion or grief was swept out with the dust of the day. The walls were lined with worn sofas and chairs. Scratched end tables with ugly lamps and ashtrays were wedged into corners. Management had not even contributed a box of tissues, and no one had thought to bring a single flower.

I closed my eyes and imagined how it should have been. We would be sitting now in a small chapel with stained glass windows, the sun streaming through them, scattering the colors of rubies, emeralds, and sapphires on the walls and floor. How much would it have cost to rent such a chapel for an hour or so and buy some bouquets of roses or lilies of the valley? My friend, Bill Hutchinson, would have gladly played the organ for nothing. I would have chosen something by Bach or Albinoni, a composer my father had loved.

The weeping of Paola, Beatrice, and Becky brought me back to reality. I respected their tears, but I was unable to join them. In fact, the longer and louder they cried, the more determined I was to remain a dry-eyed protester against this travesty. How appalled my father would have been to be dispatched with so little ceremony! Nothing had been planned. No one had been asked to speak. We just sat around in this shabby room, our eyes avoiding one another and the box of ashes.

As we continued to sit in silence, a few more people drifted in. Besides Gary Graver, exceptions had been made for two of my father's old friends, Prince Alessandro Tasca di Cuto and Greg Garrison. How many other old friends, I wondered, had been excluded because they were "Hollywood types"? On the other hand, Paola had allowed the doctor who had signed the death certificate to join us. Why not throw open the doors to Orson's dentist, his barber, his chauffeur, his accountant, his tailor, and the head waiter of his favorite restaurant? These people had seen a lot more of him than his wife and daughters. In fact, I was beginning to question my own presence there and to feel a mounting sense of outrage that I had flown across the continent to take part in this charade. That a man like my father should have less than a dozen people at his funeral was unbelievable.

For what seemed like a very long time, no one knew what to say. We just sat and sat, the awkward silence broken by bursts of sobbing from my stepmother and half sisters. Then, taking command, Skipper got to his feet and began his spontaneous tribute to Orson Welles. He recalled "the sweet kid" Orson had once been at Todd School for Boys in Woodstock, Illinois, where Skipper had been headmaster. "I knew at once that I had a young genius on my hands," he went on. "Orson liked to call me his mentor, but it was all baloney. There was very little I could teach him since he already knew everything he needed to know . . ." He rambled on, an old man lost in the intricate maze of his memories, circling around and around, retracing his steps, unaware that he was covering the same ground. At the same time, he was reluctant to surrender his command post.

I stopped listening until I heard a quaver in Skipper's voice. "There was a sweetness in him, an innocence he never lost, and that's what I loved about Orson and what I'll remember, how sweet he could be out of the public eye, when he was alone with the few people he trusted. And that's what I've lost, what we've all lost." He stopped to wipe his eyes. "But the Orson Welles the world knew, the talented actor and the great movie director, that Orson Welles will be more famous and more acclaimed as time goes on. He'll be larger in death than he ever was in life. I won't live long enough to see it, but his daughters will."

Skipper finally sat down. There were a few minutes of silence before Greg Garrison rose to speak, but I was not able to focus any longer. My mind flew back to the grief I had felt at the memorial service for Hortense Hill, Skipper's wife. Many years earlier, when my maternal grandfather had died, I had wept so uncontrollably at his funeral that a cousin had jabbed me in the ribs to make me stop. And now, at my father's funeral, I sat through the blah-blah-blah, refusing to allow so much as a lump in my throat. When was it going to reach me that I would never have lunch with my father again in the privacy of his New York hotel room, or pick up the phone and hear his thrilling voice on the other end?

("I just got the most depressing news, Christopher, another one of my ideas for a picture shot down, you know, and I thought it would cheer me up to call you." He paused while I pictured him chomping on his long cigar. "But please don't ask me what I'm doing these days, because I'm not doing anything right now that would make you proud of me."

"But I'm already proud of you, Father. You can't imagine how tremendously proud of you I am, and I'm sure you'll make another picture . . ."

"Darling girl!" he said softly, gratefully.)

It was a relief when we finally filed out of the funeral home and milled around in the parking lot while the pine box containing my father's ashes was carried out and loaded into the trunk of one of the cars. A light touch on my elbow made me turn around. There was Tasca, a courtly, elegant Italian with silver hair, smiling gently down at me. "I was the last person who saw your father alive," he told me. "We sat up half the night, talking, and he spoke at some length about you and how proud of you he was. He said that even though he hadn't been a good father to you, you'd been a very good daughter to him. It was very touching."

"Thanks for telling me this . . . but wasn't Oja with him?"

"No, she was in Croatia, visiting her family."

This left me wondering if things would have proceeded differently if Oja had been on hand. A moment later Greg Garrison, another good-looking "Hollywood type" in his designer suit and dark glasses, took me aside. "The funeral didn't have to be like this. Your father had so many friends in Hollywood, and they all wanted to come. You could have had hundreds of people here." He bit his lip, on the verge of tears. "Anyway, I wanted you to know a memorial is being planned for your father, and everyone in Hollywood will be there."

"Oh, really? Who's planning it?"

"It was Dick Wilson's idea. Do you know him? He used to work for your father."

"The name's familiar. Yes, I must have known him when I was a child, but I haven't seen him in years." Nor would Dick Wilson have any idea how to get in touch with me. I had kept such a low profile that most people considered me no more than a footnote in my father's autobiography.

"I can assure you the memorial Dick and others are planning won't be anything like this. I'm really sorry . . ."

I realized Greg wanted to console me with a vision of a public tribute to Orson Welles attended by thousands. "Thanks for telling me." We shook hands and exchanged rueful smiles. He had removed his dark glasses and was dabbing at his red-rimmed eyes with a spotless handkerchief.

"Yes siree, the public memorial will be Hollywood's grand salute to Orson, and it's about time, too," drawled Skipper, who had sauntered up and overheard our conversation. "I've been asked to deliver a eulogy. In fact, I'm going to be the first speaker on the podium." He looked more pleased with himself than usual.

"You're going?" I stared at Skipper in astonishment.

"Of course, I'm going. Wouldn't miss it for the world."

Now I was the one fighting back tears. Why had no one thought to include me? And once Skipper had been invited, why hadn't it occurred to him to take me along? Skipper who claimed me as his "honorary grandchild," just as my father had been his "foster son." Perhaps, like everyone else involved, it hadn't occurred to him that I might want to attend Hollywood's farewell to my father.

It was time to return to my real life. I looked around for the only attractive man in our gathering who was bald-headed, squinting in the sun, wearing a crumpled jacket that had not been bought on Rodeo Drive and pants that bagged at the knees. With Irwin's warm, comforting hand in mine, I would walk away from the funeral home and drive out of the parking lot where everything looked just as seedy as it had an hour ago. The sky was a mindless blue and the sun beat down relentlessly on the burger joints and pancake houses as he and I made our way to the airport. Already it seemed as though the funeral hadn't happened yet. Or might never happen.

1

Growing Up in Movieland

THE FIRST TIME I saw Rita Hayworth, my father was sawing her in half. It was the final and most spectacular trick he performed on the opening night of his Mercury Wonder Show. It was August of 1943, the summer we were at war with Japan, and the magic show was for the benefit of our servicemen who were about to be shipped to the Pacific theater. It was held in a big circus tent erected on Cahuenga Boulevard in downtown Hollywood.

I can still smell the popcorn and the sawdust, still remember my excitement throughout the show, and how, unable to contain myself, I kept climbing up on my seat, ignoring my Scots nanny Marie who kept tugging on my dress and hissing, "Now you sit down again, madam, and behave yourself!" But I had to tell the people sitting in the row behind us, "That's my daddy up there. My daddy!" I had never seen him on the stage before that night.

Billed as Orson the Magnificent, he wore a fez and a voluminous black-and-white striped robe. He might look like the genie escaped from Aladdin's lamp, a genie whose smile seemed to say, "Be careful what you wish for," but his disguise didn't fool me, and I made sure, in spite of Marie's shushing, that it didn't fool anyone else within earshot. I was five years old that night, the perfect age for the magic arts of Orson Welles, or as he preferred to call them, "hocus-pocus, mumbo jumbo, and hanky-panky." I sat there enthralled while he swallowed fire, read minds, hypnotized a rooster, pulled a rainbow of knotted scarves out of his sleeve, made a bouquet of yellow roses appear in an empty vase and a white rabbit wiggle out of a black top hat. When a man in a turban and baggy pants marched out of the wings and aimed a rifle at him, I held my breath, then screamed when the gun went off and his head snapped back. Seconds later, Orson the Magnificent turned to face the audience, and there was the bullet caught between his teeth!

Then came the moment the troops had been waiting for. A shapely young woman with copper red hair appeared on the stage. Dressed in a skimpy harem outfit, she, too, might have stepped out of the *Arabian Nights*. The moment she was in full view, the servicemen in the audience went wild, stamping and cheering for Rita Hayworth, their favorite pinup girl. Then the dazzling redhead folded herself into a long, rectangular box until only her head and her feet stuck out from either end. At that point, Orson the Magnificent began to wield a horrific saw and presto! The box split down the middle! Rita's top half went spinning to one side of the stage while her bottom half took off in the other direction. Yet the severed head was still smiling; the feet with the pretty painted toenails were still wiggling. Then bingo, bango, her two halves were reunited and she emerged in one piece! (I never did learn how my father performed this trick. All he would tell me years later about his Mercury Wonder Show was that he was as proud of it as anything he ever did.)

After the show's opening night, Harry Cohn, Rita's tyrannical boss at Columbia Pictures, forced her to withdraw. He argued that if she were performing late at night in a magic show, she would be exhausted early the next morning, when she was due on the set of *Cover Girl,* the movie she was making at the time. Rita pleaded that, after spending sixteen weeks rehearsing for Orson's show, she couldn't let him or the troops down. She was sure she could do the magic show and also fulfill her contractual commitment on *Cover Girl.* (Although she was too modest to admit it, Rita's star power was the Mercury Wonder Show's biggest draw and would have ensured it a long run.) But Cohn remained deaf to Rita's pleas, reminding her that it was not the role of a contract star to decide where she would work but to do as she was told. Not only did Cohn have no intention of letting his studio's most profitable star stay up late every night, working for free, he was even more opposed to her having anything to do with Orson Welles. (By the time my father met Rita, his reputation in Hollywood had plummeted from "boy genius" to "enfant terrible.")

Rita was so furious with Cohn she was ready to walk out on him and Columbia, but my father persuaded her not to throw away her movie career for the sake of his show. Once Rita calmed down, she worried about who could possibly replace her at a moment's notice. That was when my father thought of his loyal friend, Marlene Dietrich, the femme fatale from Germany with the husky voice and the beautiful long legs. It was said that posters of Marlene were banned in Paris Metro stations because any Frenchman who spotted her

Marlene Dietrich replaced Rita Hayworth in the Mercury Wonder Show and also performed magic tricks with Welles in the movie *Follow the Boys* (1944).

legs was in danger of missing his train. In any event, when my father called Marlene about performing in his magic show, she simply said, "Come teach me the tricks, and I do it."

If Cohn was gloating that he had managed to save Rita Hayworth from the insidious charms of Orson Welles, he did not gloat long. Hollywood's gossip columnists let it be known that "Beauty and the Brain" had been seen dining at a table for two at Ciro's, Romanoff's, the Brown Derby, and other restaurants popular with the stars. They had been caught holding hands across the table and gazing soulfully into each other's eyes. The only question was when wedding bells were going to ring . . .

They rang on September 7, 1943. During her lunch break from *Cover Girl*, Rita was whisked away in my father's chauffeured car before Harry Cohn could throw himself in front of the wheels. They were married in Santa Monica in what they hoped was going to be a quiet, civil ceremony. Joseph Cotten, my father's close friend and costar in *Citizen Kane*, stood up as his best man. However, outside the judge's chamber, a mob of press photographers stood ready to dash any hope of a quiet wedding. They had been tipped off by Harry Cohn, who, when he realized he could no longer stop the marriage, decided to milk it for every ounce of publicity he could get.

So every tabloid in the country ran photos of the newlyweds standing side by side in a happy daze, then walking out of the municipal building on winged feet. In those pictures, just-married Rita beams like a little girl who can barely contain her delight. Yet in her stylish beige suit and floppy picture hat, she carries herself with that natural dignity, that animal grace, I remember so well. As for my father, he looks uncomfortable in his banker's striped suit and bow tie, as though determined to play a part that he knows is out of character. He gazes down at his bride, his expressions ranging from grave in one photo to tender in the next. In the final shot, holding Rita's hand firmly in his, he looks overjoyed that he of all men has captured Hollywood's love goddess.

Now CAME THE brightest days of my childhood, which I owe to Rita. Almost every weekend, she invited me to stay with her and my father in their spacious home at 136 South Carmelina Drive. Rita had bought the ten-room house with its spectacular grounds and swimming pool when she realized she was pregnant. The contrast between my easygoing stepmother and my excessively strict mother only heightened my euphoria from the moment I arrived on South Carmelina Drive, the weekend stretching ahead like a round-the-clock party loaded with treats and surprises. I was also free of Marie on these occasions, which added to the holiday atmosphere. Instead of the usual routine of eating in the kitchen with Marie or being led off to bed while it was still light, knowing that downstairs the grown-ups were mixing their martinis and the fun was just beginning, I was allowed to hang around all the time and stay up as late as I liked.

Rita was everything a child could wish for in a stepmother: sweet-natured, affectionate, fun-loving, and, in many ways, a child herself. While my father buried his nose in a heavy book, Rita read "the funnies," as she called the daily comic strips in the newspapers. She read them religiously every morning while she breakfasted in bed, snuggled under the covers with my father, who was immersed in the rest of the paper. Their Hollywood-size bed had a padded, pink satin bolster studded with sparkly bits of glass I imagined were diamonds. There was something wonderfully reassuring about my father and Rita kissing and cuddling in the same bed, giggling at their own private jokes. (My mother and her second husband, the screenwriter Charlie Lederer, maintained separate bedrooms and were not physically demonstrative, at least not in front of me.) "Hello, darling girl," my father would boom in his basso profundo as I stood hovering in the doorway. "Well, am I going to get a kiss this morning?" Soon I was snuggled down between them in the warm, rumpled bed, reading the funnies with Rita and wishing I could stay there for the rest of the day.

I had no idea in those days that my stepmother was Hollywood's love goddess, the glamour girl whose pinup picture some GIs pasted on a bomb, which horrified her when she heard about it. The Rita I knew padded around the house barefoot and rarely bothered with makeup. Usually she was dressed in an old shirt and faded dungarees, which took nothing away from her natural beauty. When we played our wild, silly games, she often seemed younger than I was, which made me feel protective. I noticed how gentle my father was with her, careful not to tease her in the same, reckless way he teased me.

Horsing around the pool with Rita Hayworth and "Orsie," 1945.

Early in her pregnancy, Rita delighted in chasing me around outside with the garden hose, especially when I was fully clothed. Finally I would grab the hose and chase her, both of us whooping and hollering, until we were soaked and overcome with giggles. We would then hear my father calling out in piteous tones, "Could the two of you *please* make less noise? I'm trying to work!"

For some reason we found this hilarious, and Rita would sing out, "You can't work *all* the time, Orsie. It will make you a dull boy."

I don't think the prospect of becoming dull worried my father. He took to hiding in the bushes in a faraway corner of the garden where all you could see of him was the wavy thread of smoke rising from his cigar. When I dared to come nearer, I would catch glimpses of him hunched over in his deck chair, the cigar clamped between his teeth while he scribbled furiously on a yellow pad. Surrounded by piles of books, scripts, magazines, and newspapers, he looked like a man on his private island who had everything he needed to make him happy.

There were times we did persuade "Orsie" to join us at the swimming pool, although not necessarily to change into his swimming trunks and splash around with us. I had swum in some glamorous pools, but this one topped them all. It had a waterfall at the shallow end, and in the middle was an island with a full-grown palm tree. A rowboat was tied up at the poolside into which, when the spirit moved him, my father would jump, fully clothed, the boat staggering under his weight and rocking dangerously until he settled himself at the oars. Then he would row around the pool, loudly singing a sea chantey in a salty Irish brogue. After this impromptu performance, he would vanish once more into the bushes.

Gliding around the pool in the rowboat was much too tame for Rita and me. Our idea of fun was to race each other to the waterfall or to the island in the middle of the pool. Rita almost always won, not that I minded, and when once in a while she let me win, I knew she was deliberately slowing down, but I pretended to be thrilled, yelling, "I won! I won!" just to see her lovely grin.

Sometimes we played at being mermaids and tried to swim all the way around the island underwater. I could never hold my breath long enough, but Rita could, and in a mock ceremony I crowned her Queen of the Mermaids.

As Rita's pregnancy progressed, our hijinks came to a natural end. Now when I was invited to South Carmelina Drive, my father was often away, and I could see Rita was lonely for him. Although she was as sweet to me as ever, she also seemed listless and distracted. I did not learn until years later that whenever they were apart, Rita suspected my father of being unfaithful to her and was racked by jealousy. Not only was she well aware of my father's reputation as a lady's man, she also knew it had bewildered him to discover that in real life she was not the luscious, sexy woman she projected on the screen. Off camera she was still Margarita Carmen Cansino, born in Brooklyn to a Spanish father and an Irish mother. As she would famously say, alluding to her best-known screen role, "Men go to bed with Gilda but wake up with me."

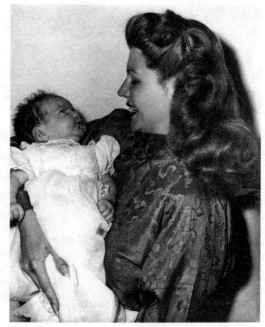

Rita Hayworth holding Rebecca, born on December 17, 1944.

To ease her loneliness, Rita acquired a large white and gold cocker spaniel. She named him Pookles, which had been my father's pet name when he was a boy. While I had nothing against Pookles, I saw no reason to make such a huge fuss over him. I felt the same way about my half sister Rebecca Welles, who arrived in the world on December 17, 1944. She was a cute baby, who smiled, gurgled, and looked exactly like our father, but what did we need her for?

Although I no longer had Rita to myself, I still lived for my weekend visits with her and my father when he was around. I was more than ready to put up with Becky, Pookles, even the Mexican bullfighter who mysteriously appeared one weekend and monopolized Rita for hours. She pretended to be a bull, pointing her fingers on either side of her head, while he danced around, snapping a red tablecloth. Rita charged, the bullfighter pivoted, and my father and I stood on the sidelines shouting "Olé." "I'll take you to a real bullfight one of these days," he promised me, and years later, when we traveled together in Spain, he kept his word.

As each weekend drew to a close, I nourished the dream that one day I would not return to my mother, stepfather, and Marie. I would live

Visiting Daddy, Becky, and Pookles on South
Carmelina Drive.

permanently with my father
and Rita. Although I never
spoke of my dream to any-
one, it was caught in a photograph taken when Becky
was almost six months old
and I was a few months into
my seventh year. We chil-
dren, barefoot and dressed
in matching pinafores with
ruffled sleeves, are nestled
in the garden swing with
our father and Pookles. The
dog licks my father's chin,
but it is Becky who claims
his lap, her baby feet kick-
ing, her arms stretched out
to embrace the world. She
gently touches Pookles, her
fingers exploring his soft, curly ear. I, too, pet the dog, strictly for the camera.
Our father is thinner than usual, having been on a crash diet, and he is growing a mustache for the part he will soon play as the Nazi spy in *The Stranger*.
But in this golden moment, he is playing Daddy, and I am smiling up at him,
my face radiant with hope.

I WAS EIGHT and a half when my mother put me on a plane to Acapulco, Mexico, where I was to join my father and Rita for several weeks. As
it was a short flight, I was traveling by myself. This was my first trip on an
airplane, and when we began to soar above the clouds, I felt it was the start
of a grand adventure.

When I arrived in Acapulco and Rita met me at the airport, I almost didn't
recognize her. Her hair had been cropped short and bleached whiter than
bone. "Why did you cut off your pretty red hair?" I wanted to know.

"I'm supposed to look evil and cold in the movie I'm making with Orsie," she
explained. "Besides, my hair isn't really red, you know. When I was your age,
it was almost black." I tried to imagine Rita as an eight-year-old, let alone Rita
with almost black hair, but at the time it was too much for my imagination.

The movie being filmed in Acapulco was *The Lady from Shanghai* in which Rita played the title role. Although she had decided to divorce my father the year before I joined them in Acapulco, she had delayed filing the papers. Making *The Lady from Shanghai* with her husband as her director and costar was Rita's last attempt at a reconciliation.

Although I knew none of this at the time, I did notice Rita was not as relaxed and fun-loving as she had been on South Carmelina Drive, but I told myself it must be very hard for her to pretend she was "evil and cold" during the long, grueling hours she had to spend in front of the camera. Also something was different about the way my father and Rita were behaving with each other. There was too much hugging and kissing going on, and every other word was "darling." One day, in Rita's dressing room, my father used up half her lipsticks scrawling impassioned words all over her mirror. I wondered if Rita would get mad and scream at him for ruining her lipsticks — my mother certainly would have — but Rita acted as though my father had filled her dressing room with armfuls of roses. The gooey red messages stayed on her mirror for days.

I don't think I had ever been bored as a child until I started hanging around my father's movie sets. Not only did it take forever to set up a shot, but then he wanted it done over and over and over. Sometimes he changed a line of dialogue or the angle of the shot, but for endless stretches of time, as far as I could see, nothing changed from one take to the next. How could they all stand it? I wondered.

The set that was in constant use during my visit was a yacht, which the actor Errol Flynn had generously loaned my father. It was anchored in the bay near our hotel. In one sequence of takes, Rita lay on the deck in her wet bathing suit, drops of moisture glistening all over her body. The Mexican sun beat down on her, the shimmering drops turned to salt, and my father began hollering, "Get some water sponges over here and make it snappy!" I was struck by Rita's patience as she lay there calmly while several assistants attacked her with waterlogged sponges. In fact, no one seemed to be getting restless but me. All eyes turned to my father with the rapt attention of musicians in an orchestra pit who stare up at their conductor. And my father strode up and down, issuing directives, joking with the actors, the crew, putting everyone at ease while he wiped his face with a bandana, booming, "My God, it's hot!"

During a break, I ran up to him, asking, "Can I go swimming, Daddy?"

"Later. We'll all go swimming."

"But I want to go now."

"I can't let you go swimming by yourself, Christopher, and nobody's free to take you right now."

"But, Daddy, in Santa Monica, I go into the ocean by myself all the time. When a big wave comes along, I just hold my nose and duck."

"We are not in Santa Monica, Christopher, and if anything were to happen to you, I would never forgive myself, so I want you to promise me that you will not go into the water by yourself. You will wait until I or Rita or someone else is free to go in with you. Do we understand one another?"

"Yes, Daddy."

I do not remember ever getting to swim in Acapulco. Instead, when I wasn't watching my father and Rita make their movie, I was exploring the winding paths and terraced gardens near the hotel. The grounds sloped gently down from the hilltop hotel to a white, sandy beach in a sheltered cove. Much as I liked being there with Daddy and Rita, I began to wish something I had never wished before: to go home to our beach house in Santa Monica before it was time. I was running out of ways to amuse myself in Acapulco—how many more times could I count the rowboats busily ferrying cast and crew members from the yacht to the shore and back again? As I stood on the hotel terrace, looking down at the sparkling bay, then following the curves of mountains that leaned against the sky, I felt homesick for *my* beach and *my* ocean with its thunderous waves, its wheeling, squawking gulls.

Yet I still looked forward to eating meals with my father and Rita in the hotel dining room. Especially at lunch, my father seemed more relaxed, expansive, and ready to laugh at almost anything I said, even when I wasn't trying to be funny. Then one day a new busboy named Pablo was assigned to our table. He was a dark-skinned boy of twelve or thirteen with coal black eyes, and I felt drawn to him without knowing why. I could not help smiling at him whenever he came to fill our water glasses, and he smiled back in an easy, natural way. At that point my father, who noticed everything, began teasing me about "falling in love with Pablo." The more I protested that falling in love was "silly," the more he insisted it was "love at first sight." Hadn't I just smiled at Pablo again, ho, ho. What was a smile from a lovely young lady but an invitation to flirt with her?

Once it had begun, the teasing went on at every meal. Finally, near tears one day, I begged him, "Daddy, please stop it! I'm not in love with Pablo. Honest . . ."

"The lady doth protest too much!" He laughed with such gusto, crinkling up his eyes, yet at times it was also the high, wheezy sound of a man close to pain.

"Do let up on her, Orsie." Rita laid a comforting hand on my arm.

I pushed the food around on my plate, my appetite gone. At last the plates were whisked away. "May I be excused, please?"

"What, no dessert? Ah, what love will do!" my father roared to one and all as I fled red-faced from the dining room.

The constant teasing left me feeling humiliated. I was not good at being teased by anyone, but when my father teased me, I was unable to laugh it off because I could not be sure, deep down, if he really loved me. I knew that he found me amusing and precocious. Unlike my moody, volatile mother, he was consistently warm with me and openly affectionate. But was he proud of me? He did not seem that impressed when I played the piano for him, or showed him my latest drawing, or gave him one of my illustrated stories at Christmas. How was I going to make him proud of me?

The answer came to me when the location for the day's shoot was moved from Errol Flynn's yacht to a dusty mountain road overlooking the bay. My father was telling the crew to move the camera here and set up the lights there, then changing his mind and making them move everything to another spot. The men were grunting, "Yes, Mr. Welles," and "No, Mr. Welles," as if lugging around heavy equipment in the hot sun was how they wanted to spend the rest of their lives. It was clear to me, young as I was, that the entire cast and crew saw my father as an exalted being. As he stood around in his open-neck shirt and baggy pants, laughing his wheezy laugh, waving his cigar, he acted as though he were giving a party. "I want everyone to have a marvelous time," he seemed to be saying, "and I'm going to have more fun than all of you put together!"

Suddenly I knew what I had to do. I ran up to my father and tugged on his shirt until he looked down at me. "What is it, Christopher?"

"I want to be in your movie, Daddy."

"You . . . what?" He stared down at me with a kind of horror.

"I want to be in the movie with you and Rita."

"Oh, no! Oh, my God, no!"

I was as taken aback by his reaction as he had been by my request. We looked each other in the eyes for a long moment. Then I persisted, "I'll do anything, Daddy, but please let me be in your movie."

"Looks like she's a chip off the old block, Mr. Welles," observed one of the crew.

Mr. Welles winced as though a fly had landed on his nose while he continued to stare at me as though he had never seen me before. At length he sighed. "Oh, all right, Christopher. You can be an American brat eating an ice cream cone."

This wasn't exactly the role I had in mind, but already one of the minions had been sent in search of anything resembling an ice cream cone. He came back with a frozen glob of fruit juice on a stick. Suddenly I was standing in a blaze of lights and being ordered by a father, turned imperious, to "whine and snivel" like the brat I was supposed to be. The camera rolled and I gave it my all while the glob melted down my arm. In less than a minute, it seemed, my father-director had yelled, "Cut!" Then he stood with his back to me, talking to the cameraman.

I waited for him to say something. Had he liked the way I had played it? "Do you want another take?" I called out. Slowly he turned and stared at me, but I saw no spark of pride in his hazel eyes. "Do you want another take?" I piped up again. Perhaps he hadn't heard me the first time.

Orson (in white suit and sailor's hat), Glenn Anders (on his right), and Chris (in front, second from right), buying ice cream in Acapulco, Mexico, while filming *The Lady from Shanghai* in 1947.

His answer came in a soft, dismissive voice on the edge of a hollow laugh. "No, that will be all, Christopher. You've had your big moment on the silver screen. Now run along and find something better to do."

Quite a few years passed before I found myself in a movie house, watching *The Lady from Shanghai* for the first time and wondering when a bratty little girl eating an ice cream cone was going to appear on the screen. She never did.

IN THE SPRING of 1947, for several months my father lived in the beach house next door to ours in Santa Monica. He had ended his relationship with Rita Hayworth and had moved in with another lovely redhead, the Irish actress Geraldine Fitzgerald. While I loved having my father next door, I did miss Rita. She had the quality, rare in Hollywood, of being herself, whether her hair was copper red or platinum blond. She was the same unaffected person in spangles and furs that she was in faded jeans and bare feet. I knew where I stood with Rita. She liked me and liked having me around.

Geraldine Fitzgerald—Aunt Geraldine to me—was a different animal. There was something elusive about her, something that made me suspect I could never know the real person hiding behind the soft-spoken Irish charm and the dazzling smile. She seemed to live in a vast reservoir of calm known only to herself. On the other hand, I had no trouble figuring out her son, Michael Lindsay-Hogg. Two years younger than I was, Michael was a lovable scamp with a mop of dark hair, eager to join in any adventure I might propose. We were in and out of each other's houses every day. Sweet and amenable most of the time, Michael was also an only child who liked doing things *his* way. The inevitable moment came when he got tired of being bossed around.

"Are they fighting *again*?" The question rose, incredulous, from the nook on the open-air porch where my father had buried himself in papers, scripts, pencils, and pads. "Can't I get any quiet around here? I *must* get this work done!" Heaving himself to his feet, sweeping up papers, scripts, et al., he vanished into the serene depths of Geraldine's house.

"You naughty children!" Geraldine descended from the porch to the sandy backyard, where Michael and I were staging our current battle. She pulled us apart as we continued to shriek and flail at each other, then pronounced the sentence we knew by heart. "You are not to play together until you can play nicely. Chrissie, you are to go home at once, and Michael, you are to go to your room."

We did as we were told, but it was not long before Michael and I had crept out of our houses and stood on opposite sides of the picket fence that separated our adjoining properties. We held hands through the fence, crying pitifully and swearing to be kind to each other, until Geraldine relented.

When I recall those sunlit days in Santa Monica, I am almost always outdoors and in my bathing suit. The houses along our strip of coastal highway were built to face the ocean, and I couldn't remember when I had not fallen asleep to the sound of waves or woken up early in the morning with the fierce desire to see the ocean emerging from the fog. It meant running out of the house in my pajamas, dashing across the backyard—a rectangular plot of sand stolen from the beach and enclosed by a high, white wall—then scrambling up the steps that led to an elevated landing and locked gate. There I would stand barefoot and shivering on the wooden platform, peering into the fog, which rolled in from the ocean like fallen clouds, listening to the rhythm of waves, how the little ones hushed as they burst into spray while the big ones boomed like faraway guns.

I remember far less about being in school, fully clothed, for the better part of the day. Life resumed when I was back home and racing through my homework so that I could run over to Aunt Geraldine's before having supper in the kitchen with Marie. My father might or might not be there, or if he was, he might or might not have time for me; but I could always go for a walk by myself on the beach. It lifted my spirits just to skip along the tide line, just to feel the wet sand yielding under my feet. It was that magical hour at the end of the day when the light turned everything to gold. I pretended the sun was a red-orange balloon that someone in the ocean—a mermaid?—was pulling down from the sky. It came down so slowly, so slowly, that it was always with a shiver of surprise that I saw it drop beneath the waves.

In those days the beach belonged to the people who lived on it. It was rarely crowded, except on weekends, and so safe that I was allowed to come and go once I grew old enough to understand that the ocean I loved with my whole being could also drown me. Yet even as a young child, with Marie standing by, I had been allowed to paddle around in the foamy leavings of waves. Later on, when the surf was not too rough, I held my nose and rolled around and around in the undertow until I came up coughing and spitting sand. This was my idea of fun. Some days the breakers were so huge there was nothing to do but sit far back on the sand in awe. I could not conceive then that my days would not always begin and end on the beach at Santa Monica.

On weekends I was more sure of seeing my father. Often on a Saturday I ran over to Aunt Geraldine's after breakfast and found him already at work, reading and scribbling in his favorite nook on the porch, unshaven and wearing only his bathing trunks. He didn't seem to hear the hush and thunder of waves, the screeching of gulls, the soothing, familiar sounds that drifted over the high, white wall. The wind uncombed his dark hair, and yet I felt he was untouchable, imagining a glass wall had risen around him. I sat down in a wicker chair, careful to be quiet, and waited with all the patience I could muster, which was not very much. I watched his every move, wondering why he slashed through some pages with a furious pencil and then smiled at others or doodled in the margins. Much as I wanted to draw closer and peer over his shoulder, I didn't dare. *If I sit here long enough,* I thought, *he'll look up and notice me . . .*

It did happen. "Hello, darling girl! How's my clever daughter today?" His voice was so welcoming that I began to tell him at once and in great detail how I was. I never felt more intelligent, more sure of myself, than when I was alone with my father and had his full attention. Then I could tell him anything, and he listened, not as one listens to a child but as though he were hearing a younger version of himself. This was heady stuff, and to have such moments with my father made me hunger for more.

DURING THE MONTHS he lived next door, my father had an open invitation to wander over to our house whenever he pleased. He and my mother seemed perfectly friendly, at least in my presence, and he also seemed to be great pals with my stepfather, Charlie Lederer. No one observing them together would have guessed that my mother and Charlie had sued my father for an increase in my child support. In fact, they had taken him to court several times, the judge had ruled in their favor, my father had agreed to an increase, and then it had never materialized. Finally Mother and Charlie had given up, and so it was back to "Orson, darling!" and a daily invitation to join them in the ritual of martinis on the front porch at sunset.

My father was well aware that Charlie Lederer was not only a highly paid screenwriter who could easily afford my upkeep, he was also the nephew of movie star Marion Davies, one of the wealthiest women in Hollywood and the mistress of the press baron William Randolph Hearst. Charlie was destined to inherit Marion's fortune, whereas my father was fated to be short of cash his entire life. It was not that he didn't earn enormous sums, whether as

Orson as Rochester in *Jane Eyre* (1944) with
Joan Fontaine in the title role.

an actor in other people's movies, a radio personality, or a lecturer traveling
around the country. For a radio appearance alone, he might earn as much as
three thousand dollars, a lot of money in the 1940s. In fact, his annual earnings were reported to be the highest in show business, which had prompted
my mother and Charlie to sue him in the first place.

As my mother saw it, "Orson's hopeless with money and couldn't save a
nickel if you held a gun to his head." In her eyes, his huge earnings were
sucked into oblivion like elephants disappearing in quicksand. She did not
want to acknowledge that it was Orson's passion for making movies and his
other vital concerns that consumed most of his income. As one example,
after making a hundred thousand dollars when he starred in *Jane Eyre* as
Mr. Rochester, one of the few times in his movie career that he played the
romantic lead, he spent every penny of it developing footage for *It's All True*,
a doomed documentary he shot in Brazil that was never released. And when
his artistic imperatives didn't empty the coffers, his altruistic impulses did.
In 1943 he had lavished forty thousand dollars of his own capital on the Mer-

cury Wonder Show, which servicemen saw for free. Before the show closed, it entertained close to fifty thousand troops stationed in the Los Angeles area. In September of 1944 he joined the Democratic Party's effort to reelect President Franklin Delano Roosevelt to a fourth term. Orson Welles gave campaign speeches all over the map, donating his fame to the cause and paying his own travel expenses.

That my father was somehow finding the money to campaign for Roosevelt while evading his responsibility to me made my mother furious. "Charlie adored you," she told me years later. "He was sweet about paying for anything you needed, including those braces on your teeth which cost a pretty penny, I can tell you!" Her blue-gray eyes flashed with an anger the intervening years had not diminished. "It was terribly unfair of Orson to let Charlie pick up the tab for you!"

"But you were all so friendly," I recalled. "Was it just an act for my benefit?"

"Yes and no. We couldn't stay mad at Orson, you see. Nobody could. He was an overgrown child, who could be maddening at times, God knows, but when he turned on the charm . . ." My mother and I exchanged a smile, both of us well acquainted with the Wellesian charm. "Then Orson and Charlie just naturally gravitated toward one another. They were both brilliant, highly sophisticated men living in a cultural desert. Marion told me Charlie had graduated from the University of California when he was only sixteen. My God, Orson and I never even *went* to college, and here was Charlie, practically the youngest college graduate in history. So my two husbands got to be great friends, and they loved to commiserate about how difficult it was to be married to me . . ." She gave her husky, ironic laugh. "But when it came to their personalities, they couldn't have been more unalike. Charlie was such a dear, sweet, funny man, and he didn't have Orson's crushing ego. He was a hell of a lot easier to live with, I can tell you."

I returned my stepfather's affection in full measure, but I never called him Charlie, not even when we reconnected later in our lives. Because he was prematurely bald and I had been two years old when he married my mother, I had concluded he must be very old and called him Granddaddy. He found this so funny he never let me call him anything else.

Charlie had the doleful brown eyes and deadpan expression of a born comedian. Known in Hollywood as a master of screwball comedy, he was famous in his private life for playing practical jokes on the unsuspecting. Whenever we visited San Simeon, the grandiose castle William Randolph

Hearst had built on a hilltop in northern California, Charlie could not resist pulling the old man's leg.

"WR is the perfect fall guy," I remember Charlie telling my father one evening while the adults were having martinis on the porch. Then, to illustrate his point, my stepfather launched into his favorite story. Late one night at San Simeon, when everyone else was asleep, Charlie stole out to the gardens and dressed the marble statues of naked women in bras and panties. Early the next morning when Hearst set out on his usual brisk walk before breakfast, he was brought up short by the underwear adorning his Greek nymphs and Roman goddesses. Who on earth would dare do such a thing? He began shouting for his companion, Marion Davies, who rarely emerged before noon, to come and see what had happened and to help find the culprit . . . as if he didn't already know who it was. "The grand old gentleman stood there bothered and befuddled as each of his guests stumbled half-asleep into the garden and began to howl with laughter." Charlie gave us his doleful, deadpan look, our cue to laugh as hard as the stumbling guests.

During the months my father was our neighbor, he became Charlie's willing accomplice. There was the night my mother and Charlie were giving an important dinner party for some high-powered studio executives and my father suddenly appeared outside our dining room windows. He had traded his bathing trunks for a dinner jacket, shirt, and tie. Freshly shaved, his wavy dark brown hair slicked back, he stood with his nose pressed against the glass like a wistful boy shut out of a candy store. My mother pretended not to notice. Then, dramatically clutching his stomach, my father began to whimper and groan.

"Oh, do make him stop, Charlie!" My mother was near tears. "He's ruining dinner for everyone!"

"But, Virginia, you can see the poor wretch is starving."

"Make him go away!"

"Well, I can't turn away a man in a dinner jacket. It wouldn't be civilized. We'll have to invite him to join us."

"Oh, all right." My mother had finally caught on that it was a gag. So had the dinner guests, who had fallen into an embarrassed silence but now erupted in gales of laughter, while Charlie calmly examined his fingernails, then looked up in mild surprise as if to say, *Is it really that funny?* And that, of course, made it even funnier.

My NEXT FORAY into motion pictures began in June of 1947 when I was nine years old. My father was still staying next door with Aunt Geraldine, and he was about to film his freely adapted version of Shakespeare's *Macbeth*. One afternoon I came home from school to find the entire cast assembled in the living room and getting ready to read through the shooting script. I ran up to my father standing at the front of the room like a benevolent teacher who waits for the class to settle down. "Can I stay and listen, Daddy?"

"Yes, if you're very quiet."

Our homey living room was stuffed with actors. Most were Mercury Theatre regulars who had first worked with my father on Broadway and then followed him to Hollywood, but there were a few new faces: Jeanette Nolan, a well-known actress in radio about to make her film debut as Lady Macbeth, and Dan O'Herlihy, fresh from the Gate Theatre in Dublin and playing Macduff. Then there was a lean young man of nineteen who called himself Roddy McDowall. He had won fame as a child actor in *How Green Was My Valley* and *Lassie Come Home*, and now he was about to make his Shakespearean debut as Malcolm in my father's *Macbeth*. Although I recognized Roddy from his *Lassie* movies, which Marie and I had wept through more than once, he was ten years older than I, which, as far as I was concerned, put him on another planet.

I found myself some space on the floor and was prepared to be mute for the next hour when, to my surprise, Charlie sauntered into the room and was handed a script. He sat down on the floor next to me. "Are you going to be in the movie, too, Granddaddy?" I asked in a whisper. Then, when he nodded, "Who are you going to be?"

"One of the three witches."

I thought he was kidding me. How could a bald man play a witch? On the other hand . . . before I could stop myself, I scrambled to my feet and ran up to my father, the only person left standing in the hushed room. "May I have a script, too, please? I want to be one of the three witches." To my dismay, everyone laughed.

"We have all the witches we need, Christopher." Although my father spoke with measured calm, the look he gave me was one of irritation. "Now please sit down like a good girl and don't interrupt us again."

"Please, Daddy, can't I be in the movie? Please, can't I, Daddy—"

"There are no parts for little girls in *Macbeth*!"

"Let her read a few lines, Orson," Charlie put in mildly. "She reads pretty well for a kid her age."

"Oh, all right." My father handed me a script with the sigh of a man submitting to an unreasonable demand against his better judgment. "Christopher, if you insist on being in *Macbeth*, you'll have to be a little boy."

"Okay!" I sang out with an alacrity that made everyone laugh again. And that was how I landed the part of Macduff's son.

Having satisfied my father that I could rattle off my lines with aplomb, even though I had little understanding of what they meant, I began my movie career in earnest. First I was fitted for my costume. I was used to wearing not much more than a swimsuit or summery dress, and now, beginning with the wool hat on my head, I was layered in heavy clothing meant for unheated castles and windy Scottish moors. Under my long wool tunic, I wore a woolen shirt and tartan plaid trousers. Then a tartan shawl, which matched my trousers and the headband on my hat, was draped over the tunic, tied around my waist, and held in place by a metal ornament pinned to one shoulder. My costume was made still more uncomfortable by the scratchy feel of wool against my skin, yet every morning, when Marie helped me into it, I was merry with excitement. It was cool and crisp that early in the day, and soon my father's chauffeured car would come to collect me, and I would ride beside him all the way to the studio.

My mother had readily agreed to my accompanying my father every day during the three-week period it would take to film *Macbeth*. "I can't think of a better way for you to spend your summer vacation or to get to know Orson," she told me. Then I overheard her telling Charlie, "I think Orson's finally taking an interest in Chrissie."

So it was with high hopes that I stood shivering in the driveway, listening to the ocean pound through the morning fog, and waited for Shorty, as we called my father's driver, never wondering if the name might offend him. Shorty was a hunchbacked dwarf who drove with blocks of wood strapped to his feet so he could reach the pedals. His real name was George Chirello, and he would also have a part in *Macbeth,* which was fast becoming a family enterprise. I was a bit afraid of this sour little man who rarely spoke to me, though he always jumped down and held the door until I had plopped myself in the backseat beside my father. Seat belts had not yet been invented, and the opening and shutting of windows still required a human hand to turn the handle. As I tended to get carsick, especially when the car reeked of cigar

"Christopher, if you insist on being in *Macbeth*, you'll have to be a little boy."

smoke, I could not open a window fast enough. I rode with my nose sticking out the window as though I were a dog instead of a nine-year-old girl dressed up like a Scottish lad from the time of the Druids.

So we set out from Santa Monica and tore along to the studio, the sun barely risen, the highway almost deserted. Except for a grim-faced Shorty at the wheel, I was alone with the big, handsome man I called Daddy. I had been saving up so many things to tell him, things that would make him laugh. Here was my chance to shine, and he was staring out the window or making doodles on the script on his lap. I had not known until that moment that a person could be sitting right next to you and yet be as far away as the moon. Was he displeased that I had clamored for a part in *Macbeth* and, before that, in *The Lady from Shanghai*? I did not know how to tell him what I really wanted: to move from the periphery of his attention to the center of his world.

At the time I was too young to understand that my father had much to preoccupy him on our daily drives to the studio. After the box-office failure of his masterwork, *Citizen Kane*, followed by the equally unpopular *The*

Magnificent Ambersons, most of the major Hollywood studios wanted nothing to do with the art films of Orson Welles. They had all turned down his proposal for *Macbeth*. Anything by Shakespeare was far too highbrow for the average moviegoer. Then Welles's notion of turning this antiquated tale into a horror movie was "just plain screwy," even if there was a ghost in it, along with a series of grisly murders.

To be able to make his *Macbeth*, my father had struck a near impossible deal with Republic Pictures, a small, low-budget studio that churned out Grade B Westerns. He had agreed to film his picture in twenty-one days. The result was pandemonium on Republic's Stage 11, where most of *Macbeth* was shot, and yet—and how this amazed me as a child—my father remained calm and in full command throughout it all. Though he often had to yell to make himself heard, he was the unflappable general issuing orders to the troops in the din and smoke of battle.

My notions of moviemaking had been formed the year before in Acapulco, where shooting had moved at an easy pace, with midday breaks for five-course lunches and an afternoon siesta. Sometimes, between takes, my father had told ribald stories that made everyone laugh but that I was too young to understand. If I had been bored at times, I had also been outdoors in Acapulco and free to wander around most of the day. Here in Hollywood, I was confined all day long in a hot, stuffy sound stage. At least eight sets were crammed under one roof, and they seemed to be in continuous motion, pieces being hauled from one spot to another, like a gigantic jigsaw puzzle pulled apart and reassembled. The crew never stopped hollering, "Look out! Watch your backs! Coming through!" At least three scenes were being shot at the same time, just one of the Wellesian ways to make a picture in twenty-one days. There were no long breaks for meals, no time for racy jokes, and boredom was a liability. I had to be alert every minute not to trip over a cable or be knocked to the floor by a piece of heavy equipment "coming through."

I had never seen my father work so intensely or sweat so profusely. Where did all his joyous energy come from? How was he able, at one and the same time, to direct the picture, play the title role, and hand-hold any actor who needed a word of encouragement? How, in the midst of nonstop frenzy, did he know exactly what was going on at every moment in every corner of the studio? One day, as I was watching him perform in one of his scenes with Lady Macbeth, he suddenly yelled, "Cut!" and rushed over to a set on the other side of the sound stage. Out of the corner of one eye, he had seen something he didn't like. "Your daddy has eyes in the back of his head," one crew member told me with a mock grimace. "I don't think he's human."

"Yeah, he's the human fly," joked another. "Watch your back now, little lady . . ."

Of all the scenes I watched in the making, I was most impressed by the banquet scene attended by Banquo's ghost. The heavy wooden table was piled high with platters of real food, pewter pitchers, and goblets. Suddenly the ghost appeared, and in terror Macbeth sprang to his feet, upended the table, and sent the food and dishware clattering to the floor. Then he did the scene again. Again. And yet again. Between takes, assistants scrambled to collect the scattered food, pitchers, and goblets and put them back on the table exactly as they were before. How was my daddy able to upend that heavy table take after take without showing any sign of exhaustion? I was awestruck.

When I came to realize the rocky cliffs were made of cardboard, the wind came from a wind machine, and the sky was a painted backdrop, I understood how Dorothy must have felt when she discovered the Wizard of Oz was a fake. On the other hand, the horses were very real and they peed all day long on the flimsy sets. By the end of the day, the stench was unbearable.

So this was life in the movies: waiting out the day in a hot, itchy costume while holding my nose from the stink of horse pee. "When are they going to do my scene?" I kept asking anyone who would stop long enough to talk to me, but no one seemed to know, not even my stepfather. Barely recognizable in his creepy makeup as one of the three ghouls, Charlie delighted in pouncing on me with a fiendish cackle that never failed to make me scream. I was beginning to wish I had never begged my father to give me a part in *Macbeth*.

I was thankful when another young actor arrived on Stage 11 and soon became my boon companion. A few years older than I was and several heads taller, Jerry Farber had been engaged to play the part of Fleance, Banquo's son. "I've been in lots of pictures already," he told me with undisguised pride, "because I'm a professional child actor." I did not envy him. The time he had spent on sound stages had given Jerry a pale and spindly look. Now he studied our barely controlled commotion with a practiced eye and decided *Macbeth* was going to be "a big flop." Even if you could figure out what was going on, you couldn't understand half of what the actors were saying. They were speaking in a heavy Scots brogue. (My father maintained that if Shakespeare were alive today, he would not understand the overly refined English accents cultivated by Old Vic actors. "It's marvelous when a well-spoken Irishman or a Scotsman does Shakespeare," he told me. "Why shouldn't all the Scotsmen in *Macbeth* sound like Scotsmen?") I knew a few Scots words from Marie, who called me "lassie" and "my wee bairn" when she was pleased with me — and "madam" when she wasn't — but even Marie might have had a hard time understanding Lady Macbeth. Her famous line, "Out, damned spot. Out, I say!" sounded more like, "Oot, demmed spat. Oot, ay seh!"

Jerry and I began sneaking out of our sound stage and running over to a nearby lot where the filming of a B Western was in progress. What a swell picture this was! Why couldn't my daddy make a Western? I must remember to ask him on a day when I was feeling especially brave. Meanwhile, we kids in our tartan plaids watched the hero on the white horse thunder into town in a cloud of dust. We watched him shoot it out, alone and unafraid, with the bad guys in the black hats. Through countless takes we held our breath while he knocked out one of the bad guys and then threw him like a sack of rotting onions through the saloon's swinging doors. Each time the villain landed in the dust, we cheered. After the gloom and confusion of *Macbeth,* what a relief to be in the Wild West. Here was a Main Street we knew by heart, with its noisy saloon, its barbershop with the red and white striped pole, its wooden Indian, and its hitching posts for the horses peeing in the great outdoors.

Finally I was called to do my scene with Lady Macduff, who was played by Peggy Webber, known in her radio days as "the Girl with One Thousand Voices." She was an attractive blond with corkscrew curls, and our scene went smoothly. It was all a lark to me, and I felt quite at home in front of the camera.

The following day my father explained to me that I was to run as fast as I could down a corridor, because a murderer was chasing after me, knife in hand. I was to scream and look terrified. At the end of the corridor, I was to fall facedown on a mattress while the murderer plunged a rubber knife into my back. "Have you got all that, Christopher?"

"Yes, Daddy."

"Okay. Let's roll 'em. Take one." I did everything he had told me to do, but at the end of the take, he was yelling, "No! No! No!" Luckily, he wasn't yelling at me but at the actor playing my assassin. "You're handling her much too gingerly. You've got to make it look like you're *killing* her!"

"But, Orson, I don't want to hurt your kid," the actor protested.

"Forget she's my kid and remember you're a *murderer,* not Margaret O'Brien touching a hot stove!" my father thundered. "Now hit Christopher hard this time. Take two!"

As I listened to this exchange, a chill came over me. Didn't my father care if I got hurt? We did the scene several more times. I got pounded on the back but not so hard that I couldn't take it, and finally my father-director was satisfied. I scrambled to my feet and looked up at him expectantly, but already he was turning away and talking with his assistant. At that moment, the fun and excitement I had felt at being in Daddy's movie drained out of me.

I asked myself: *Do I really want to spend my life cooped up on a sound stage, waiting for the director to get around to my scene?* Were weeks of being bored worth the few moments of elation when I stood before the camera, putting my whole heart into it? Maybe I didn't have to be in the movies like my father, Rita, Aunt Geraldine, and most of the grown-ups I knew. There must be some other way I could make my father proud of me . . .

2

Orson's Kid

"WHEN'S DADDY COMING TO see us again?" I had bounded into my mother's room early in the morning and settled myself at the foot of her huge double bed. The best time to approach her was while she was having breakfast on a tray. She looked wan and a bit frail without makeup, her fine blond hair in a tangle.

"I don't know, Chrissie."

"We haven't seen him in such a long time. Can we call him, Mommy?"

"I *have* called him!" She smashed out her cigarette in the ashtray by her bed, then immediately lit another, her blue eyes glittering through the smoke. "But don't worry, darling. I'll call again and you *will* see your father, I promise you!"

Yet it was not in response to my mother's pestering that my father appeared in our beach house in Santa Monica and later, after we moved to Beverly Hills, in our mock-Tudor house on Bedford Drive. He was more likely to arrive unannounced and then madden the cook by staying for lunch or dinner. Always casually dressed in summer slacks and an open shirt, he behaved as though he were a member of our household, coming and going as he pleased with no need to give an account of himself.

From the moment my father walked through our front door, everything seemed more vibrant. I could feel his exuberant energy swirling around him and giving off sparks. After the bear hugs, the kisses, the joyous greetings—"How's my darling girl today?"—I was giddy with excitement, and all he had done was say hello and ease himself into an armchair.

"Shall I play the piano for you, Daddy?" My heart was pounding so hard that I wondered if I would be able to play.

"Not now, Christopher."

"Do you want to see a drawing I did?"

"Later." Puffing out his cheeks, he busied himself with the ritual of lighting and relighting his cigar.

"Shall I make you a martini?"

"What?" He turned to my mother in disbelief. "Virginia, did our daughter just offer to make me a martini?"

"Chrissie makes a damned good martini," Charlie drawled, winking at me. "You should try one, Orson. It'll put hair on your teeth."

"Are you two raising her to be a barkeep, or is this your idea of a practical joke?"

"Oh really, Orson, don't be a bore!" my mother snapped. "Most people think it's terribly cute when Chrissie offers to make them a martini."

"Well, I don't!"

"Would you like some lemonade, Daddy?"

"Dearest child!" He held me in his gaze for a lovely, long moment. Then he glowered at my mother. "If I may be permitted to say so, Virginia, there are more than enough alcoholics in your family without enlisting Christopher while she is still in pigtails."

"*My* family. I like that! What about *your* family?"

A moment of tense silence. Then my father gave a hollow laugh. "Did you say there was some lemonade?" he asked me, and when I nodded vigorously, "Then bring me a nice tall glass with plenty of ice. That's my darling girl."

I ran to the kitchen as though my life depended on it.

ALTHOUGH I WAS a sunny child with a strong capacity to enjoy myself, I was not nearly as high-spirited in Beverly Hills as I had been in Santa Monica. Now, instead of dashing out in my pajamas to greet the ocean every morning, I stared out the window at the pool in the back garden. Swimming in a pool seemed awfully tame after ducking ocean waves and rolling around in the undertow. I missed the ocean and wandering along the beach, chasing sandpipers or hunting for sea glass in clumps of seaweed. I still had a shoe box filled with my treasures: They had looked like rubies and emeralds when they first glistened in my palm, but once away from the ocean, they had turned strangely dull.

I also missed a number of important people who disappeared from my daily life once we moved away from Santa Monica. These included Aunt Geraldine and my constant playmate, Michael Lindsay-Hogg, who no longer lived next door. At times I found myself thinking of Rita and my half sister, Rebecca, and wondering why I didn't go to visit them anymore. Although I knew Rita had divorced my father, I didn't see why that should prevent me from seeing her. Besides, I was curious to get to know my half sister now that she was a toddler beginning to talk. When I asked Marie about her, she tartly observed, "Ach, she's the spitting image of Mr. Welles, which is more than we can say about you, thank the Lord."

One morning I asked my mother if I could visit Rita, which made her frown and nibble on her fingernails. Then, summoning a smile, she exclaimed a little too brightly, "*Of course* you want to see Rita. She's an absolute darling, and she's been so good to you. But . . . well . . . I hate to have to tell you this, Chrissie, but Rita doesn't want to see you anymore."

"But why, Mommy?" I was stunned.

"Because she's mad at Orson, and she has every right to be."

"But what does that—"

"Rita can't separate you from Orson, you see."

I didn't see.

"Orson should never have married her," my mother rushed on. "He's *hopeless* at being married, as I could have told her, and now I hear he couldn't care less about poor little Becky. Orson's seeing even less of Becky than he is of you, if that's any comfort to you."

It wasn't.

To cheer me up, Mother and Charlie turned half of the attic into an enormous playroom. In spite of their good intentions, it was here, for the first time in my life, that I felt lonely, isolated from the rest of the household. It was an airy, light-filled room with a carpeted floor and floor-to-ceiling shelves that held my dolls and toys, more than one child could ever play with—and I am sorry to say I didn't let visiting children play with them either. The superfluous dolls and stuffed animals sat collecting dust on the shelves like unsold goods in a toy store. The playroom was so huge that it dwarfed the full-sized puppet theater that Charlie had built and given me on our first Christmas in Beverly Hills, along with a dozen marionettes in colorful costumes and several changes of scenery painted by my mother. I could have easily invited thirty children up to the playroom to watch an impromptu puppet play, but most of the time I performed for the benefit of Marie, as well as the cook and the other servants. Sometimes I pretended my father was in the audience. "Now that's my talented daughter!" I imagined him saying with a delighted laugh.

"She takes after me, of course." After all, the play was written, directed, produced and performed by Christopher Welles, who also played every role.

Sometimes, alone in my playroom, the sound of rain drumming on the windows, I missed my father so much that it felt as though a hole had opened up in my chest—a dark emptiness that might never go away. In the Santa Monica house, I had kept a suitcase packed and hidden away in my closet, awaiting the day my father would arrive and announce, "Christopher, you're coming to live with me." How often I had rehearsed the scene in my mind. I would haul out the suitcase, grab a favorite doll, the book I was reading, a sweater in case it got cold, and almost fall down the stairs in my rush to join my father, towering in the hall. Then, as he took my suitcase, I would remember. "Can Marie come, too?"

"Yes, of course," he would boom. "I wouldn't dream of separating you from Marie."

"And what about Grace?" Grace was Marie's sister, who worked for us as a cook.

"Yes, she can come . . ."

"And Frankie?" He was Grace's handsome teenaged son on whom I had a crush.   "They can all come," said my magnanimous father. "Even Charlie can come, but not your mother. She has to stay here." Just before I threw myself into my father's car, I turned and saw my mother, all alone and weeping in the doorway . . .

In Beverly Hills it was harder to kid myself. Not only was I never going to live with my father, I was seeing less and less of him. Did I occupy such a small corner in his mind that he needed someone to remind him I was his daughter?

Of course, Daddy loves me! Didn't he fall to his knees the moment he saw me, fling his arms wide open and sing out in his bass baritone, "Here comes my darling girl"? When I arrived for a daylong visit doggedly arranged by my mother, didn't he parade me in front of fellow actors, cronies, and hangers-on? "This is my daughter, Christopher, you know, my eldest, my firstborn. Isn't she wonderful?" And after the hugs and greetings bordering on euphoria, didn't he immediately hand me over to his secretary, his assistant, or whoever volunteered to look after me?

"Your daddy is really sorry he can't spend more time with you . . ."

"I know. He has to work."

Orson Welles could not be my daddy for more than a moment here and there. That was all I could expect of him. Moments that dazzled and then vanished like fireflies on a summer night.

A CONSTANT STREAM of people visited our house on Bedford Drive. Directors and producers came to see Charlie, closeting themselves for hours in his study. Screenwriters came to work with him. Actors dropped by for a drink or a swim. Before I was sent off to bed, my skill as a maker of dry martinis was much in demand. Usually I fell asleep to the sounds of raucous laughter and thunderous splashing as people dived into the pool, with or without their clothes. Sometimes drunken party guests stumbled into my quarters, such as the time I walked into my bathroom and found two naked bodies contorted on the floor. They stopped whatever they were doing long enough to smile up at me, "Oh, hello, Chrissie. What are you doing here?"

"You're in *my* bathroom," I told them in the icy voice my mother would have used.

"Oh, are we? Then be a good girl and let us use it for a while. Close the door behind you . . ."

Then there were Charlie's bridge cronies, all of them male and as serious about winning as though they were fighting World War Three. The slightly sinister crew began arriving in the late afternoon and usually stayed until three or four in the morning. Sometimes they stayed well past sunrise, and when I came down the stairs in the morning, I found grizzled bodies snoring on the sofas.

Mother had installed gaming tables in an alcove off the living room, and Charlie was forever urging her to be his partner, but she declined the honor. Normally the most mild-mannered of men, he had been known to shout, curse, and threaten divorce when she played the wrong card. So the war games began without her, and before long the air was so thick with tobacco smoke that it was difficult to make out the cards. Still, I did my best, but after the time I ran around the tables, announcing the cards in each player's hand, I was no longer allowed within ten feet of them.

The well-known screenwriter Ben Hecht often came to our house to work with Charlie. A dour, self-important man, he rarely said more than a terse hello to me, and if I hung around more than a few minutes, he would turn to Charlie with a weary sigh and ask when "Orson's kid" was going to leave them in peace. It was clear from his tone that his dislike of Orson Welles had become attached to me.

It had never occurred to me before the move to Beverly Hills that being "Orson's kid" might be to my disadvantage. In my new public school, derisive cries of "Hollywood brat! Hollywood brat!" followed me down the hallways, and a bunch of older bullies took to cornering me and stealing my lunch money. "Where you'd get a name like Christopher, you little snot nose!" they jeered. "Oh, your daddy gave it to you? Did he think you were a boy, yah, yah . . ."

While I was learning not to reveal to anyone who my father was, the words "Orson's kid" might as well have been branded on my forehead. One day, as school was letting out, a teacher I didn't know stopped me in the hall and asked, "Are you Christopher Welles?" I nodded, anticipating her next question.

"Is it true your father is Orson Welles?"

"Yes." I looked down at my shoes as though I had admitted to something shameful, hearing my inquisitor suck in her breath.

"Oh my," she said rather lamely, then gushed, "I would *love* to have his autograph." When I did not offer to get it for her, mumbling that my father was out of town and I did not know when he would return, she let me go.

It wasn't just the teachers. The same kids who hollered "Hollywood brat!" also wanted my father's autograph. "Autographs are silly," I told them.

"So you won't do it?"

"No. I'm not going to bother my daddy to get you a stupid autograph."

"Listen to her! Stuck-up Hollywood brat!"

I didn't tell the autograph seekers that the real reason for my unwillingness was that I had no idea when I would see my father again.

My MOTHER MAY have given up the battle to get my father to increase my child support, but she held fast to her determination that he was to see me as often as he could manage it. First thing in the morning, even before Marie brought her breakfast tray, she called my father's secretary. "What do you mean Mr. Welles doesn't have the time to see Chrissie! Tell him to *make* the time!" The crack-of-dawn calls continued until I had been squeezed into my father's calendar. Then, on the morning of the appointed day, Mother was once again on the phone with the beleaguered secretary. "Now you be sure to remind Orson he's having lunch with Chrissie and to send his car for her at noon."

How many times did I change my clothes that morning? I drove Marie crazy, demanding she braid my hair this way and that way until I was satisfied. When the clock struck twelve, I waited in the front hall. And waited. At the slightest noise, I darted out to the driveway thinking Shorty had come for me at last, only to trudge back to the hall. Hours slid by, but I refused to move from my lookout post. The sun was setting the tops of the palm trees on fire, and I was concluding that Daddy must have meant dinner, not lunch, even though it was usually lunch and not dinner. Wait! Wasn't that crunch on the gravel his car after all?

All that long afternoon, Marie appeared from time to time, shaking her head. I pretended not to see her familiar, comforting shape. She was short, plain, and stout, my Marie, and her wiry hair stuck out from her head as though her finger were permanently lodged in an electric socket. "Will you come to your senses, Madam," she asked in her soft brogue, "or are you going stand there until the cows come home?"

"There are no cows in Beverly Hills," I informed her.

"Ach, you're a stubborn one, you are. You'll be the death of me yet!"

When darkness fell, and still the phone hadn't rung with an excuse, an apology, or a dinner invitation from "Mr. Welles," I began to cry. And there was Marie, hands on her hips, announcing, "We've had quite enough nonsense for one day, we have!" And with that, she led me unresisting to the kitchen where she gently dried my eyes and we ate our cold supper with no need of further conversation.

SEVERAL TIMES A year and always at Christmas, our household moved up to San Simeon, or Hearst's Castle as it is known today, where Charlie's aunt, Marion Davies, lived with William Randolph Hearst. Aunt Marion, who had lost most of her relatives, was extremely close to Charlie. Nor were they that far apart in age: Marion had been thirteen when Charlie was born on December 31, 1910. "We're more like partners in crime than aunt and nephew," he liked to say. They certainly shared the same irreverent humor and irresistible urge to tease "Pops," Marion's affectionate name for Hearst. During a long, dull evening at San Simeon, Charlie and Marion would exchange a wicked glance and then begin turning somersaults in unison on one of Hearst's priceless Persian rugs.

Marion Davies was past forty-five when I knew her, and was growing pleasantly plump. No longer the stunning young blond Hearst had plucked from a Broadway chorus line, she was still warm and bubbly and had an infectious laugh. Marion reminded me of Rita because she was so genuine, so incapable of artifice or pretension. I liked her for not trying to conceal her slight stammer. When Aunt Marion threw her arms around me, stuttering, "Chrissie d-d-darling!" I knew she was sincerely glad to see me. She wasn't batting her false eyelashes at me or looking over my head and flashing her teeth in a phony smile because someone more important had walked into the room behind me.

On the other hand, I dreaded having to stand before the tall, imposing man I was instructed to call Mr. Hearst. No matter how many times we had already met, I shook his hand and dropped a curtsy as though it were the first time. Something in his manner suggested I was not being formal enough, and, if I knew what was good for me, I would kneel before him and put my forehead to the floor. He looked so old to me—well over a hundred, I figured—that I couldn't meet his gaze. His hand felt as cold as his blue eyes bearing down on me. "How do you do, Miss Welles?" He had a high-pitched, squeaky voice that didn't go with the rest of him.

"How do you do, Mr. Hearst?"

"I hope you will enjoy your stay at San Simeon." He attempted a smile, and I assured him that I would try my best.

I was too young to appreciate the irony of my position—both the child of the man who had made *Citizen Kane* and the stepchild of Marion Davies's beloved nephew. Marion, Charlie, and my mother feared that the mere sight of "Orson's kid" might give Pops apoplexy, and so, whenever we stayed at San Simeon, I was kept out of the way as much as possible. Not understanding why I was being isolated made it hard for me to enjoy myself during these visits.

Years later, of course, I knew along with the rest of the world that *Citizen Kane* had so enraged William Randolph Hearst that he became determined to wreck my father's career and drive him out of Hollywood. What is still not clear to me is whether Hearst ever saw the offending movie himself. My father told me that while in San Francisco for a showing of *Citizen Kane*, he happened to find himself in the same elevator with Hearst. "I invited him to come to my picture, and he pretended not to hear me." While the story might vary each time my father told it, it was inevitably accompanied by a burst of wheezy laughter and the lighting of a fat cigar.

Mother told me she had seen a pre-release print of *Citizen Kane* with Hearst and Marion at San Simeon a year after she and Charlie were married.

It was customary to show pre-release features after dinner in Hearst's private movie theater with its red plush seats and wood-paneled walls lined with gilded statues. "The theater looked like a small version of one of those garish, overdone movie palaces from the 1920s," Mother recalled. "After the screening, WR and Marion retreated to their private suite without saying one word to anyone, while Charlie and I held our breath in horror."

Yet Charlie had no memory of this screening. He insisted to me on several occasions that neither Hearst nor Aunt Marion ever saw *Citizen Kane*. Their condemnation of the picture rested on the outraged reactions of loyal friends who saw it as a cruel and unwarranted attack, particularly on Marion. In Charlie's view, Hearst was more distressed by the movie's insinuation, through the character of Susan Alexander, that Marion was a failed and pathetic alcoholic than he was by any unflattering references to himself.

So who was telling the truth? I'll put my money on Charlie.

Certainly the San Simeon I knew bore little relation to Xanadu, the fictitious castle in *Citizen Kane*. While we sometimes drove up to San Simeon—Mother, Charlie, Marie, and I—we usually took the train from Los Angeles to San Luis Obispo, a distance of some two hundred miles. We were met at the station by one of the hired cars Hearst used to ferry his guests to the castle. The last leg of the journey took about an hour and a half over bumpy dirt roads. It didn't matter how many times I had made the trip. Each visit I felt as excited as a child on her first African safari.

We entered the wilderness of foothills, valleys, and open plains that was San Simeon, at the time a vast estate of about 240,000 acres. From the edge of the property to the castle on the hill, Hearst's private road stretched more than six miles, but even from far away, we could see the twin towers of the main house, La Casa Grande. In poor weather when the towers were wrapped in mist, it looked like a hilltop castle in a fairy tale. As our car bumped along in low gear, we had to roll up the windows to keep out the dust.

At one time Hearst had owned the largest private collection of wild animals in the world. Arriving guests had seen giraffes nibbling on treetops, impala leaping across the road, and yaks lumbering down to a water hole. Except for the bears, lions, tigers, and other dangerous animals that were kept caged in San Simeon's zoo, the animals roamed free, which made our approach to the castle feel like a daring adventure in the wild. I was fascinated by the llamas grazing near the road, lifting their heads to watch us pass—they looked so haughty and full of themselves—but I also liked the zebras galloping across

Virginia and her second husband, Charlie Lederer, at
San Simeon, 1940.

the plains, the prancing ostriches, and the leaping kangaroos. The road was
marked with signs reading ANIMALS HAVE THE RIGHT OF WAY, and I remember
that one time we sat in the car for close to an hour, waiting for a bison to
move out of the road.

When at last we pulled up in front of the castle, we were met by the shouts
and hammering of workmen. "When is WR going to *finish* San Simeon?"
Charlie asked of no one in particular. We all knew the answer: "Never!" The
building and remodeling would go on until Hearst's failing health forced him
to leave San Simeon forever on May 2, 1947. Until that day, some part of the
castle was always covered in scaffolding; the guest villas, swimming pools,
and gardens continued to evolve; and the entire castle complex changed from
one visit to the next like an epic in endless revision. We might arrive in time
to see a fountain being ripped out or a terrace being moved because the newly
planted flower beds needed to be in the shade and not in the sun. Whatever
we had admired the last time was bound to have changed. An entire floor
might be redone to accommodate some works of art Hearst had just acquired,
or what had been an overstuffed room a few months ago was now an open
space filled with statuary and leafy plants. Yet the overall effect was one
of opulent rooms bathed in light, offering unlimited comfort and pleasure.
There was none of the gloom my father evoked in Xanadu with its sinister
front gate, its lonely, gargantuan rooms.

As soon as we arrived, Mother and Charlie went off to their guest villa, and I would see even less of them than I did at home. Marie and I were put in "the tower," which seemed all the more remote because we had to take an elevator to reach our rooms. Mine had a trundle bed and round walls covered in a mural depicting *The Massacre of the Innocents.* It showed Roman soldiers hacking off babies' heads, blood spurting from mutilated bodies. Now I realize it was probably a Renaissance masterpiece, but at the time, it filled me with horror.

During the day I spent as little time as possible in my room. Each morning, Marie and I went down to the dining room where we had breakfast by ourselves. It must have been festive at night, when the immense chandelier was lit and dozens of guests sat around the fifty-four-foot-long table, talking and laughing. In the early morning only Marie and I were there, dwarfed at one end of the table.

After breakfast we went out to see the gardens, the pools, the fountains, and all the delights of the castle grounds. In fine weather Marie and I spent most of the day outdoors. We might go farther afield and stroll under the mile-long pergola covered with grapevines. The air was fragrant with flowering bushes and the fields bright with lime, lemon, and tangerine trees. Yet, in spite of the loveliness around us, I often felt sad and out of place. The only children at San Simeon were made of stone and stood in the middle of fountains without their clothes on.

Several times a day I asked Marie when we could go to see Aunt Marion. If it was before lunch, Marie reminded me, "Now you know Miss Davies spends the morning in her room and doesn't see anyone before lunch." After lunch Marie's predictable answer was, "We had best keep to ourselves." When I persisted that I didn't see *why* we had to "keep to ourselves" *all* the time, Marie sighed. "Now, Madam, I've told you a hundred times if I've told you once. We're to stay out of Mr. Hearst's way and everybody else's for that matter. You are *not* to go and bother the big people until they ask for you."

"Yes, Marie."

There was only one time Mother, Charlie, or Marion asked to see me, and that was before dinner, usually served at nine p.m. By then I was in my pajamas and ready for bed, but Marie led me to the door of the assembly room, where "the big people" were gathered. Hearst permitted his guests to have one alcoholic drink, and only one, before the evening meal, but as I later learned from Charlie, Marion was adept at hiding bottles of gin in toilet tanks, which accounted for the inordinate number of "powder rooms" at San Simeon. Her friends smuggled bottles of booze in their luggage and hid them in their rooms, but if they were caught, they were likely to find their bags packed and out in the driveway. In any event, by the time drinks were handed around in the assembly room, everyone except Hearst had already had a few. Laughter was loud and long as Charlie demonstrated his skill at standing on his head.

I stood in the doorway, watching. Finally Mother noticed me and called out, "Hello, Chrissie darling!" Then Marion rushed over, flushed and out of breath, dropped to her knees, and gave me a welcoming hug. "How are you, darling? Are you having fun? What did you do today? Tell me everything." I started to, but she was already on her feet, talking to someone else. So I made the rounds, saying good night, shaking hands, smiling at whoever came lurching forward, drink in hand, to holler as though I were deaf, "Good night, Chrissie!" Then Marion, Charlie, and several others began to sing "Good night, Chrissie!" to the tune of "Good Night, Ladies!" The "big people" were howling with laughter when Marie led me away to the tower.

THE LAST LUNCH I had with my father at the Brown Derby, a popular eatery in Hollywood's heyday, is the one I remember the best. "I'm going to Italy in a few weeks," he told me, after we had made our way through the throng of autograph hunters, waiting to pounce on the stars who ate here, some so often they had their designated booths in the lively, smoky interior of the restaurant, shaped like a bowler hat. We were given a less prominent booth near the kitchen, a sign of my father's lowered status in Hollywood, although it didn't register on me at the time.

"Do you know where Italy is, Christopher?"

"No, Daddy."

"No? What on earth do they teach you in that school of yours? What grade are you in now?"

"Third grade, Daddy. They skipped me again."

"Don't they teach geography in the third grade?"

"Yes, but we've only studied the geography of California."

"What? This is appalling!" His thunderous voice made the people in the next booth jump as though they had been shot. Then they swung around and stared at us, open-mouthed. To add to my embarrassment, the waiter appeared, shook out a napkin, and tied it around my neck as though I were a baby in a highchair. "We will have to do something about your education," my father rumbled, but soon he was lost in the delights of studying the menu and conferring with the waiter. "Hmmm. How is the lobster bisque? Is it made with fresh cream? And how are the oysters served." I could see him tasting each dish in his mind, lost in delicious hesitation, as though his well-being depended on whether he ordered the bisque, the oysters, the steamed mussels, or something called *gazpacho*. Meanwhile, I kicked my legs against the hard underside of the booth and studied the signed caricatures of movie stars that covered the walls, looking for people I knew. In the end, I predicted, my father would order what he usually did when we ate here: a Cobb salad, followed by another and another. He would tell me once again that the dish had been invented by the owner of the Brown Derby, David Cobb, and that whenever I ate in restaurants—not a frequent event in my nine-year-old life—I should order what the restaurant was famous for, listed on the menu as *the specialty of the house*. Now he lowered the menu and bathed me in one of his marvelous smiles. "What will you have, darling girl?"

"A hamburger and a vanilla milkshake, please."

"Again?" The smile faded.

"Yes, please, Daddy."

"Why don't you be more adventurous today? How about some oysters?" I made a face. "Have you ever eaten one?" I shook my head. "Then how do you know you won't like it? You may not know where Italy is, but we can certainly do something to educate your palate." A burst of wheezy laughter and a con-spiratorial wink at the waiter. "Bring my daughter a dozen oysters, please."

"Oh no, Daddy, I'll be sick."

"Nonsense. Oysters are good for you."

The next ten minutes were misery. To distract myself from the impending disaster of gagging on the oysters and then having to run to the restroom to throw up, I asked him why he was going to Italy.

"To be in a movie," he said, sighing. "Not mine, unfortunately. Someone else's. But if I want to keep working as an actor, I have to go where the work is, you know."

"Oh."

"Is that all you have to say? Just 'oh'? Don't you want to know *what* movie or what part I'm going to play?"

"Yes, Daddy."

"I see you're as blasé as all the other Hollywood kids, and how I make my living doesn't really interest you."

I didn't know what *blasé* meant, but from his tone, I could tell it was a disappointing quality for me to have. At such moments, the euphoria of being with my father became infused with anxiety. What if I didn't measure up? Could I be myself and also be Orson's kid? At that moment the waiter set before me a plate of oysters, so fishy-smelling my nose began to twitch. I stared down at the fat, grayish white globs stuck to their shells and told myself I might be able to get them down if I closed my eyes and pretended they were raw eggs.

"Now use that small fork to dig one out . . . That's right, Christopher. Now sprinkle a little lemon juice on it. There you go. Don't sniff it, for God's sake. Eat it!"

"Do I have to chew it, Daddy?"

"Down the hatch!" He watched while I poured one down my throat and felt it wiggle as though it were an eyeball blinking open. "Now isn't that delicious?"

"Yes, Daddy," I lied. Then, after a nervous pause, "Do I have to eat them all?"

"Just one more. That's my girl. Now was that so terrible?"

"No."

"You have to *try* things in life, Christopher. There's a great big world out there that has nothing to do with Hollywood. Geography doesn't begin and end with California, you know. Now what shall we order next? I'm going to have another Cobb salad . . ."

"I'll have a hamburger and a vanilla milkshake."

"Dear God, it's hopeless!" He laughed, good-humoredly, though.

The people in the next booth kept gawking at us and whispering among themselves, which meant they must be "civilians" (as movie people referred to anyone who wasn't "in pictures" like themselves). While our neighbors made me uncomfortable, my father paid them no more attention than if they had been flies buzzing on the other side of a screen door. He was between his second and third Cobb salad when one of them approached our booth, armed with a menu and a pen. "May I have your autograph, Mr. Welles?"

"Certainly. Where would you like me to sign?"

"Right here, Mr. Welles, and I just wanted to say . . ." Eager to spout his opinions of *Citizen Kane* and *The Magnificent Ambersons*, the stranger lingered while my father continued smiling, nodding, murmuring, "Thank you so much. That's so kind of you."

Why does this always have to happen when I'm alone with Daddy?

"Autographs are stupid," I burst out after the interloper had returned to his booth.

"Shhh!" My father put a finger to his lips. "I happen to agree with you, but you can't tell a person that something he wants is stupid. That would be very rude."

"But, Daddy," I babbled on, "kids at school have autograph books, and they go around showing them off to other kids and boasting they've got Elizabeth Taylor or Clark Gable, and sometimes they get into fights about who's got the biggest stars in their book. It's so *stupid*!"

"Now I know what to get you for Christmas!" He gave me a twinkling look. "An autograph book!"

"You know, Daddy," I rushed on, "one of my teachers asked me to get your autograph, but I told her you were away, making a movie, and I didn't know when you'd be back."

"You shouldn't have said that." He looked at me reproachfully, then sighed. "What is your teacher's name?" After I told him, he scribbled a message on the back of a menu. "Now you give this to your teacher the next time you see her, and don't ever refuse another request for my autograph."

"All right, Daddy."

"When someone asks for your autograph, they're paying you a compliment, don't you see?"

"But why do they have to bother us when we're having lunch? Why don't you ask them to come back later?"

He laughed though I hadn't meant to be funny. "Well, Christopher, I hope for your sake that you never become famous."

"Oh, I don't want to be famous, Daddy."

"You don't? Why not?"

"I want to be a civilian, like Marie."

"So you're going to grow up to be a nanny. Well, now I've heard everything," and he laughed so long and with such gusto, throwing back his head, his chest heaving, that he had to wipe his eyes with a napkin.

When my father hugged me goodbye that day and told Shorty to drive me home, neither one of us realized that the next time we met, it would not be in Hollywood. In going to Italy, my father assumed he would not be there any longer than it took to shoot his scenes in *Black Magic*. While abroad, he also hoped to find financial backing for a movie of his own based on Shakespeare's *Othello*. He had no idea that his jaunt to Europe to appear in a movie would stretch into years of wandering from country to country, hat in hand.

So ended the Hollywood chapter of our lives.

3

Going to Daddy's School

"If I have to go to Daddy's school in Woodstock, why can't Marie go with me?" I demanded of my mother during the "safe" hour when she was having breakfast in bed. How fresh and beautiful she looked in the early morning, her skin glowing as though a thousand tiny candles had been lit inside her.

"You're too old to have a nanny, Chrissie." She lit an unfiltered Camel cigarette, her hand trembling.

"I'm not too old. I know lots of kids my age . . ." I was not yet ten.

"Besides," my mother rushed on in a too bright voice, "you're going to be living with Hortense and Skipper, and you know how much they love you. Orson lived with them when *he* was a little boy. Why, the Hills are practically your grandparents."

"I don't want to live with them, Mommy."

It was as though she couldn't hear me. "They'll take *marvelous* care of you, you'll see, darling, and after a while you'll love being with them and you won't miss Marie at all."

"I *will* miss her! I will!" I had not meant to shout and stamp my foot. "I want to stay here with Marie and Granddaddy!"

"But not with me, is that it?" Suddenly her voice was icy and her eyes were flashing like blue knives. I started backing toward the door.

"No, Mommy, I didn't mean . . ."

"Whatever you meant, it doesn't matter, because you *can't* stay here." She pushed the breakfast tray off her lap with such force that an empty juice glass fell over. "You know Charlie and I are getting divorced."

"But why, Mommy? Why do you have to get divorced?"

"Oh, really, Chrissie, what a little bore you are!" I could not decide if she was going to leap out of bed and shake me until my teeth rattled or bury her head in the pillows and burst into tears. "Who gives a damn what you want anyway?" she exploded. "You're going to live with the Hills until I can put my life back together again, and that's that. And if you're going to cry, go and do it somewhere else! My nerves are shot to hell this morning!"

I was not going to cry—she was—but I knew better than to rush back to the bed and throw my arms around her. She was no longer the amenable mother of the morning but the edgy woman with the volcanic temper who ruled the rest of the day. I pretended I was leaving, but hovered outside her doorway, listening to her muffled sobs. Soon I would be living in some-place called Woodstock, Illinois, where my father had gone to school, and my mother would be living in New York City. Without me. What would her bedroom in New York look like? Would she decorate it in soft shades of lavender, pink, and gray to match the one she was leaving behind in Beverly Hills? Would I visit her in New York and perch again at the foot of her bed in the early morning? And who would carry in the breakfast tray now that Marie was being "let go"?

I tried to imagine some future time when I would find my mother pound-ing on her portable typewriter at her elegant antique desk, or stretched out on her pink velvet chaise longue, her head raised on a mound of lacy pillows, reading a novel while she nibbled on her nails. *Why can't I live with you in New York? Or with Daddy in Italy? How long are you going to leave me with Granny and Skipper?* Unasked and unanswered, my questions hung in the air, which smelled in equal portions of her spicy perfume and the cigarette butts piled up in crystal ashtrays.

I HAD NOT been a student at Todd School for Boys very long when Skipper, the school's headmaster, wrote to my father in Rome: "A much too efficient secretary ruins approximately every tenth day of a fast ebbing life by placing on my desk a list of parents to whom I owe letters . . . Today your name appears on such a list! I owe you an orientation report. My God!" While Skipper feared "this may herald the end of a beautiful friendship," he went on to report that I was "pretty damn well oriented" and that "if Hortense can stand it . . . I'm now quite certain it will prove really grand for Chrissie." He then repeated to my father what he had written my mother the week before: "The initial cold plunge into her new environment has drawn from Chrissie none of the squeals of terror I anticipated, rather prolonged shrieks of exuber-ant delight."

Left: Roger "Skipper" Hill. *Right:* Hortense Hill.

While I liked living with the Hills in their cozy, rambling farmhouse far from the campus, being the only girl in a school for boys left little room for exuberance. It was with relief that I returned to the farm at the end of the school day and to the unfailing source of warmth and support I found in Granny Hill. Looking back, I doubt that I could have survived my years at Todd without her, and she was to remain, throughout my life, a far more loving mother than my own.

The farm was a soothing place for a high-strung child whose previous world had collapsed without explanation. I liked to sit in the empty barn and listen to the whoosh of wings when barn swallows flew in and out, or lie on my back in fields of alfalfa and listen to the wind rustle through them. If I closed my eyes, I could pretend it was the sound of the ocean on that long-ago beach in Santa Monica, where my father had been close by, and which seemed to me now the only place where I had been truly happy.

Yet I was quite happy when I dashed into Granny and Skipper's bedroom early in the morning and snuggled down between them in their messy bed. (It brought back those sun-drenched mornings I had spent sandwiched between Daddy and Rita in their bed.) Although the Hills looked ancient to a child of ten, they were enjoying a vigorous middle age. Granny was growing stout and matronly but glowed with good health. Skipper's unruly hair had turned bone white, but his unquenchable energy kept him younger than Peter Pan.

On school mornings, I steeled myself when it was time to get into Skipper's dusty, old rattletrap of a car. Hunched over the wheel and humming under his breath, he took the turns as though we were in a stagecoach being chased by bandits, but it wasn't the car ride that bothered me. It was the prospect of walking into my fifth-grade class and hearing someone hiss at my back, "Here comes the *girl!*" This invariably set off a chorus of moans. They could not have sounded more miserable if they had heard all school vacations would be cancelled for the next year.

It was useless to discuss my predicament with Skipper, who thought being the only girl in his school for boys conferred a high degree of distinction on me. "You should be mightily proud of yourself," he had told me more than once. "How many girls get a chance like this?"

"But the boys don't like me, Skipper."

"They will, honey, they will. Just give 'em time to get used to you."

They'd had plenty of time, it seemed to me, and my situation was not improving. If being a girl wasn't enough of a crime in their eyes, I was also the child of Todd's most famous alumnus, a fact I had hoped to keep secret but which everyone on campus had known long before I set foot in the place. During recess some older boys lay in wait for me and began bruising my ears with "Yah! Yah! Orson's little brat. Go back where you came from!" *If only I could . . .*

My efforts at playing first baseball and then football with my classmates failed to win me any converts. Then a bighearted boy named Louis Bernhardt appointed himself my friend and protector. One afternoon after class, we walked around the football field, discussing my predicament. "You can't help being a girl," sympathized Louis, shaking his head, "or having a famous father. It's really a shame . . ."

"What can I do to make the boys like me? There must be something." We trudged on a while in silence.

"I know!" he finally exclaimed. "You can give a party and we'll invite . . ." He reeled off the names of the few boys in our class who were beginning to waver in their opinion of me.

So we went into town, where I spent my entire allowance on candy and other treats. When school let out the next day, Louis and I held our "party" behind some bushes in a secluded corner of the campus grounds. The three boys we had invited started to talk excitedly about the Superman movie they had seen the previous Saturday, and to speculate about what was going to happen when the sequel was shown this coming Saturday. "Shall we let her come with us to the movies?" The hands helping themselves to the last of the candy froze in midair. The boys looked at one another, tentative, while I held my breath. Then, slowly, one by one, they nodded. "Okay, she can come, if she doesn't scream or anything. Girls always start to scream when . . ."

"Chrissie won't scream," Louis assured them. "I'll sit next to her and hold her hand so she won't be scared."

So ended my days of taunts, snickers, and hissed insults in the schoolroom. My new friends saw to it that the other boys left me in peace.

On Saturday mornings, we insatiable fans of Superman, Batman, and Spiderwoman trooped to the picture show in town, stopping first at the candy store to stock up on Mars bars. And I am proud to say I watched these movies with as much gusto as the boys around me, stamping and yelling when our heroes triumphed over evil, falling silent during the suspense-ridden scary parts, and though I had to clutch Louis's hand from time to time, not once did I scream. Not once.

SKIPPER CONTINUED TO send reports of my activities to my father in Rome in which he indulged his love of hyperbole. "Last Saturday, in my innocence," he wrote him, "I suggested she write a play for Valentine's Day presentation. Now her once beloved ice skates lie in the corner like empty saddles in the old corral. I rather expected this activity would open up a new vista of delight, but I was unprepared for the completeness, nay violence, of her ecstasy. Over the weekend Hortense had to resort to force-feeding her while her hand still clutched a poised pencil and her brain still clutched a dancing ballerina's problem of outwitting a horrible giant. She couldn't possibly have been as thrilled and excited if she had just discovered the ultimate rewards of sex. Where this will lead, God knows. And when she tells me she plans to be: Author, Producer, Director, and Principle [sic] Actor, you will sympathize, I trust, with my solemn wonder."

Did Skipper really believe I was growing up in my father's likeness, or was he merely flattering his former protégé? In any event, I was experiencing, as my father had before me, Skipper's remarkable ability to instill confidence in the young and make them believe they can do anything.

One day he took me to the airfield where he kept his own cub plane. Once aloft, he turned over the controls to me and said, "Now it's your turn to fly, honey."

"But I don't know how," I wailed.

"Now, Chrissie, there's nothing to be scared of. You're a smart gal and flying is a cinch. Look, put your hands here, that's right, move this a little to the left, that's it, hold her steady now . . ."

How calm he sounded, how sure of me. He had moved out of the pilot's seat to sit behind me, and a sudden suspicion made me swing around. "Am I flying this plane, Skipper, or are you?" As I spoke, the plane took a sudden dip downward.

"Lesson number one," drawled Skipper in his Midwestern twang. "Don't look over your shoulder when you're piloting a plane. Keep your eyes fixed on the horizon, that's the girl, and use it as your guide."

"I'm flying! Look, Skipper, I'm really flying!"

"Told you it was a cinch."

Skipper took the same breezy approach with me when I wanted to be in the school talent show. "Of course, you can be in the show," he assured me. "You were born for the stage like your dad. How old are you now?"

"Ten."

"Well, then, you're a year ahead of him." Skipper showed me some stills from 1920 productions of the Todd Troopers, as the show was called in my father's time. I was amazed to see a chorus line of young Todd boys sporting wigs, makeup, dresses, and silk stockings. "Folks found it hilarious in those days," Skipper explained. "Believe it or not, we weren't the only all-male school putting on a girlie show."

"Did Daddy dress up like a girl, too?"

Skipper laughed, shaking his head. "By the time he was eleven, Orson was just the right shape and size for the chorus, but once you heard him speak, it was out of the question. He had that *same* remarkable voice back then, and he already had an adult stage presence. No, we gave our prodigy the juvenile lead in our show called *Finesse the Queen* even though he was shorter than his leading lady." And Skipper fished out a photo of my chubby, eleven-year-old father, radiating confidence in his dress suit, white shirt, and tie as he stands surrounded by female impersonators looming over him in veils and harem outfits.

By my day, the Todd Troopers had evolved into the Bach to Boogie Show, which included anything and everything except boys imitating girls. Once a year Skipper took the show on the road, and we played to full houses in Chicago, Detroit, and other Midwestern cities. It was an incredible opportunity for a young person to experience the theater in a professional setting.

I had my own act impersonating Ethel Merman, the star of *Annie Get Your*

Gun. I had seen the musical during a visit with my mother in New York, and for the rest of my stay I had amused her and her friends by imitating Merman's brassy voice, swagger, and sass. As a parting gift, my mother gave me a recording of the show, which I played until I knew every song by heart.

Dressed in buckskins, boots, and a cowboy hat, I toted a rifle and belted out two of Merman's hit songs: "You Can't Get a Man with a Gun" and "There's No Business Like Show Business." Accompanying me were half a dozen Todd seniors in cowboy outfits, forming a half circle behind me, crooning and strumming on guitars. I threw myself into my Ethel Merman impersonation with the same enthusiasm and lack of self-consciousness I had felt playing Macduff's son. And what fun it was, being on the stage, much better than being in the movies. There was no waiting around day after day, wondering when they would get to my scene, no endless takes when they finally did. I could stride out in my cowgirl outfit, do my act once, and then bow to waves of applause. What would Daddy think of me now?

"YOUR FATHER'S HERE, Chrissie . . ."
"He's come all the way from Rome to see you . . ."
"He's busy with Skipper now, but you'll see him later at the farmhouse."
The school day passed in a delirium. A teacher helped me find Rome on a spinning globe, but I had no clear idea of how far away it was from Woodstock, Illinois. Rome might as well be in another galaxy. Nor did I dare believe that when the school day was over at last and I burst through the farmhouse door, I would smell cigar smoke and hear a bass voice booming, "Is that my darling girl?"

And yet that is exactly what happened.

There was my father in Granny's kitchen, more handsome and imposing than ever, seated at the head of the oak table as though he sat there every day. "Daddy!" I shrieked, flinging my arms around his neck. At that precise moment, the door of the Swiss cuckoo clock on the wall flew open, the wooden cuckoo popped out, and sang its two notes, making us laugh. (I was to wonder in later years if the speech about the cuckoo clock that my father contributed to the character of Harry Lime in *The Third Man* originated in Granny Hill's kitchen.)

How strange it was to be eating dinner with my father as if no time had passed since our last meal together at the Brown Derby in Hollywood! He had put on weight since then, and his eyes were bloodshot, but he was still a vital presence. As old as he looked to my ten-year-old eyes, he was barely thirty-three. "How's my darling girl?" he asked, but before I could tell him the story of my life, he began talking to Granny and Skipper as though I were not there. That, at least, was familiar.

Flushed in the face, an apron tied around her ample waist, Granny was bustling from oven to table and back again. "Now this is what I call real food," my father exclaimed each time she set down a dish before him.

"Oh, get on with you," Granny scoffed, wiping her hands on her apron. "There must be plenty of real food in Rome by the look of you."

"Now Horty, let's not have any cracks about my weight." He gave one of his loud laughs that had no humor in it. "Let's talk about Christopher instead. I hear she's been pounding the boards in your variety show. May a concerned Todd parent ask why he was not informed of your theatrical designs on his child?"

"You should have seen her, Orson," Skipper enthused. "She was a real trooper. Brought down the house, too." Then turning to me. "Come on, Chrissie, show your dad what you can do."

"Now, Skipper, don't make the child sing for her supper."

"I don't mind, Daddy."

"Well, I do." He laid a restraining hand on my arm. "Pay no attention to Skipper, whatever he tells you, and stay away from the stage."

"Why, Daddy?"

"A life in the theater will only make someone like you unhappy."

"But it was such fun . . ."

"What did I tell you, Orson?" Skipper grinned.

"Well, I can see I'm outnumbered here." He paused to spear another piece of Granny's fried chicken. "Seriously, I wish you two would point Christopher in another direction. She's much too bright to be an actress. I tell you, she'll be *miserable* in that kind of life."

"But *you're* not miserable, Daddy, and *you're* an actor."

"How do you know I'm not miserable? As a matter of fact, I *hate* acting and I only do it because I have to." He held me in his gaze, and I wondered if he could see I did not believe him.

"Chrissie does like to write stories," Granny put in. "You should hear what her English teacher says."

"There you go!" my father roared delightedly.

"She also loves to play the piano. She's taking lessons with—"

"No, no, a musician's life is almost as bad as an actor's. Frankly, I don't care what she does as long as she doesn't end up in Hollywood with all those cretins."

"What's a cretin?" I asked without getting a response.

"Well, acting does run in the family," Skipper drawled, surveying me with his keen, sailor-blue eyes. "Chrissie gets it from her mother, too."

"Virginia was all ambition and no talent," my father rumbled. "Thank God she finally came to her senses and gave it up."

"You didn't think so once," Granny observed. "The way I remember it, the two of you set off for New York to make theater history, and God himself couldn't have stopped you . . ."

The adults went on to talk of other things. "May I be excused, please?" I asked.

"Yes, honey, run along now."

In the doorway, I turned to look one last time at my father, closing my eyes and then opening them again to make sure he was still there. Then I lingered

"All he had to keep him company . . . was his dog, Caesar."

long enough to catch Granny's loving smile and Skipper's approving wink—long enough to feel them reassuring me that I could be anything and anybody.

I LIVED WITH the Hills for almost two years while my mother was between marriages. Along with unstinting love and encouragement, they gave me my first taste of being part of a family and living a normal life. As an adult, whenever I presented Skipper with my gratitude, he would drawl, "You weren't with us nearly long enough," but those few years had been crucial to me, and the relationship they began with the Hills would have meaning and importance for the rest of my life.

The Hills were also my major connection to the young Orson Welles. As an adult I often visited them in their Woodstock farmhouse. Over the years they brought alive for me the remarkable boy my father had once been. Typically, I sat beside Granny, the two of us pouring over her scrapbooks and photo albums while she exclaimed, "If only you could have known him back then, Chris. Your dad was such a sweet boy before fame spoiled him."

"Now, Horty," Skipper never failed to correct her, "you know damned well he was a ham and a phony even then." Too restless to sit with us on the sofa, Skipper was invariably pacing up and down, combing his mane of white hair with an impatient hand, picking up this and that and putting it down again. "Don't you remember Orson told us he was born at six a.m. in Kenosha, when all the factories are supposed to open up? The moment he was born—he got this from his mother, he says— every factory bell and whistle went off for miles around." Skipper snorted. "Well, I believed this malarkey until Doctor showed me Orson's birth certificate, and it turns out our boy was born at 7 a.m." (Doctor was the way we referred to Maurice Bernstein, a Russian émigré who practiced medicine and had insinuated himself into the Welles household.)

"Well, Orson *was* born in the morning and in Kenosha," Granny observed with a chuckle. "That much is true anyway."

We were all agreed that George Orson Welles came into the world on May 6, 1915, the second child of Beatrice Ives Welles and Richard Head Welles. Beatrice was thirty-three when Orson was born and Richard forty-two. Orson's only sibling, Richard Ives Welles, was ten years older and, for reasons even the Hills could not explain, a profound disappointment to his parents. At the age of eleven, brother Richard was packed off to Todd School, leaving the field clear for baby Orson.

"Orson told us when he was a child that he didn't have any friends his age,"

Granny recalled, pointing to a photo of an intense little boy in a sailor suit, leaning against a mongrel taller than he is. "All he had to keep him company, he said, was his dog, Caesar."

"He looks so sad and serious," I commented, thinking he could not have been more than five when this picture was taken. "You'd think everyone had deserted him except Caesar."

Granny chuckled. "No wonder Orson has always been crazy about dogs. I suspect he likes them a lot better than people."

"Dogs don't let you down," Skipper observed with a wry laugh.

ANOTHER RELIABLE SOURCE of information about my father's early life was Ada Henderson, a cultivated, elderly widow I knew in Chicago through my maternal grandmother. Ada, who had been a close friend of Beatrice Ives Welles, described her to me as "a cool, self-centered woman who had little tolerance for children in their natural state." It was customary in the 1920s, she explained, for well-to-do parents to leave their children in the custody of nannies and see them, at most, once a day. In any case, Beatrice did not have much time for her younger son. A gifted pianist and composer, she devoted herself increasingly to her music.

From Ada, I also learned that Dick Welles was a remote figure, not often home, and it did not take long for the charming émigré, Maurice Bernstein, to fill his place. Whether to flatter Beatrice or console her for her disappointment in her older son, Doctor pronounced Orson a genius.

Armed with this information, I had more questions to put to the Hills on my next visit with them in their Woodstock farmhouse. "Is it true, that story Doctor tells about how he knew my father was a genius when he was two years old?" I posed the question to Skipper

Hailed as a genius at the age of two.

roaming about the room. Doctor claimed that on first meeting Orson in his crib, the toddler had solemnly declared, "The desire to take medicine is one of the greatest features which distinguishes men from animals."

Skipper hooted. "Doctor's the only person I know who can go one better than your dad when it comes to myth and obfuscation." Only an English teacher, I thought, could blithely drop a word like *obfuscation* into a casual conversation. "We'll never know, one way or the other, since no one but Doctor was on hand to hear this astonishing proof of genius."

My own impression of Doctor, whom I had met as a child, was that he was an oily, silver-tongued phony. Now, aware it was none of my business, I asked Skipper, "Did Doctor really have an affair with my grandmother Beatrice or is that more myth and obfuscation?"

"Well," Skipper drawled, "Beatrice was Doctor's patient all right. She was in poor health for a long time before she died, but maybe she was able to go to bed with him all the same. Does it matter? Whether Doctor slept with Beatrice or not, he wrecked her marriage, which Orson never forgave him for."

I had learned from Ada that my father was four years old when his parents separated. He and his mother moved to Chicago, where they were quickly followed by Maurice Bernstein. Dick Welles, who stayed behind in Kenosha, was now financially independent, having been handsomely rewarded when his manufacturing firm was sold to a larger concern. He promptly retired from his job as the company's treasurer and began a life of drinking, gambling, and womanizing. Increasingly, Maurice Bernstein took over the role of Orson's father, to the point that the boy started calling him "Dadda."

"Orson never talked about it," Granny mused, "but he had to feel as every child does when his parents separate and his mom takes up with someone new."

In one camp stood Orson's tall, dark-eyed mother, a strong woman ahead of her time, more handsome than beautiful. "She had a voice like an oboe," my father once told me, "and she could mesmerize you with her charm." In the other camp was Orson's father, a diffident man who drank too much.

"What was my grandfather like?" I asked Skipper, who had met him many times.

"Kind of dull, to tell the truth. Also kind of pathetic once the drinking got heavy. And he was dead set against Orson having anything to do with the theater. He'd come to Todd to see Orson in a play, and then he'd stand in the back of the auditorium and sneak away before the final curtain. That really hurt your dad, that his father wouldn't come backstage. Damn it, Dick should have gone backstage and said hello to his kid!"

"Maybe he was too drunk," I offered, but Skipper would accept no excuses.

"No, he was a lousy father, but I have to say this for him. He was a class act, a real gentleman. Orson loved him a lot more than he deserved and never stopped trying to turn him into something he wasn't."

True. Whenever I asked my father to tell me about *his* father, I was treated to another tale about Dick Welles, the brilliant inventor, or Dick Welles, the business tycoon. Warming to the subject, he went on to describe his father as the urbane world traveler relaxing in first-class limbo on ocean liners; or the international playboy who broke the bank at Monte Carlo; or the witty raconteur who kept bars and pubs throughout the British Empire open until dawn.

On the other hand, Ada had told me the *real* Dick Welles would have preferred that his wife give up her musical aspirations after their marriage and devote her mornings to the dressmaker and her afternoons to bridge games and ladies' teas. He was dismayed by reports from Chicago that Beatrice was holding weekly musical soirees and exposing young Orson to a bunch of "long-haired arty types."

"It was my mother who wanted me to learn the piano," my father once told me when he was reminiscing about his childhood. "She made me practice for hours on end every day—scales, scales, and more scales. She hired a wretched spinster lady who stood over me and made sure I did it. You have no idea how I *hated* the piano—not like you, Christopher. You owe your musical gifts to your grandmother Welles, you know." One day, my father went on, he was so fed up with practicing that he climbed out the window and stood on the narrow ledge, threatening to jump if he was made to play another scale. "The spinster lady screamed hysterically for my mother who was in the next room." He paused dramatically.

"And . . . what happened?"

"I heard my mother say, as cool as you please, 'Well, if he wants to jump, let him jump.'" He began to laugh uproariously.

"She said that?"

"If she hadn't, I wouldn't be here to tell about it." When I still looked disbelieving, he explained that his mother, who knew him "inside out," understood how the melodramatic gesture of "stepping off into space" would have appealed to him. "So, she had to kill my act, you see. When I realized she wasn't going to rush to my side, fall on her knees, and weep and plead with me not to take my life, I climbed back into the room."

"Then what did you do?"

"I sat down at the piano and started playing those dreadful scales again."

Unlike the endless practicing, my father recalled how much he enjoyed mingling with the musicians and theater people who flocked to his mother's home in the evenings. At these gatherings he was treated like an adult, encouraged to recite epic poems by heart or otherwise amaze his mother's friends. The moment he became "boring," it was back to the nursery. So young Orson learned to be nimble-tongued and entertaining—traits he would retain long after he had escaped into fame and adulthood. "I was always determined," he told me in the voice of one who had thrown off a terrible illness, "to rid myself of childhood."

Beatrice Ives-Welles, as she billed herself, became a performing artist of some renown, devising a unique one-woman show in which she played her own compositions on the piano while reciting poetry. Unfortunately her career was cut short by increasing bouts of ill health. On May 10, 1924, just four

Beatrice Ives Welles—"his mother and his muse."

days after Orson's ninth birthday, Beatrice Welles died at the age of forty-two. "Ever since then," my father confided, "I've never wanted to celebrate my birthday."

Granny believed he never got over losing his mother at such a young age. "She had been dead two years when he came to us at Todd, and already he was making up stories about her."

It no longer mattered who Beatrice Welles had been in real life. In her son's eyes, she grew ever more beautiful, brave, and amazing, until she became a crack shot who could shoot straighter than Annie Oakley, and a suffragette who had staged more protest marches than Susan B. Anthony. True, she had not loved him enough; she had exiled his father and thrown open the door to Doctor, the fox in the chicken coop; but she lived on in his memory as tough, exciting, glamorous. The woman, real and invented, who had opened his ears to music, his eyes to art, and his mind and heart to the theater. His mother and his muse.

TODD SCHOOL WAS a strong point of connection between my father and me. "You were the lucky one," he laughed during one of our reminiscences in later years, "because when you went to Todd, Skipper was the headmaster and the place had become a paradise for boys." I didn't want to point out that when I went to Todd, it was not exactly a paradise for girls. "I had to contend with Nobel Hill, you see," my father went on, referring to Skipper's stern, Bible-pounding father, "the same headmaster who'd expelled my older brother, Richard. You have no idea how terrified I was when I heard they were sending me to Todd."

(Fortunately for Orson the schoolboy, by the time he arrived at Todd, Nobel was becoming a figurehead, and Skipper was in the process of assuming command, a job he later said he took on with deep reluctance, having envisioned a big-city life in Chicago and a sprightly career in advertising.)

"Do you know what my greatest coup was at Todd?" my father asked me with shining eyes. After an expectant pause, he answered his own question: "Winning Skipper's love. I was just a kid in knee pants, and Skipper was a married man in his midthirties, but it was what the French call *un coup de foudre*. We were fatally attracted to one another, you see. The difference in our ages didn't matter, because Skipper was always younger than me. He had the kind of youth I never had."

"There *is* something ageless about him," I agreed.

"Oh, he'll never grow old. He'll outlive us all!"

"You've often joked that he's a leprechaun in disguise."

"What makes you think I was joking? You know what? I've decided he's really a troll. The kind who lives under a bridge and lies in wait for unsuspecting travelers." He laughed delightedly at his new and improved metaphor, which called up for us both the mischief in Skipper's smile and in the way he crinkled up his sky-blue eyes as he stared off into the distance at something known only to himself. Then my father's face clouded as he remembered what it had cost him to "win" Skipper, universally popular on campus and in constant demand as future headmaster, teacher, and family man. "When Skipper began spending more time with me than anyone else, everyone hated me."

"Not everyone," I suggested. "What about Granny?"

"Hortense resented me, too."

"But Granny loves you like her own son. I know she does." How much like a little boy he looked when the hurt showed through, a little boy with a round, chubby face and a button nose, but he hadn't heard me. He was looking through me, back to a time I couldn't envision, when he had felt the first lashes of hostility, the first stings of envy, when he had learned this was the price he must pay, again and again, for having been born with a superabundance of gifts.

"They all hated me," he said with the sadness of one who believes nothing can alter his fate, "and they still do."

"They may not like you as much as they should, but they don't hate you."

"Dear child! If only it were so . . ."

THE HILLS' THREE children, all of whom I had come to know well, viewed Orson Welles much as he himself viewed Maurice Bernstein: an interloper grabbing love that didn't belong to him. From them I learned that Orson the schoolboy did not find many friends among his peers. Although he was widely admired, he was also seen as imperious and full of himself. He was envied because his close relationship with Skipper gave him privileges not conferred on any other Todd boy before or since. These included a room of his own and permission to cut any class that didn't interest him. Pleading asthma and flat feet, he excused himself from gym and most forms of physical exercise except swimming, which he happened to like. Thus the budding young director was able to devote most of his time and energy to putting on an astounding number of plays. His talent for self-promotion was equally evident: Under an assumed name, he touted his own productions in the school newspaper.

As for Granny Hill, while she did not resent my father as he believed, she did wonder in retrospect whether she had been too permissive, allowing him to take advantage of her easygoing hospitality. Almost every night, to the consternation of the Hill children, young Orson could be found holding forth at the dinner table. And after dinner, he moved into the Hills' bedroom, making himself comfortable on their bed and continuing, as Granny recalled "to talk his head off until we had to throw him out." By that time, it was often two or three in the morning.

"I was always exhausted back then," Granny remembered, "what with staying up every night with Orson and then having my two girls and baby boy to take care of the next day, not to mention all the school stuff I had to do for Skipper."

"Then why did you permit it?" I asked her.

"I should have laid down the law more—I see that now—but if you could have heard your dad, Chris, the way he talked at that age. The ideas he had. The words he used. Skipper couldn't get over it. We'd never had a boy like Orson before. He was so far ahead of himself, it kind of scared us . . ." And she chuckled, remembering those sleepless nights, then heaved a deep sigh. "It's never been easy, loving Orson. You know, whenever he came to see us, he expected to be the center of attention, and our own kids were supposed to take a backseat. I couldn't talk to anyone but him, and if I did, if I turned away or ignored him, he'd look hurt. Why, sometimes he got so upset, he walked right out of the room!"

"Then what happened?"

"Oh, he'd be back before you knew it, ready to charm us again and make us laugh at his stories. Some of them were so preposterous, we couldn't help laughing."

"Orson was a born storyteller all right," chimed in Skipper, who had been listening to our conversation, "but there were times I used to wonder if he was really a kid or a premature old man. Then I'd see how easily his feelings got hurt or how much he wanted everyone to like him, and I'd realize there *was* a kid inside that ancient gent he pretended to be." Skipper fell silent, conjuring up the boy he had lost.

The Hills, I learned, were not the only adults enthralled by Orson the boy. Among the papers my mother left me after her death, I found the journal entries of a woman who had met the prodigy during a school vacation when he was staying with his father. After their initial meeting, she wrote:

> I listened to Orson . . . just home from school, talk. He seems to me to be a precocious child, very gifted in his use of words and interested in art. I can't say he is a very lovable child, but it is no doubt because he has been made so much over that he is too desirous of being the center of attention and has that know-it-all attitude. He's quite interesting, tho, for it's my first experience with anyone of the kind. Mr. [Dick] Welles just dotes on him, calls him "lamb." He is so crazy about him that it's almost pitiful.

The next day, she wrote:

> Orson . . . & I have just come in from a delightful walk. I think it is about 9 [o'clock]. Orson is a great boy—such a complex [mind]. He uses the longest words and talks about things that are most unusual for a boy so young—religion, the universe, etc. He has a great sense of humor, however, which offsets some of this peculiarity, & I like him much better than when we first met. He says even psychologists haven't been able to figure him out. . . .

How my father loved the idea that no one could figure him out; yet it is not so difficult to peer through the fog of "myth and obfuscation" and catch a glimpse of the boy torn between the doting father who called him "lamb" and the wily doctor who called him "Pookles." A boy already troubled by insomnia, who spent a portion of every night measuring how alone in the world he was: his mother dead; his father and Dadda fighting for possession of him but incapable of understanding him; his older brother, Richard, drifting around somewhere, continuing to disappoint his elders.

"That left the burden of achievement on me," my father remembered, "and I couldn't let them down, you see. My parents were larger than life to me, wonderful, mythical, almost fantastical creatures, and more than anything I wanted to please them . . ."

"But your mother was dead," I reminded him.

"They were both dead by the time I was fifteen," he said, "but that didn't change anything, not at all, because the wish to please them has never left me." Lighting a cigar, he puffed on it thoughtfully, while we shared a moment of silence and, I felt, a rare moment of truth.

"EVERY SCHOOL VACATION, I'd get these pathetic calls from Orson's dad, begging me to let his kid spend it with him," Skipper remembered. "Then Doctor'd call me in a tizzy and give me an earful about Dick Welles's drinking and womanizing and what a bad influence he was on the boy." Skipper shook his head with a rueful laugh. "Doctor wanted Orson to spend all his vacations with him and see pratically nothing of his father. The tug-of-war between those two made it really tough on the poor kid."

"Where did my father want to spend his vacations?"

"With his dad, of course. He adored him."

"So what did you and Granny do?"

Orson Welles at fourteen.

"Well, Horty and I couldn't prevent Orson from seeing his father, but we did swing the contest in Doctor's favor. We believed he was a better influence, you see." Granny and Skipper were also impressed by Doctor's new wife, Edith Mason, an opera singer well known in her day.

The Hills might have seen the situation differently had they been privy to Doctor's predilection for creating domestic triangles. I learned from my father that during one school vacation spent in Edith Mason's apartment in Chicago, he found himself living not just with Dadda and the glamorous Edith but with her former husband, the Italian conductor Giorgio Polacco, and their daughter Graziella, all of whom were yelling at one another in several languages. "I couldn't wait to get back to my lonely room at Todd," he recalled with his wheezy laugh. "It was only at Todd that I could be my own person."

He went on to confide in me that much as his father and Dadda despised each other, they were united in their disapproval of the theater as a career. "God forbid that I should become an actor!" he boomed. "My father wanted me to go into business or high finance, and Dadda wanted me to become a musician like my mother."

"And you didn't want to go in either of those directions."

"You bet I didn't!" A burst of laughter. "I was passionate about the theater — putting on plays was all I ever wanted to do with my life — and Skipper, God bless him, was the only one of my elders who encouraged my theatrical ambitions. That's why they call him my mentor, you know." ("Hell, I was never his mentor," Skipper would scoff in his old age. "There was nothing I could teach Orson about acting or the theater that he didn't already know.")

Yet as time went on, Todd was not always the refuge young Orson needed it to be. His father began appearing on campus unannounced and invariably drunk. "Sometimes Orson was so embarrassed, he hid in his room," Skipper remembered. "It got to where Dick Welles was drunk pretty near all the time — the main reason Horty and I didn't think Orson should stay with him. After that hotel burned down, Horty was convinced Orson put his life in danger every time he stayed with him. Well, you know what a mother hen Horty is . . ."

Skipper was referring to the Sheffield Hotel, which my grandfather Welles ran for a time in Grand Detour, Illinois. It had burned to the ground in May of 1928, soon after my father turned thirteen. There are conflicting reports about the fire. The most colorful one occurs in a memoir my father began toward the end of his life at Skipper's urging, only to abandon it after a handful of pages. ("I hate writing about myself," he confided to me at the time. "It's so difficult. I'd much rather write about all the fascinating people I have known.")

In the surviving fragment, eventually published in a 1983 issue of Paris *Vogue* that featured Orson Welles, he is up to his old trick of scattering a few shards of truth among the newly polished myths. And how he leads us on a merry dance as we try to catch him out! He himself had missed the fire, he tells us, having been packed off to boarding school "for the last of my three years of formal education." *But Father Orson, you were only thirteen when the hotel caught fire. You had three more years ahead of you at Todd before you would graduate at sixteen, remember?* Never mind. He describes the scene as though it had unrolled before his eyes, as though he were leaning forward in his director's chair, hunched on the edge of the seat, the air around him echoing his roar of "Action!" Look! The gracious old hotel has just caught fire. Smoke is billowing out of windows and doorways. Upper floors begin to teeter and crumble. Monstrous flames lick the night sky like the yellow tongues of dragons. The cold intensifies the harsh light and the "Christmassy fall of snow." *Christmas in May, Father Orson?* Wait! Here comes Dick Welles, "the suspected arsonist," who looks so much like Errol Flynn that he probably is. He is staggering out of the flames, wearing only a nightshirt. In one hand he carries a parrot cage; in the other, a hand-tinted photograph of "a lady in pink tights," a former sweetheart named Trixi Friganza. Close-up of the *empty* parrot cage. Cut!

Two years after the fire, his father took Orson to China on an ocean liner. They had not been at sea very long before the fifteen-year-old boy realized that his father was in an advanced stage of alcoholism. Dick stayed in his cabin, either too ill or too drunk to function, leaving his son to fend for himself. Touchingly, Orson wrote the Hills that he wished he could "find a drink that wouldn't make him sick." While he took no moral position about his father's drinking, it wasn't easy to travel with a man so drunk that at one point he lost his pants in public.

The Hills maintained that the trip was "pretty much a disaster from start to finish," but my father told me he did not agree. "That trip introduced me to the exotic theater arts of the Far East, and I can't tell you what a strong impression they made on me at the time." When he hadn't been looking after his father, he had been going to the Chinese opera and every other theatrical entertainment he could find. "I'll never forget the elaborate costumes, the masks, the revolving stages . . ." It had been a crash course for him in brilliant stage tricks and exotic effects.

On his return, the Hills made him promise he would not see his father again, unless, by some miracle, Dick Welles reformed. "So I promised," my father recalled, "not because I agreed with them — I didn't think my father's drinking was a terrible thing — but because I wanted to please them."

On December 28, 1930, Dick Welles died alone in a Chicago hotel at the age of fifty-eight. Orson had stayed away from his father during the half year that had elapsed since their return from China. Now he blamed the Hills for exacting such a promise and blamed himself for ignoring his father's entreaties to come and see him. "If I'd gone to see him, he might still be alive," he reproached Skipper. It did no good to point out that the causes of death listed on Dick Welles's death certificate, ironically signed by his arch rival, Maurice Bernstein, did not include filial neglect.

DICK WELLES'S WILL stipulated that Orson choose a legal guardian who would be in charge of him and his inheritance until he came of age. My father immediately approached Skipper, never dreaming the older man would refuse. ("I wasn't even tempted," Skipper confided in me. "I had enough on my hands already.") Although it took some doing, Skipper persuaded Orson to make Maurice Bernstein his guardian, pointing out that "it would break his heart" if he didn't. He made the boy swear he would never let Doctor know he hadn't been his first choice.

My father's sixteenth summer was a turning point in his life. He graduated from Todd, which in those days did not go beyond tenth grade, and then he was in limbo. Doctor was adamantly opposed to his having anything to do with the theater and determined to send him to Harvard or Yale as soon as he could be admitted. Why not spend the summer in a college preparatory school, he suggested? That was the last thing the teenager wanted to do since college held no appeal for him. He enrolled instead in painting classes at the Art Institute of Chicago. While he had a flair for art, particularly the quick, humorous sketch or watercolor, he was far more interested in finding work as an actor or painting scenery for a summer stock company. He placed several advertisements in the Chicago papers and made the rounds of theatrical agencies, but nothing came of it.

Meanwhile, the aspiring young actor was learning to his dismay that he had saddled himself with a wily, tightfisted guardian. Dadda Bernstein made his Pookles plead for every dollar, nor did he spare a penny for Orson's older brother, Richard, who had been locked up the year before in the state asylum in Kankakee, Illinois. One of Dick Welles's last acts had been to commit Richard at the age of twenty-four for reasons that have never been clear.

"Why did they put your brother in a nuthouse?" I once had the temerity to ask my father, bringing a reproving scowl to his face.

"It would behoove you, Christopher, out of respect for your unfortunate uncle to call it an asylum." Subject closed.

However tightfisted Doctor may have been with my father, he had no compunction about using his ward's money to build a lavish home in the leafy town of Ravinia just outside Chicago. The house was for Pookles, he maintained as he moved in his new lady love, Hazel Moore, and her husband Ned, creating yet another domestic triangle. Now that Pookles had a real "home," why was he avoiding it? Doctor professed to be hurt and offended when Pookles preferred his old room at Todd which Skipper had let him keep. Todd would remain my father's base of operations for several years.

During the summer, though, Skipper had little time for him, and in the end young Orson was forced to stay with his guardian's ménage in Ravinia. "It was not a happy feeling to be living in a house furnished mainly with the belongings of my late mother," he recalled to me. In fact, the threesome in Ravinia made him as uncomfortable as he had been during the screaming matches in Edith Mason's apartment. "But Ravinia was even worse," he told me, "because I felt the adults were all against me."

To add to my father's misery, the ragweed was rampant that summer and he was suffering from hay fever and asthma. It became clear to everyone that he could not stay much longer in Ravinia. One torpid night, the subject of what he should do for the rest of the summer was hotly debated, and as my father later wrote Skipper, "Dadda arrived at a momentous decision." It was agreed that Orson should go on a sketching tour of Ireland and Scotland. "Going abroad alone is not quite as unthinkable as joining the theater."

Little did Dadda know that in allowing his beloved Pookles to go to Ireland that summer of 1931, he was also allowing the unthinkable to happen. It was in Dublin's Gate Theatre that Orson Welles, at the age of sixteen, made his professional stage debut. And never looked back.

4

My Father Lost and Found

"I DON'T WANT TO leave you, Granny," I told her through helpless tears, my arms tightly wound around her waist. "Why do I have to live in Rome with Mommy and her new husband? I'm sure they don't want me. I'm sure if you ask Mommy, she'll say—"

"Now, Chrissie, you know your mother loves you and wants you to live with her—"

"No, she doesn't, Granny. She doesn't!"

"There, there, dear, don't get yourself worked up. Just think, you and Orson will be living in the same city again—"

"Daddy's living in Rome?"

"Well, of course he is. You knew that."

"Will I get to see him, Granny?"

"Of course you will, dear. There now, dry your eyes. There aren't many little girls who get to fly to Rome all by themselves on a great big airplane—"

Summer was ending in 1949 when, at the age of eleven, I was put on the plane to Rome with my new passport securely pinned to my undershirt. All the way across the Atlantic, I made up fantastic stories about my life, which I poured into the indulgent ear of the kindly, gray-haired gentleman sitting next to me. He looked at me with growing amazement until, exhausted by my performance, I fell asleep.

En route to Naples, the plane touched down briefly in Rome. When I did not get off with the other disembarking passengers, my frantic mother talked the sympathetic Italian officials into allowing her to board the plane. She found me sound asleep in my seat. It seems my seat companion gave her such an astonished look that when we were out of the airport, she demanded, "What on earth did you tell that man, Chrissie? I won't have you making up stories about me to strangers." I knew it was pointless to explain that my "stories" weren't about her at all.

My first week in Rome passed in a daze. I could not yet believe I had left behind me, like a room abruptly locked in my absence, the bucolic town of Woodstock, Illinois—the town my father once likened to "a wax flower under a bell of glass in the paisley and gingham county of McHenry." Surely I would go back there soon and live again among people who thought well of me—the Hills, their children and grandchildren, the many friends I had made at Todd among the faculty and their children. The conviction that my true home lay among decent, caring folk in small-town America kept me going during the early bewilderment of Rome.

What disconcerted me at first was not the change of locale—the shift from the flat farmlands of Illinois to a lively metropolis filled with history, monuments, and deafening traffic. It was my anxiety about my new stepfather, Major Jack Pringle, and whether or not we were going to get along. When I wasn't worrying about that, I found it exciting to be in Rome. I could see how grand and beautiful it was, unlike anything I had known. We were living in the heart of the city on the Via del Corso, just steps away from the Piazza Venezia. Home was now an elegant second-floor apartment with a ceiling that my mother said belonged in a Renaissance palazzo and looked as though it had been painted by Raphael. In the early morning while I sat alone in the dining room, sipping hot chocolate with steamed milk, I stared dreamily upward at the baby angels flying through rosy clouds and wished hard that I might join them. The frescoes had been discovered by the previous tenants when their maid, dusting for cobwebs, had poked a hole through the false ceiling with her broom, and there they were, as fresh as the day they were painted.

After breakfast I often accompanied Rosina, the woman who cooked and cleaned for us, to the open-air market within walking distance of our apartment. She was stouter than Granny and had a front tooth missing, which did not stop her from beaming at me at every opportunity, and she dressed in black from her head scarf down to her scuffed, lace-up shoes. Although she spoke not a word of English, somehow we communicated with smiles and body language. It was at the noisy, bustling market that I learned my first words of Italian—*pesce* (fish), *peperoni* (green peppers), *pomodori* (tomatoes), and whatever else Rosina was buying that day. How I loved walking through the market, lugging a large, open wicker basket filled with our purchases, admiring the piles of apples or heads of lettuce heaped on the stands, all the vibrant colors, the warring smells of fish and cheese and freshly baked bread. Around me shoppers were haggling at the top of their voices, vendors were yelling back and throwing their hands in the air, then the shoppers edging toward the next stall, the vendors erupting again in a torrent of emotion, and all this commotion over a kilo of onions or a fat wedge of parmesan cheese.

I could enjoy living in Rome, I thought, if only I could live here with Rosina instead of my new stepfather. Many years would pass before I could finally acknowledge his considerable intelligence and charm, but even on our first encounter, I saw how attractive he was, without being handsome. Slim, dark-haired, with a trim mustache and a military bearing, he was an elegant dresser verging on being a dandy, an upper-class Englishman who aped the prejudices of his class and yet was something of a maverick. Firmly believing women were inferior, he nonetheless treated them with the utmost gallantry. "When Jackie lights my cigarette," my mother liked to say, "I feel like I'm a member of the British aristocracy."

My stepfather was a World War Two hero renowned for his six daring escapes from high-security prisons, an accomplished horseman, a crack polo player, and a gifted linguist. While a prisoner of war, he had taught himself Italian, German, Spanish, and French, all of which he spoke fluently. There was much to admire and respect about the man, but I was not his contemporary, nor was I meeting him at a cocktail party when he could have lit my cigarette. Life had cast him as my stepfather, a role for which he had neither the aptitude nor the desire. When Charlie Lederer had married my mother, he had not seen me as a liability, but Jack Pringle's one thought about me was how to get rid of me so he could have my mother to himself.

The battle lines were drawn on my first morning in Rome. Soon after I woke up, I ran into my mother and stepfather's bedroom, just as I used to do when I lived with Granny and Skipper, threw my arms around Jack, gave him an affectionate hug and kissed him on the cheek. Then I bounced out again to have my breakfast in the dining room under the cherubim and seraphim. Later that morning, my mother took me aside. "Jackie doesn't want you rushing into our bedroom in the morning and giving him hugs and kisses, so please don't ever do that again."

I stared at her in bewilderment. "But why not, Mommy?"

She sighed. "I don't know how to explain it to you, Chrissie, but he's English and he went to Sandhurst."

"What's that?"

"A top military academy in England. So, you see, he's not used to being hugged and kissed by a little girl. What you did embarrassed him . . ."

"Don't people hug and kiss one another in England?"

"Don't be exasperating, Chrissie." This was said quietly with a sigh, as though my being exasperating was something she had come to expect, but the cold edge to her voice, the old glint in her eye, were gone. "The point is that Jackie doesn't like it coming from you. He says it's wet."

"What does he mean it's wet?"

"Just don't do it anymore, okay?"

"Okay."

I was left alone in my room to reflect that the mother I had found in Rome was not the same person I had last seen in New York. Here she was fluttery, girlish, and a lot more nervous. I wondered why. Most disconcerting of all, she was beginning to sound vaguely British and to use expressions like "jolly good" and "old chap." She might suddenly come out with a remark like, "I say, we had a ripping time last night at the so and so's, didn't we, Jackie darling?"

Soon after I arrived, we all went for a stroll around the Piazza Venezia, Jackie leading the way and pointing out the sights for my benefit. We began at the foot of the enormous monument to Victor Emmanuel II that dominates the square, a frothy confection in white marble of fountains, statues, and a majestic staircase leading up to the monument itself. I craned my neck to see the colonnade that ran its length and on top of that, at either end, a chariot driven by an angel with outstretched wings. "This was put up fifty years after Italy became a unified country, but the Italians don't like it very much, and I can't say I blame them. It is a bit overdone," Jackie was saying. "They say it looks like a wedding cake. What do you think, Chrissie?"

"I suppose it could be a wedding cake . . . for giants."

Jackie laughed. "Why don't you climb to the top and have a look around? You'll get a splendid view from the terraces. Your mother and I will wait for you here."

I did as I was told, but the "splendid" view was mainly of the traffic careening around the square and of two people who had shrunk in size, my mother and Jackie, seated at the bottom of the staircase and locked in an embrace. Suddenly I remembered Granny's warning before I left Woodstock, which now seemed to have happened a long time ago. "If your mother and Major

Pringle don't want you around all the time, it's because they're still on their honeymoon, and you mustn't let that hurt your feelings, dear." But it did.

On the way back to our apartment, Jackie pointed to a balcony of an imposing building. "Look, Chrissie. That's where Mussolini used to stand and deliver his speeches to the crowd below."

"Who's Mussolini?"

Jackie looked at me aghast, then turned to my mother. "What on earth did she learn at Todd School?" Then back to me. "Didn't you study World War Two in your history classes?"

"No," I mumbled. I could see it would not help to mention that I *had* studied the American Revolution and Civil War since Jackie hadn't fought in either of those wars.

"This is absolutely appalling!" he went on to my mother while I walked glumly behind them, the sidewalk being too narrow to walk three abreast. "No wonder you Americans are so ignorant" (a remark she would not have let pass in the old days).

That evening, while my mother and Jackie were having their cocktails before dinner, my stepfather asked me to draw a freehand map of the United States and then put as many cities as I could on it. I had never drawn such a map before, and it was soon apparent that it was not one of my skills. The only places I was able to include with any certainty of where they were located were New York, Chicago, Woodstock, Los Angeles, and Reno. "Reno!" laughed Jack derisively as he surveyed my pathetic map.

"Well, I did live there twice, you see, to get a divorce," my mother explained in her new, overly bright voice.

"Oh, I see." How the two of them laughed while I sat silently by, wondering why it was *that* funny.

Shortly after that evening, Jackie devised his plan to educate me while we lived in Rome. Even though I was learning more Italian every day, enrolling me in a local school was out of the question. It was also unclear how long we were going to be living in Rome. So Jackie gave me an "assignment" every day: I was to visit one of the city's spectacular sights in the morning, pay close attention to everything I saw there, note my impressions in a notebook I was to carry with me, then come home and write an essay about what I had seen.

I began with the Colosseum, continued with the Forum, which required several visits to explore thoroughly, and gradually progressed to St. Peter's where I spent day after day in the Sistine Chapel, enchanted by Michelangelo's frescoes. There were no lines in those days, no mobs of tourists straining at the ropes, and an eleven-year-old girl could spend hours undisturbed in the chapel, craning her neck toward the magnificent ceiling and scribbling away in her notebook. It amazes me now to recall that in all those solitary days and hours spent wandering around the monuments and splendors of Rome, no one ever bothered me: not a single child molester came forward to interrupt my reverie or note taking for the dreaded essay. At first Rosina accompanied me to the place appointed for my assignment that day, and then came back later to collect me; but once I knew my way around the city, I went every-where alone. I felt as completely safe walking the streets of Rome by myself as I had in that lost and long-ago time, walking the beach of Santa Monica.

I worked hard on my essays, rewriting and copying them several times before I was satisfied. At Todd School, I had excelled in English composi-tion, and I wanted to show Jack Pringle what I could do. I was still bristling at his reference to "ignorant Americans." So, knowing I had done my best, I waited expectantly while he began reading my composition aloud to my mother during their usual cocktail hour before dinner. He had not finished two sentences before he was convulsed with laughter. My errors in spell-ing, which he delighted in pointing out to my mother, who assured him she couldn't spell either, produced fresh gales of merriment while I sat there, crushed and humiliated.

This performance was repeated every time Jackie read one of my essays, and each time it sapped my confidence a little more. His need to put me down, which he would have called "taking me down a peg," was as strong as his need to remove "Orson's kid" from the scene by sending her all over Rome with a notebook. In his eyes I was too full of myself, too forward with adults, too quick to join in the conversation instead of sitting quietly in my corner. Major Pringle lost no time in trying to turn me into a model of manners and British reticence, and on the surface he succeeded. I soon learned to curb my natural exuberance and silence my tongue, but in my heart I fought him like a tiger.

I HAD BEEN in Rome long enough to write several essays about its historical and cultural treasures when one day my mother invited my father to lunch. From the moment he walked through the door, I was struck by the contrast between my burly father with his tousled hair, his crumpled slacks and open-neck shirt, and my suave stepfather with his trimmed mustache, his corduroy pants hot off the ironing board, and an ascot knotted around his neck. How strange it was to see the two men together and feel the tension between them. There was none of the easy camaraderie I had observed between Orson Welles and Charlie Lederer, who had remained good friends. In fact, shortly before my mother and Jackie got married in Paris in May of 1949, my father and Charlie were also in Paris, collaborating on a script for a French film.

While I sat silently at the dining room table, learning to be "seen but not heard," the adults' conversation ranged from the discovery of the extraordinary ceiling in our apartment to what Orson was doing in Rome. "I'm shooting some scenes for my *Othello* at the Scalera Studios," my father told us, then turned his radiant smile on me. "Would you like to come and watch one afternoon, Christopher?"

"Oh yes, Daddy!" I exulted. Jackie gave me a reproving glance. "Yes, *please.*"

Jackie leaned forward in his chair with a feigned show of interest. "Orson, I didn't know you were filming *Othello*. Will it be anything like your *Macbeth*?"

"*I* was in *Macbeth*," I loudly volunteered, ignoring the stony look from my stepfather. "I played Macduff's son," I added, ready to brave anything with my *real* father close at hand.

"We all know that, Chrissie," said my mother in a tired voice.

"Well, *Othello* and *Macbeth* are very different plays, you know, so I could hardly treat them in the same way." My father spoke softly, with careful courtesy, as though addressing a complete idiot.

"Yes, *of course!*" Jackie gave his self-deprecating laugh. "What I meant was, will your *Othello* be in the same marvelous *style*?"

"If you mean, will the picture look as though I directed it, then I guess the answer is yes. It's like asking: Does Ella Fitzgerald always sound like Ella Fitzgerald when she sings, or does she suddenly open her mouth and sound like Bing Crosby?"

I laughed delightedly at this, and my father joined me, his great guffaw of wheezy laughter making the dining room feel so alive that I imagined I saw the baby angels on the ceiling flutter their wings. Then, all of a sudden, he rose from the table, signaling to my mother and stepfather frozen in their chairs that the interview with Orson Welles was now at an end. "You'll forgive me if I eat and run but I must be getting to the studio. We start work around two in the afternoon and I don't like to keep my actors waiting."

"Oh, won't you stay for coffee, Orson?" my mother pleaded.

"Well, all right, but just one cup to be sociable."

My father eased himself into the sofa and I perched on the arm nearby, asking him in a whisper, "When can I come with you to the studio, Daddy?"

"Any time you like," he boomed.

"Tomorrow?"

"Fine. Is that all right with you, Virginia?"

"Of course. Will you send someone to fetch her?"

"'Fetch'? Did you say 'fetch'? I say, old girl, we *are* getting veddy British all of a sudden." My father delivered this remark in a perfect imitation of an upper-class English gentleman while I watched Jackie stiffen and suck in his breath.

Recovering his composure, he turned to my father. "Before you go, Orson, there's something I'd like to show you." He left the room and came back with my freehand map, which he gave my father, holding it at arm's length as though it might be contaminated.

"You asked her to draw a map of the United States?" My father sounded incredulous. "I don't think *I* could draw a freehand map of anything, even though the word 'genius' was whispered in my ear from the time I began to walk."

"You may be right about that, Orson, but I still found it shocking that Chrissie couldn't put more than a few cities on her map. What do they teach American schoolchildren?"

"Why don't you ask an English child to draw a freehand map of Great Britain and see what you get? I think Christopher did very well, considering . . ." A wonderfully warm feeling had begun in my toes and was working its way through my whole body.

"Then have a look at these essays she wrote." Jack thrust them into my father's hands, explaining how they had come to be written.

"You're sending her to the Forum and all the way to St. Peter's by herself?" My father sounded incredulous again.

"Please just read the essays, Orson," my mother put in.

"I haven't got time to read them all, you know . . ."

"Then just read the first one."

He did. And he didn't laugh. "I think this is very good!" he announced. "As you Brits would say, 'Well done.' 'Jolly good.' 'Yoicks, tally ho!'"

"Oh, really Orson," my mother sighed.

"What about Chrissie's spelling mistakes?" Jackie asked, very stiff and British.

"What about them? Emily Brontë couldn't spell either, you know. What's important is that Christopher expresses herself in an original way. Surely originality is more important than *spelling*, but perhaps you don't agree."

"Who's Emily Brontë, Daddy?"

"Ask me, tomorrow, darling girl. Now I really must go."

The glow brought on by my father's visit lasted for the rest of the day. It had given me a song I would sing under my breath whenever my spirits sagged. The lyrics were simple and to the point:

> *Daddy doesn't like Jackie.*
> *Jackie didn't make a hit and Daddy doesn't like him,*
> *doesn't like him, doesn't like him one bit!*

THE NEXT DAY was mellow with September sunlight. I sat beside my father in the backseat of his chauffeur-driven car, breathing in gulps of air from the open window to ward off the nauseating smell of his cigar. "I want to tell you about the actors you're going to meet today," he was saying in confidential tones as we left the center of Rome and its honking horns behind us. "There's my old friend from the Gate Theatre in Dublin, Micheál MacLiammóir, who's known me since I was sixteen. You may find him a little fey."

"What's *fey*, Daddy?"

"Someone not quite of this world, like a leprechaun or magical being. But you know, for all his exaggerated mannerisms, Micheál is a very perceptive and intuitive person—he notices *everything*—and that, of course, makes him the superb actor he is."

"What part is he playing in your movie?"

"Iago. The evil courtier who tricks Othello into believing his wife Desdemona has been unfaithful to him."

"And who's playing Desdemona?"

"A very pretty Canadian actress called Suzanne Cloutier. You'll meet her as well."

"Is she nice?" Something in his voice had suggested that she wasn't.

My father sighed and thought a while. "Suzanne is so stubborn and resistant to everything I tell her to do that I've started calling her 'the Iron Butterfly.' But I know that if I can just get through to her, she'll be the greatest

Desdemona the world has ever seen! God knows her *looks* are perfect for the part, and I ran through several Desdemonas before I found her."

As I would later learn, the first Desdemona had been the Italian actress Lea Padovani, who dropped out to make another film. She was followed by the American actress Betsy Blair, who did not last long, because my father found her looks "too modern" for a Renaissance maiden. Cloutier, on the other hand, was a delicate, wide-eyed blond with an air of innocence that seemed irreproachable. In her period costume, she was such a perfect Desdemona it was impossible to picture anyone else in the role.

We were now driving along the Appian Way, which my father was explaining to me was the most important of the ancient Roman roads because it linked the capital of Rome with the south of Italy. "There are catacombs all around here," he said, gesturing out the car window at the hulking ruins to the left and right of us. "On another day we'll come back and have a look at them." I stared happily out the window at the pines arching over the road, the stands of cypress, and the gentle countryside bathed in the honey-colored light of early autumn. For the first time since I had arrived in Italy, I felt myself again, as though I had never set foot in Jack Pringle's kingdom of cool restraint.

At a country restaurant in a garden overlooking the Appian Way, we were joined at lunch by Micheál MacLiammóir who *did* seem "not quite of this world." Slight and angular, he looked as though a puff of wind might carry him off at any moment. I had never met a man before who powdered his face white and lined his dark, expressive eyes in black, turning himself into a tired ghost. But his manner was so genuinely warm and his sense of humor so nimble that I liked him at once. The attraction seems to have been mutual, for in the journal he kept on the making of *Othello* and later published as *Put Money in Thy Purse,* he noted:

> Orson's little daughter Christopher has appeared: an enchantress of the very first order. Not beautiful, which surprises me because her mother Virginia is lovely, and she resembles her closely, except that she is dark instead of fair. And Orson himself, though admittedly no Hermes, is not without a certain lunatic radiance; maybe Christopher will turn into a beauty, or at least a siren, because she already has merely to glance your way (which she frequently does if you're near enough, whoever you are) and you melt.

As lunch progressed I grew increasingly sure of myself, especially after my father told Micheál with evident pride that I had done an impersonation of Ethel Merman in Todd School's talent show. "She also knows all the songs from *South Pacific*," added my beaming father.

"And *Brigadoon*," I could not resist adding.

"Oh, do sing for us, Christopher," Micheál implored.

"Do you want me to, Daddy?"

He had *not* wanted me "to sing for my supper" in Granny's kitchen, I remembered, but now he nodded, and I launched into my repertoire of songs and impersonations. Later Micheál would record in his journal, with some exaggeration:

> She sang "Some Enchanted Evening" and did some shattering imitations of various celebrities beginning with Ethel Merman, making hay with several Barrymores and a few famous political figures, and finishing with her own Daddy.

After lunch we drove back to the studio in Rome where some indoor scenes in *Othello* were being shot on a set of a hallway in a castle. My father introduced me to everyone, actors and technicians, their names and faces a blur while I smiled and shook hands. *I'd like to come here every day*, I wanted to tell them. *You all make me feel so welcome.*

That afternoon I watched them filming a scene between Othello and Iago; my father more handsome than ever in blackface, transformed into the tortured Moor, and Micheál unrecognizable as the cunning villain with a gaunt, lined face and spindly legs. I watched take after take but found myself unable to stay in the moment. In my mind I was already in the car, being driven back to the apartment on the Via del Corso, and it was too late to fling myself on Othello's metal-plated breast and cry out, *Why can't I live with you, Daddy? Please. I won't be any trouble. Please let me stay here with you . . .*

Several days after my visit to the Scalera Studios, my father ran out of funds. Not for the first time, the production of *Othello* was called to a halt and the cast disbanded. Finding himself at liberty, my father turned his attention to me. We spent one afternoon prowling through the dank, smelly catacombs littered with ancient skeletons. My father was bent over the whole time to avoid hitting his head on the low ceiling, but this did not stop him from filling my ears with grisly tales of Christians being fed to the lions.

"Now that you've been to the Colosseum, Christopher, you can imagine it perfectly." I shuddered. "And while all the horror and bloodshed was going on, the spectators were howling and cheering and the Roman matrons were doing their knitting . . ."

On another day he took me to his lovely villa in nearby Frascati where we had lunch at a refectory table—"a monks' table," he called it—in an airy white dining room. Afterward, he showed me around the villa, and what a welcoming house it was, with its spacious, light-filled rooms, comfortable furniture, colorful rugs scattered on stone floors, wood-burning fireplaces in all the rooms, and from every window and terrace an enchanting view.

In the late afternoon, we stood on the upper terrace, gazing down at the luxuriant garden and at the valley beyond. With his hand on my shoulder, my father murmured in a wistful baritone, "It's so beautiful here in the spring. You should see it when the fruit trees are in bloom. Look, Christopher." He pointed out the almond and cherry orchards nestled in the valley among stands of cypress, pines, and olive trees. "But I am so rarely here," he sighed. "We were shooting *Othello* in Venice, you know, and before that in Morocco, and God only knows where the next location will be or where the next pot of gold is coming from . . ."

More than ever, the question was on my lips, the question I longed to ask, but never would, because I already knew the answer.

AFTER SPENDING SEVERAL months in Rome, I traveled with my mother and stepfather to Johannesburg, South Africa, where we were going to live for the foreseeable future. Jackie had connections with the South African gold-mining industry, although how he made his living, once he transformed himself from a military man into a businessman, is not any clearer to me now than it was then. What worried me, in any case, were not Jackie's mysterious dealings in gold. Rather it was how, if we were living a continent away from Rome, I was ever going to see my father again.

We traveled to South Africa on "a flying boat," an airplane that took off and landed on water. It was a strenuous journey that began in Sicily and took four days. It was also a bumpy ride because the plane flew at a low altitude like a floundering whale. The air pressure in the cabin was so erratic that we were given oxygen masks and advised to keep them on at all times, except, of course, when we had to use the airsick bags, which were soon in short supply. Day after day, the sound of retching filled the cabin. I was miserably ill for the whole trip, a combination of airsickness and asthma, and lay on the cabin floor, gasping for breath. Jackie tried to buck me up by drawing funny pictures of me in my oxygen mask, or with my head stuck in an airsick bag, but only he and my mother were laughing. Although the low-flying plane afforded spectacular views of the pyramids, the Sahara, the dense, ominous stretches of jungle, and the majestic Victoria Falls, I did not cheer up until the trip came to an end.

Soon after we arrived in Johannesburg, we drove south to Cape Town to visit some of Jackie's friends. I stared out the car window at huge termite hills dotting the dusty landscape, thorn trees with flat tops, a herd of impalas leaping gracefully over the road. These flat, open grasslands were called "the veld," Jackie explained, and covered most of the Transvaal, but once we left the interior and reached the Cape, there would be orchards and vineyards, mountains and the sea. "It will remind you of California," Jackie told me.

Meanwhile, nearing a township, we passed Africans gaily dressed in tropical colors and walking on foot in single file. The men carried staffs and the women walked behind them, balancing enormous bundles on their turbaned heads. They were blacker than coal, blacker than any Americans I had ever seen, and when they smiled, the whiteness of their teeth was dazzling. Half-naked children with spindly legs and runny noses ran shrieking after our car, which quickly enveloped them in clouds of dust.

My first look at South Africa convinced me I had been transported to an alien planet. Everything was strange and turned upside down, beginning with the weather. It was summer when it should have been winter, and there was "a rainy season" followed by "a dry season." We ate a weird-tasting fruit called "pau-pau" that looked like cantaloupe but tasted nothing like it. And Cape Town, with its rows of Dutch gabled houses clinging to the mountainside, its vistas of the Atlantic Ocean and flat-topped Table Mountain, looked nothing like California.

Back in "Jo'burg," as the locals called it, we moved into a modest house with a small garden in a white suburban enclave. It had a thatched roof weathered to a charcoal gray and a veranda where tea was served in good weather by the African houseboy in his white, starched uniform and white gloves. This daily ritual took place at eleven in the morning—"elevenses"—and again at four in the afternoon. The houseboy glided wordlessly in and out with the tea tray containing a pot of strong tea, another pot of hot water, a pitcher of milk, lemon slices, lumps of sugar, and a plate of "biscuits." We were allowed to say thank you and to ask for more hot water, but Jackie made it clear we were not to get familiar with the servants or speak to them any more than was strictly necessary. This made me feel very uncomfortable, especially in the early morning when the houseboy awakened me with a knock on my door, brought a cup of milky tea to my bedside, and opened my bedroom curtains. All I could say to him was "Good morning" and "Thank you." It didn't seem right to me that a grown man, especially one as tall and dignified as our houseboy, should be waiting on a young girl.

We acquired a puppy resembling a Great Dane except that she had a ridge of fur growing in the wrong direction along her back and so was called a Ridgeback. She was my dog, I was told, which meant that it was my job to sit outdoors with her and pluck the ticks off her coat. These I smashed with a stone, blood spurting in all directions, and after a week or so, I came down with a bad case of tick fever.

Lying ill in bed, I could hear the servants' lively chatter outside my window as they passed back and forth between the house and their separate quarters in the backyard. They spoke a lilting language punctuated with clicking sounds, which I later learned was Zulu. I learned to distinguish between the voices of our houseboy, our male cook, the "girl" who cleaned, and the "boy" who worked in the garden but was not allowed in the house because he had not been issued a white uniform and gloves. At mealtimes I could smell the cast-iron pot of "mealie meal," or corn mush, simmering over an open fire in the yard, and sometimes late at night, I was awakened by whoops of unrestrained laughter and loud explosions of talk—sounds that made me uneasy. What if these native people, so polite and reserved by day, rose up in fury one night and turned us out of our house? Why should we live in comfort while they were crammed into rickety shacks with tin roofs and had to wash in the yard, filling a bucket from a coldwater spigot?

Appalled by the servants' living conditions, my mother made curtains for their tiny rooms, covered the bare floors with rugs, and installed a radio. The result: The servants left in the night, taking the radio with them. "That was extremely foolish of you, Virginia," Jackie scolded her, "and I hope you've learned from your mistake."

"But . . ."

"You frightened them away, you silly woman, with your rugs and curtains and American notions of how to treat them. These natives aren't used to our amenities. How do you think they live in the bush?"

"I have no idea . . ."

"You'd better smarten up, Virginia, before you make utter fools of us both."

To hasten the process of converting my mother to the racist views Jackie held in common with the majority of white South Africans in that era of apartheid, he arranged for a group of white women to visit Virginia at teatime and "smarten her up."

"You must never treat them as your equals," one told my mother, "or they will rob you blind!"

"You hire them to do a job, and if they don't do it, or annoy you in any way, you sack them at once," another advised.

My mother was also instructed to "sack" any "native" who was lazy, spoke out of turn, or showed the slightest sign of being "uppity" or impertinent. The houseboy could get drunk every night and beat his wife on his own free time, but if he was caught helping himself to the master's liquor cabinet, it was back to the bush with him. Before they left, I heard one women advise my mother to lock up her jewelry, the silverware, and the liquor, since even a "good boy" was not to be trusted. It struck me as curious, listening in my corner, that the mature African men and women working for these white South Africans were referred to as "boys" and "girls."

During our first year in South Africa, my mother changed from the open-minded American woman who had treated African-Americans as her equals, the woman who had loudly cheered and danced around the living room with Charlie Lederer when we heard on the radio that Franklin D. Roosevelt had been elected to a fourth term. She became a female clone of Jack Pringle, and the two of them teamed up against me, because I refused to change my essential self and blend in seamlessly with my surroundings. I was not a chameleon like my mother. And, strangely, the absence of my father made me realize how much he had already shaped me and that his power did not depend on his presence. I was Orson's kid—not Virginia's and certainly not Jackie's—now and forever.

MY TWELFTH BIRTHDAY had come and gone without my hearing from my father. That evening my mother came to my room to say good night and found me slumped in a chair. "Now look here, Chrissie," she said, "you can't expect Orson to remember your birthday when he's in Europe and you're in South Africa." It was uncanny how one look at my long face had been enough to tell her why I was sad.

"Marie's in America," I pointed out, "and she sent me a birthday card with five dollars in it. She isn't even my nanny anymore."

"Marie's a dear and you must be sure to write and thank her."

"What I mean is everyone except Daddy remembered my birthday even though I'm living in South Africa." I had received cards and presents from Granny and Skipper, Aunt Caryl, Grandmother and Grandfather, even Charlie Lederer.

"I see what you mean, Chrissie, and I can see it's upset you, but it's nothing to cry about."

"I'm not crying!" I might, though, if I let myself think about how far away my father was and how little hope I had of seeing him again. "I don't care about getting a birthday present from Daddy," I went on, keeping my voice cool and steady. "What bothers me is he didn't call me today or even send a telegram."

"He obviously forgot."

"He never forgot before!"

"There's no law saying he has to remember every one of your birthdays, is there? Oh, don't look so tragic! It was different when we all lived in Hollywood and you were more in Orson's life." She brushed my hair out of my face, then stood hovering over me as though she wanted to be warm and motherly but didn't know how. Then, in a softer voice: "Instead of sitting there feeling so sorry for yourself, why don't you think about all the birthdays he *did* remember?"

With that she left, gently closing the door. Now I was alone, I could cry as much as I wanted without being accused of feeling sorry for myself, but what good would that do? I sighed, thinking over my mother's last words. Then, as though she had flung open the doors of an old toy cupboard, I suddenly saw the doll my father had given me on my fifth birthday—the most beautiful doll dressed in old-fashioned velvet and lace. She had a porcelain face, real hair, and pretty blue eyes that opened and closed when I rocked her in my arms. I saw the stack of Land of Oz books; the recordings of *Peter and the Wolf* and *The Nutcracker Suite,* which I had played until I knew every note by heart; the fluffy, pink bedroom slippers with the pom-poms on top, a smaller version of Rita's slippers. I had worn mine until they fell apart. One by one, they came back in a joyful parade, all the birthday gifts from my father. Gifts that were always exactly what I wanted.

But wait! How could I have forgotten the most special gift of all? On the evening of my seventh birthday, my mother told me to sit by the radio. "Your father has a wonderful surprise for you." She tuned in his half-hour evening program on his *This Is My Best* series, and I heard his unmistakable voice as clearly as if he were in the same room: "Good evening, this is Orson Welles." After announcing that tonight's special guest was the singing star Jane Powell, he went on, "My eldest daughter, Christopher, is seven years old today, and like most ladies and gentlemen of her age, Christopher likes her father to tell her a story. Well, I don't know of a better one than 'Snow White and the Seven Dwarfs' . . . ."

I clapped my hands in delight. He *knew* it was my favorite story! On our last visit, having seen the Walt Disney movie, I had amused him by singing Snow White's song, "Some Day My Prince Will Come." Now Jane Powell was going to sing it for me on my birthday. My father's radio play moved forward in a fast-paced, thrilling way. The wicked queen was as scary as Snow White was innocent and beautiful . . .

For a long time after the program ended, I had sat by the radio, lost in a magic world of poisoned apples and happy endings. Five years had elapsed since then, but no one—not even Jack Pringle—could take that memory away from me.

So now I knew what I had to do. Whenever being without my father began to hurt too much, I would come and sit quietly in my room, close my eyes and remember.

ONE MORNING WHILE my mother and I were having our "elevenses" on the veranda and Jackie was away at his office, she announced that I was going to boarding school. "But why, Mommy? I thought I was going to live with you and Jackie."

"You *are,* silly. You'll be home for the hols." She was beginning to sound more British than Queen Victoria.

"But why can't I live at home and go to school during the day?"

"Jackie thinks the discipline of boarding school will be good for you. It will smarten you up, he says." She smiled gaily and gave me an extra biscuit with my tea, but I was not fooled. Jackie had found the perfect way to remove me from the scene and, at the same time, convince my mother that the banishment was for my own good.

There followed months of misery at Kingsmead College, an all-girl school modeled on the English system of treating young girls like military recruits. We wore hideous green tunics that had to be two inches above our knees—we would periodically kneel on our desks while a teacher came around with a measuring tape—pale green bloomers to protect our modesty when it was windy, and opaque brown stockings. No makeup or jewelry was allowed. While kneeling meekly on her desk, a girl might have a ribbon or barrette yanked out of her hair and be sharply reprimanded by the teacher with the measuring tape. On Sunday mornings, when we marched two abreast to the church in town, wearing brown bowler hats and green blazers over our uniforms, the boys from a neighboring boarding school leaned out the windows, shouting, "Here come the frogs!"

Up to this point in my life, whenever I found myself in a new place, not too much time passed before I made at least one friend. Kingsmead was the exception. As my first term wore on, the girls continued to treat me as an outsider and a freak. They made fun of my American accent and the hours I spent practicing the piano. At night, I would find my bed short-sheeted. Worse, I would find it crawling with the infinite variety of insect life that thrived in South Africa. I knew better than to report these activities to the matron, a scrawny, bespectacled woman who ran our dormitory like a boot camp.

One evening, to my surprise, the matron summoned me to her office and handed me the telephone. "Your mother wants to speak to you personally," she sniffed, communicating how highly irregular this was.

"How are you, darling? Are you liking school?" At the sound of my mother's voice, I burst into tears and the matron yanked the phone away from me.

"Hello, Mrs. Pringle, this is the matron speaking. Chrissie is quite overcome, hearing from you, but some of our girls *do* get weepy when they hear from home. They need time to adjust to being here, so it *would* be better if you didn't call her again, since it will only upset her and she *is* such an emotional child, isn't she?"

IT WAS NOT until my second term at boarding school that I made my first friend, a sweet-natured Jewish girl named Wendy Miller. On Saturdays, Wendy and the handful of other Jewish girls at the school went to synagogue, and I would have liked to accompany them. Having been brought up with no religion, I was curious about all of them. The Christian girls in my class were attending confirmation classes, and I wondered if being "confirmed" would make me more acceptable. Then, in his sermon one Sunday, the priest ranted on that only the members of the High Anglican Church had any hope of going to heaven; everyone else was headed straight for hell. I wanted to leap to my feet and shout, "How dare you people send Wendy to hell?" It was the end of my flirtation with the Church of England.

During the "hols," I found a haven with the Epsteins, a family Jack Pringle did not altogether approve of—they were unusually liberal for white South Africans. However, he did not object to the great amount of time I spent at the Epsteins or to anything that kept me out of his own home. He and my mother had now adopted two children in their infancy, a girl and a boy they named Angela and Simon. They had formed a family unit of four that excluded me.

While my mother and Jackie would have protested that of course I was a welcome member of their family, their unceasing criticism delivered the opposite message. I was fat, lazy, ignorant, selfish, inconsiderate. Nothing I did was good enough. Even my obvious gift for playing the piano came under attack. How "frightfully boring" of me to want to be a music teacher instead of a concert pianist. Was I really serious about making a career out of giving piano lessons? In that case, they might as well sell the grand piano they had bought especially for me. My mother actually carried out this threat, but then bought another grand piano as she liked to play show tunes by ear, in between sips of her martini and puffs on her cigarette. "Your mother has a real gift for music," Jackie made a point of telling me, "not like you."

When I was home from boarding school, what a relief it was to stay with the Epsteins. Harry Epstein was our doctor. He was a good-hearted man with whom I felt at ease. His wife Iris was pretty and fun-loving, but it was their daughter, Barbara, who was my special friend. Barbara was extraordinarily gifted, musical, brilliant, and precocious. We were united in our passion for classical music and the piano, Barbara's knowledge of music and her skill at the keyboard far exceeding mine. It was she who introduced me to madrigals, Bach cantatas, and Handel operas at a time when they were rarely performed, igniting an intense love of early music that has never left me. When we weren't lying on our stomachs on the living room rug, listening to recordings, we were pounding out duets on the Epstein's upright piano.

Most of my good memories of Johannesburg took place in the Epstein household. Along with the hours of glorious music, here I found warmth, spontaneity, humor, and just plain nonsense. Much as I thrived on Barbara's sharp mind and the lively discussions that went on at the Epsteins' dinner table, after a day of being serious, we girls collapsed with the helpless, unstoppable laughter that came over us for no good reason other than our age. The frivolity continued when I stayed overnight in Barbara's room and instead of sleeping, we were whispering in the dark, making up silly jokes and stifling our giggles in our pillows. We were soul mates, Barbara and I, enjoying the passionate friendship of young girls. How innocent we were in those long gone days! Yet we could begin to imagine our future as women—the first glimpse of a ship in full sail rounding the horizon.

OVER A YEAR had passed with no communication from my father, and I was finding it painful to talk about him—or even to think about him. When asked, "Is it true you're Orson Welles's daughter?" or "What is your father doing these days?" I looked away, mumbling, "Yes," or "I don't know." Then, on March 27, 1951, my thirteenth birthday, I was home from school and reading in my room when I heard my mother calling me. "Chrissie, there's someone on the phone for you." To my surprise, she suggested I take the call in her bedroom and close the door.

When I picked up the phone and heard my father booming, "Hello, Christopher," I could hardly believe it. For a moment, I didn't know how to respond. "Is this my daughter Christopher?" he asked, louder than before.

"Is that really you, Daddy?"

"You bet it is. I'm calling from London, and you can't imagine how difficult it's been to get a clear connection to Johannesburg. I've had to move heaven and earth."

"Then you've tried to call me before?"

"Many, many times. I was beginning to think I'd never get through to you . . ."

"I'm sorry."

". . . but I've finally reached you, and what luck that my call went through today. Happy birthday, darling girl."

"Oh, Daddy!" *He'd remembered!* Swallowing hard, I went on, "It's just wonderful to hear from you and I . . . I miss you so much."

"I miss you, too. In fact, that's another reason why I'm calling. How would you like to come to London and stay with me for a while?"

"Oh, could I, Daddy? When?"

"Just as soon as we can arrange it."

I hung up the phone in a happy daze. My father had done it again. Somehow he always knew exactly what I wanted for my birthday.

5

The Visits

I WAS OVERJOYED WHEN my mother arranged a month's visit for me with my father in Europe. He and I would begin our time together in Rome and then travel to London, where we would stay for several weeks. "Now you're thirteen, I think you're finally old enough to cope with Orson's blazing intellect," my mother declared, "but you'll need a chaperone. You're too young to fly to Rome by yourself."

In those days the trip took more than thirty-six hours as the plane had to land several times to refuel, but that didn't count the delays en route. When engine trouble developed, we passengers had to sit for hours in steamy waiting rooms, watching flies blacken strips of flypaper pasted on grimy walls, listening to the whir and creak of slow-turning ceiling fans. We were offered tepid tea with condensed milk or ghastly soft drinks made with bottled lime juice. At one refuelling stop the engine trouble grew serious enough that I had to stay overnight in a rickety hotel room that was little more than a tin shack. I could feel the nearness of the jungle as I lay awake in the torpid air, watching the mosquito net draped over my bed sag with the steady accumulation of exotic insect life.

My chaperone, June Besso, was a long-faced woman in her late twenties, shy and gentle. She was tall and gangly with a loping walk that made me think of a giraffe. My mother had befriended "poor June" after an unhappy love affair led the young woman to an attempt to take her life. "Poor June's had a rotten time of it," my mother had confided before we left, "so a trip to Rome is just the thing to cheer her up. She's terrified of meeting Orson, but I'm sure you'll smooth the way for her, won't you, Chrissie, and do take good care of her in Rome."

"Isn't poor June supposed to be taking care of me?"

"Oh, really, Chrissie, you *are* so tiresome!"

My father saw through my mother's ruse of wangling a trip to Rome for her friend, all expenses paid by him. He was furious. The first moment we were alone, he reminded me I had flown by myself from Los Angeles to Acapulco when I was only eight years old; more recently I had made a solo flight from New York to Rome. "There is absolutely no reason on earth why you need a chaperone," he thundered. "So I'm sending her back to Johannesburg on the first plane."

"Oh, Daddy, she'll be so unhappy if you do that, and Mummy will be upset, too." (In spite of myself, *Mommy* had become *Mummy,* and other anglicisms had crept into my speech.)

"The round-trip fare for your chaperone has already cost me a bundle, you know, and now your mother expects me to shell out for her hotel room and three meals a day." He stopped when he saw my stricken face. "I'm not blaming you, darling girl, but I can't afford to pick up the tab for May."

"June," I whispered.

"Whatever her name is. Oh, all right, she can stay a week, but no longer, or I'll end up in the poorhouse!"

"Oh, thank you, Daddy!" I flung my arms around him, but my relief did not last long. In the days that followed, my father subjected June to relentless teasing. The moment she appeared, he began to hum the tune from *Carousel,* "June Is Bustin' Out All Over," and each time he did, he had the satisfaction of watching her grow red in the face and flail about, more awkward and gangly than ever. He made fun of her South African accent, her dowdy clothes, her ignorance of all things Italian. Too late I wished I had not played a role in keeping June in Rome. This desperately shy woman who lived on the edge of depression must have been wondering how she could ever have wanted to meet handsome, glamorous Orson Welles. It was the first time I had seen him be cruel to anyone — not that he was aware of it. As far as he was concerned, June was fair game and it was all in good fun.

I, at least, was glad of June's company, especially on those days my father was not able to spend much time with me. Although he was always working, he would sandwich me in whenever he could between long-distance phone calls, interviews with journalists, and the many solitary hours he spent working on treatments and giving visible form to the latest "ribbon of dreams" that glistened in his imagination.

Usually he was able to make time for me at lunch and dinner. In fact, when

I recall being with my father anywhere in Europe, we are invariably eating our way through a five-course meal in an excellent restaurant. These meals were long, leisurely affairs during which I discovered what my mother had meant about "Orson's blazing intellect." His conversation was so dazzling that I felt my mind was being bombarded by shooting stars. More often than not, I had to confess my ignorance of the subject he had raised, which never failed to astonish him. Why hadn't I heard of such-and-such or so-and-so? What on earth were they teaching me in that English school in Johannesburg? Not very much, he concluded. That was why most schools were a waste of time, in his opinion, and I should take my education into my own hands as he had done.

While my father was tied up with work during the day, I took June to my old haunts—the Colosseum, the Forum, St. Peter's—and showed her around. She was impressed by how much I knew. She was also terrified of Roman traffic. "How do you know they'll stop?" she asked me, quavering on the curb. It was true that most Roman drivers tore around the piazza, wheels screeching, horns blaring, and stopped only if you threw yourself in front of them with the utmost confidence that their brakes were working. "Don't look," I ordered June. "Just start walking and they'll stop, I promise." So she covered her eyes with one hand, gave me her other one, and let me drag her across the intersection, more like a blind, balking mule than a gentle giraffe. In the middle of one of these maneuvers, I suddenly noticed blood on the bottom half of her dress and streaming down her legs. "What's wrong, June? Did you hurt yourself?"

"It's the curse," she whispered. "It's come so early, I wasn't prepared." I had heard about "the curse" from girls at school but had never expected to see a woman menstruating in the middle of a Roman intersection, inspiring every male driver who had braked in time to add to the serenade of catcalls and obscenities. "I've got to get back to the hotel as quickly as I can. Please help me, Chrissie."

Perhaps, I thought, frantically hailing a taxi, June *would* be better off back in Johannesburg. When the day came for her to leave us, I did not protest. With June gone, my father made an effort to spend more time with me. He was delighted by my love of art and took me to many of the museums and art galleries in Rome.

"What Italian artists do you like the most?" he asked me on one of these excursions.

"Michelangelo," I responded without hesitation. "He's my favorite."

"Good choice, Christopher, but why Michelangelo and not Leonardo da Vinci?"

"Well, Daddy, it started when I saw his frescoes in the Sistine Chapel."

He immediately broke into a wide grin. "That's my girl!"

The very next day, we spent hours studying the ceiling of the Sistine Chapel, my father helping me identify what was happening in every inch of it: "Look up there, Christopher, that's God creating the sun, the moon, and the planets, and there he is creating the first man. Isn't it lovely, Christopher, how that act of creation is shown by the fingers of God and man about to touch? What an inspired idea that was! There's Adam and Eve being driven from the Garden of Eden—do you see the serpent with the woman's face coiled around the Tree of Knowledge? And there's Noah lying in a drunken stupor. Now look very closely at the Great Flood right next to it. Isn't it marvelous what Michelangelo did with that?" My father was so boyish at these moments, so filled with enthusiasm, that I wanted to laugh out loud for the sheer joy of being with him and sharing his passion.

For the rest of our stay in Rome, we made it our project to see any work of art we could find by Michelangelo. I had already admired his *Pietà* in St. Peter's; in those days you could walk right up to the statue of the Madonna tenderly holding the dead body of Christ on her lap. You could even lay a cautious finger on the cold white marble robes of the Madonna or the foot of Christ. It amazed me that every vein showed in Christ's foot, and my father explained that Michelangelo had stolen corpses from the city morgue in order to perfect his knowledge of anatomy.

After St. Peter's, my father took me to the church of San Pietro in Vincoli. It houses the enormous tomb of Pope Julius II, which Michelangelo designed but never completed, and his famous statue of Moses is seated at the base of the tomb. "Moses looks so alive," I exclaimed, staring at the muscles bulging in the statue's arms and the prominent veins in his hands, "but why does he have horns on his head?"

"I can't remember the reason, but art critics are always complaining about those horns. They *do* make Moses look like a goat." We both laughed at this, my father's hearty laughter echoing up and down the church's dim interior.

Before we left Rome, my father bought me two art books, one of Michelangelo's paintings and the other of his sculptures. In one of these

For
Christopher
(the ART-LOVER)
from her
ever-loving
Daddy

"... he drew a charming cartoon of the two of us standing at the base of a statue."

books, he inscribed the flyleaf: "For Christopher (the art-lover) from her ever-loving Daddy." Then he drew a charming cartoon of the two of us standing at the base of a statue. Looking much too serious, I am holding a lorgnette to my eyes, and towering above me is my fabulous father, puffing away on his Havana cigar.

FROM ROME WE flew to London where we were to spend several weeks before I was due back at school in Johannesburg. I look back on those whirlwind weeks, as I do on all the times I spent with my father in Europe, as both the pinnacle of my life up to that point and the foundation of my life to come. In our often fleeting times together, Orson Welles did more to shape my character, values, and aspirations than Virginia and Jack Pringle could have accomplished in a lifetime.

Wherever my father went in London in those days, he was instantly recognized as Harry Lime, the character he had played in the British thriller *The Third Man*. The role had made him more famous than anything he had ever done, including *Citizen Kane*. When I told my father I had not seen *The Third Man*, he immediately arranged for a private screening at Shepperton Studios. There we were in the darkened projection room, just the two of us, enveloped in cigar smoke and watching the credits roll.

"That's you!" I cried, when the name of Orson Welles appeared on the screen. He put a finger to his lips, but I was irrepressible. "What part do you play, Daddy?"

"The villain."

"But Daddy, I want you to be the hero."

"Villains are a lot more fun, Christopher."

My father's close friend, Joseph Cotten, played Holly Martins, an American writer who goes to Vienna in search of his old school chum, Harry Lime. The beautiful Italian Alida Valli played Harry Lime's girlfriend. The film was directed by Sir Carol Reed from an original screenplay by the novelist Graham Greene.

"Why didn't *you* direct it, Daddy?"

"Shush, I'll tell you later, darling girl."

As the movie began, I leaned forward eagerly in my seat, but long moments passed and still my father had not appeared on the screen. "Daddy," I whispered, "why aren't you in the movie yet?"

"Shush, my love. Be patient."

Almost an hour into the film, when I thought I could no longer bear the suspense, I watched as a cat rubbed itself against a pair of highly polished black shoes. A man's shoes. Who could be hiding in the darkened doorway? Suddenly a light flicked on in an upstairs window, catching a man in its beam for an instant: slim, smiling, sardonic, devilishly handsome. It was "the third man" of the title, who had faked his own death to escape from the law and continue his life of crime. It was Harry Lime, an American black marketeer in postwar Vienna who spread illness and death by selling inferior penicillin. But was it also my father? For once he was not wearing a false nose or anything else that disguised his looks, and yet he was nothing like his real self. He had turned into the heartless, unscrupulous, wickedly charming Harry Lime. I was so fascinated by the transformation that I paid scant attention to the story or the hypnotic zither music in the background. I was mainly impressed by Harry Lime's long-awaited first appearance in the doorway, and the heart-stopping chase through the gritty sewers of Vienna that ends in his capture. In the final scene the wounded Lime hauls himself up the sewer's iron staircase. He struggles to remove the manhole cover but does not have the strength. In a last attempt at salvation, his fingers reach imploringly through the grating. It made me think of the damned souls in Michelangelo's hell reaching toward heaven.

"Well, what did you think?" my father asked as the lights came up in the screening room. I told him I'd found the movie very exciting, especially the chase through the sewers. "But what did you think of Harry Lime?"

"I know he was bad and deserved to be caught, but I still felt sorry for him at the end."

"You did?" He broke into a broad grin. "You mean you couldn't help liking him, in spite of the terrible things he'd done?" I nodded vigorously. "Well, that's wonderful, Christopher. That's what makes this movie work and any other one, for that matter — that you can feel sympathy for the villain." From the way he was chomping his cigar, I could tell he was pleased with me.

"What about you, Daddy?" I asked as we left the screening room. "Do you like Harry Lime?"

"Like him? I *hate* him!" He spoke with a vehemence that startled me. "He's utterly cold and without passion."

Orson playing the villain Harry Lime in *The Third Man* (1949).

As OLD AS my father seemed to me at the time, he was actually at the peak of his youthful vigor and optimism. Tall and burly, he was not yet the monolith he would become in later years when his flat feet and delicate ankles could no longer support his enormous weight and he had to be ferried about in a wheelchair. Now he was fully capable of shepherding me around on foot. Just as he had deepened my love of art during our visits to the churches and museums of Rome, so in London he brought to life the Tudors and the Stuarts. It would remain my favorite period in English history.

We began at the Tower of London, the grim fortress on the Thames where so many were imprisoned and executed during the reigns of Henry VIII and his daughters, "Bloody" Mary and Elizabeth I. We stood looking down at the Traitors Gate, the entry point from the Thames where boats unloaded new prisoners. "Just think of the thousands who passed through here," my father intoned, "never to return to the world."

Then he told me about Anne Boleyn whose personal tragedy appealed to our shared romanticism. King Henry had been so determined to marry pretty, high-spirited Anne that in order to divorce his first wife, Catharine of Aragon, he had split with the Roman Catholic Church and founded the

Church of England. Then, Anne, not knowing when she was well off, had dared to cuckold the king and been sent to the Tower. Only twenty-nine years of age, she lost her lovely head on the Tower Green.

On another fine day, my father took me to Hampton Court. It had been built by the archbishop of York, Thomas Wolsey, he told me. On completion, the manor house and its grounds were so grand that Wolsey feared King Henry might suspect the archbishop was trying to outdo his sovereign and live above his station. So, to save his neck, Wolsey made a gift of Hampton Court to the king. My father led me through the palatial rooms, pointing out the fine antiques, chandeliers, and paintings. We lingered in rooms with leaded windows that looked out on the serene gardens and the Thames beyond. What fascinated him the most, though, was the vast kitchen complex with its three fireplaces and adjoining pastry house, confectionery, saucery, spicery, boiling-house, larders, and sculleries. "Think of the banquets they prepared here for the king," he murmured with more than a touch of envy.

Our next excursion was prompted not by English history but my father's memorable role in *The Third Man*. The moment he appeared in a public place, anyone with a musical instrument struck up the theme from the movie. It seemed that the face of Orson Welles had become synonymous with the zither's insistent tune. It also seemed that every musician in London knew the tune, and every restaurant, lounge, tearoom, or hotel lobby possessed a piano, gypsy violin, or three-piece band. So there was no escape since my father was not about to give up his leisurely lunches and dinners, a hearty tea with scones, raspberry jam, and clotted cream at four in the afternoon, cocktails before dinner, brandy after dinner, and a pint of stout at any time of the day.

Each time we were subjected to yet another rendition of the theme from *The Third Man*, my father would heave a sigh. Patient as he tried to be — and in dealing with his fans, he showed remarkable patience and courtesy — the breaking point came when we were waiting to cross Piccadilly Circus one afternoon. An organ-grinder on the corner spotted Harry Lime and began to play the tune my father never wanted to hear again. "That does it!" he roared. "We're getting out of London!"

The very next day, a chauffeured limousine drove us into the English countryside. A lavish picnic hamper, lap rugs, cushions, a folding table, and chairs occupied the trunk. About an hour out of London, a suitable grassy knoll was found by a winding stream in open country. It was a glorious late spring day with not another human in sight and no car but ours parked to one side of the country road, bordered by tall hedges. The table and chairs were set up under a shade tree, the picnic hamper unpacked, and we settled down to the serious business of eating. My father was wolfing down the gull's eggs he loved, while the chauffeur, in impeccable uniform and white gloves, uncorked the vintage wine. "Can I have a sip, Daddy?"

"Absolutely not!"

As I was debating which bottled soft drink to choose, along came a man on a bicycle, pedaling furiously along the deserted road, then stopping short when he saw us. The man grinned, waved—"Oh, dear God, no," groaned my father under his breath—and whipped a harmonica out of his jacket pocket. On this he proceeded to play the theme from *The Third Man*.

OUR STAY IN London coincided with the 1951 Festival of Britain. The stars of the festival were the reigning king and queen of the English theater, Sir Laurence Olivier and Vivien Leigh. On successive nights at the St. James's Theatre, they were appearing in the title roles in Shakespeare's *Antony and Cleopatra* and in George Bernard Shaw's *Caesar and Cleopatra*.

Also performing in London that May was the irrepressible, red-haired comedian from Brooklyn, Danny Kaye. His movies were among the few that were shown on Saturday nights at my boarding school. I had found him irresistible in *The Secret Life of Walter Mitty*—funny, charming, and vulnerable at the same time—and I had laughed myself silly during his manic routines in *The Inspector General*. So when my father asked me which I would like to see first—the Oliviers' classical offering at St. James's Theatre or Danny Kaye's one-man show at the Palladium—I had no trouble making up my mind.

I loved everything about Danny Kaye: his rapid patter songs, his hilarious impersonations, his dazzling display of foreign accents, his nonstop clowning. While he couldn't be called handsome, I found him extremely attractive. He was a slim, well-built man as graceful in his movements as a classical dancer. Whether on stage or off, he exuded an engaging warmth and openness.

During the interval, as intermission is called in England, my father told me, "Sam Goldwyn wanted Danny to have a nose job, but he refused." *Good for him*, I thought. My father gratified a stranger's request for his autograph before continuing. "Danny is Jewish, you know. He was born Daniel Kaminski, and his father was a tailor, I think, from somewhere in Russia.

Anyway, Danny grew up poor. He dropped out of school when he was your age, Christopher—something you might consider doing yourself, by the way, if you continue to be so miserable at that school in Johannesburg—and then he became a stand-up comic at those Jewish resort hotels in the Catskills. The borscht belt, they call it. That's where he learned his trade, and that's where he still might be working today if he hadn't met Sylvia Fine."

"Who's Sylvia Fine?"

"The woman he married and the woman who made him. She writes his songs and most of his material. A very clever woman. She also manages his career. So he's completely dependent on her, you see, and can never divorce her."

"Does he want to?" I asked hopefully.

"Even if he did, he couldn't. Besides, they have a daughter."

That didn't stop you, I almost said.

It was time to return to our seats for the second half of the show. Before long I was laughing until I felt weak and my eyes were tearing. After the final curtain call, the last explosion of applause, foot stamping, and cheering, my father rumbled, "Would you like to go backstage and meet Danny Kaye?"

"That would be nice," I forced myself to respond in a calm, grown-up voice. *I mustn't let Daddy see what a crush I have on Danny Kaye, or I'll never hear the end of it.*

Moments later we were ushered into Danny's dressing room, and he and my father were exchanging hugs and warm greetings.

"Hey, Orson, great to see you. I didn't know you were in London."

"Danny, you were great. My daughter couldn't stop laughing."

"This is your daughter?" Danny swung around, dropped to his knees and flung his arms wide to receive me. "Rebecca!"

"No, I'm Christopher, Mr. Kaye. Rebecca is my younger sister."

"Christopher!" he cried without missing a beat. Still on his knees and with his arms wide open, he smiled up at me as though he had been waiting his whole life to embrace me. The situation was beginning to feel false and theatrical to me, but seeing no way out of it, I leaned over and, to my surprise, Danny hugged me with unmistakable warmth. Then he was on his feet again, agile as a cat and all charm, grinning down at me and ruffling my hair. He clearly liked children and felt comfortable with them, but at thirteen, I no longer saw myself as a child.

"I really enjoyed your show, Mr. Kaye," I told him, trying to sound like a matron of forty. "You were wonderfully funny."

"Wonderfully funny, was I? My, my." His blue eyes were mocking me. "Then you must come again and watch the show from the wings. Would you like that?"

"Oh yes, Mr. Kaye!"

"Good. You can come back whenever you like, but only if you stop calling me Mr. Kaye. I'm not old enough to be called anything but Danny. If you can call me Danny, then we'll get along just fine. Let's hear you do it."

"Danny."

"That's swell." He ruffled my hair again, making me feel about three years old.

A few days later, I returned to the Palladium and saw Danny's show again, from the wings. How privileged I felt to be standing there with the backstage crew, as though I, too, were a member of the company. Every time Danny bounded off stage in my direction, as soon as he was out of the audience's sight he wiggled his nose at me or chucked me under the chin, cooing, "Hi there, little girl. Having fun?" And I assured him I was. *Just give me five more years,* I wanted to tell him. By that time Sylvia Fine will have fallen off a cliff, and *I'll* be writing your tongue-twisting songs.

After I'd seen Danny's show twice, my father took me to see the two Cleopatras being performed on consecutive nights. As I sat enthralled through both productions, no one had to tell me that Laurence Olivier was the greatest actor in the English-speaking world. It was apparent from the moment he appeared on stage, a handsome, commanding presence, so sure of his every word and movement, so at home in the play that one could hear the collective sigh of the audience relaxing into the moment. We were in the hands of a master, whether he gave us Shaw's Julius Caesar in his world-weary fifties or Shakespeare's Marc Antony in his ardent youth.

On the other hand, in her two versions of Cleopatra—Shaw's headstrong child-woman and Shakespeare's smoldering femme fatale—Vivien Leigh was mainly remarkable for her beauty. At thirty-eight, she was so petite and vivacious that in Shaw's play she created the illusion of being only sixteen. In the interval my father boomed, "Believe me, Vivien's a lot more convincing as a young Cleopatra than Katharine Cornell was when she tackled Juliet in her forties."

He began to tell me how he had toured the United States with Katharine Cornell in Shakespeare's *Romeo and Juliet* when he was still in his teens, his first professional engagement in the American theater, but several times he had to interrupt himself to oblige the autograph hunters. One fan leapfrogged over the seats in his frenzy to reach Orson Welles, only to present him with a pen that was out of ink. While my father behaved like a gracious host welcoming unexpected guests, I resented the intrusion. These people we didn't want to know came crashing into our space and then felt free to hang around and ask questions that were none of their business.

"Vivien Leigh is very lovely as Cleopatra," I told my father when we were alone again, "but she doesn't come across the way Laurence Olivier does."

My father gave me a delighted smile. "You're right! Vivien is much better in the movies—in fact, she's superb. Some actresses can't project on the stage but have a magical relationship with the movie camera. Larry is the opposite, not nearly as thrilling on the screen as he is on the stage, but I do wish he wouldn't wear tights. If I were directing the Cleopatra plays, I would do them both in modern dress so we wouldn't have to see Larry's legs."

"What's wrong with his legs?"

"What's wrong?" He glowered at me. "They're so thin they look like matchsticks. For years Larry starved himself, you know, because he was too poor to buy food, and now it doesn't matter how rich and famous he is, he looks *dreadful* in tights. Someone ought to tell him . . ."

On the second night, when my father took me backstage to meet the Oliviers, I prayed he wouldn't raise the subject of tights. Still in their stage costumes and makeup, the incredibly good-looking couple greeted us with the easy smiles and warmth of theater people, creating an aura of instant familiarity. I wanted to pull up a chair in their cozy dressing room and talk to them for hours. Although I didn't realize it at the time, I was no better or worse than the autograph hunters who besieged my father.

"Orson, you must come to lunch this Sunday," Vivien was saying, "and bring Christopher, of course." There was something birdlike about her, her hands fluttering in the air as she spoke, her head cocked to one side, her darting, luminous eyes that took our full measure.

"That's very kind of you, Vivien, and I'd be delighted to bring Christopher if she's still with me on Sunday . . ."

"Still with you?"

"By then she may have run off with Danny Kaye. She's madly in love with him, you know."

"Daddy!" So he had found me out after all! I turned crimson and wanted to rush out of the theater and vanish into the night, never to be seen again.

Vivien turned to her husband, who had begun to remove his makeup. "We can't have her running off, now, can we, darling?"

"Of course we can't," Sir Laurence agreed, scrubbing his face with cold cream. As neither one of them seemed to be making fun of me, I lifted my eyes from my shoes.

"I know what we'll do," cried Vivien, giving me a dazzling smile. "We'll invite Danny to lunch, too. Would you like that, Christopher? Of course you would!"

So it was all arranged. On Sunday my father hired a chauffeured limousine and we were driven about fifty miles north of London to Notley Abbey, the Oliviers' palatial country home in Buckinghamshire. My father had boned up on the house's history, which he imparted to me on the way there. Named for an Augustinian monastery, the thirty-two room house had been an abbot's lodge in the thirteen century. Then, in 1539, when Henry VIII abolished all monasteries in England, the building and its extensive grounds—over seventy acres of rich farmland, orchards, and gardens—were surrendered to the crown. By the time the Oliviers bought Notley Abbey in 1943, it had fallen into disrepair.

"Larry fell in love with the place and its history," my father told me as our limousine snaked up the driveway and the abbey loomed before us, an austere Gothic presence of gray stone and leaded windows. "Larry has played so many kings on the stage and screen, you know, that he wants to live like one in his private life." A wistful note had crept into my father's voice, making me think of a small boy pressing his nose against the window of a pastry shop. At that point in his life, Orson Welles had no home to anchor him, and even though he was living in Europe by choice, he was a man without a country. "Larry could afford all this," he rumbled on, as though thinking aloud. "He made a fortune with *Henry V,* the most popular movie ever made of a Shakespearean play, and that's exactly what it is, a play slapped onto the screen."

"Notley Abbey looks awfully gloomy," I remarked, peering out the window. "Does it have a dungeon?"

"Dear child," he laughed.

"Well, *I* wouldn't want to live here."

"Wait until you see the inside, Christopher. Vivien has done wonders with it. She has a talent for decorating—and for entertaining. She likes nothing better than to invite carloads of people on weekends, which drives Larry crazy." He went on to tell me that Olivier was an intensely private man who would have preferred to spend the day reading in his study or working in his rose garden. "Larry's out of luck today, all right." My father gestured at the lineup of fancy cars parked in the driveway. "Looks like we're not the only ones invited to Sunday lunch."

The overcast sky and a brisk chill in the air made us hurry indoors, where we found lamps lit and fires crackling in the succession of rooms on the ground floor, which included three large living rooms, a library, and a dining room. A feeling of warmth and coziness pervaded these rooms, in spite of their high-beamed ceilings and leaded-glass casement widows. There were piles of books and bowls of flowers fresh from the garden on the antique tables, brightly colored cushions on the slipcovered sofas, reading lamps and comfortable arm-

The celebrated couple of stage and screen Vivien Leigh and Laurence Olivier, 1941.

chairs everywhere. After seeing Notley Abbey's grim exterior, I could never have imagined I would feel so at home once I had walked through its doors.

Vivien greeted us with cries of delight and introduced us to Suzanne, her eighteen-year-old daughter from her first marriage, who was visiting that weekend. I could hardly believe they were mother and daughter. Somehow Vivien — so petite, lively, and exquisite — had produced a tall, stolid daughter who was painfully shy. I tried to draw Suzanne out, but she had the sullen air of a person determined to keep her problems to herself, and she seemed particularly ill at ease with her mother nearby. I wanted to tell Suzanne that I knew how hard it was to have a famous parent who only saw you now and then, and maybe, if you had to lose a parent to fame, it was worse to lose a mother, but what could we children of fame do but make the best of it? We might as well enjoy our parents while we were with them . . . But there was no breaking through her British reserve.

Before long we trooped into the dining room and took our places around the long table. There must have been at least fourteen of us. Among the guests, I recognized the actors Spencer Tracy and Katharine Hepburn. Tracy looked sunk in gloom and hardly said a word to anyone. After Vivien seated herself at the end of the table, she invited my father and Danny Kaye to sit on either side of her. Before taking his place at the head of the table, Olivier seated me to his left, graciously holding out my chair. Being the youngest and least important person in the room, I felt extremely honored. Then Olivier put Robert Helpmann, the great Australian dancer, next to me.

The forty-two-year-old Helpmann had recently retired as a principal dancer with the Sadler's Wells ballet. Although I had never seen him dance on the stage, I recognized him at once from *The Red Shoes,* a movie I had seen twice. This was the film that inspired many girls of my generation to take up ballet. It also turned lovely, auburn-haired Moira Shearer, a relatively unknown dancer with Sadler's Wells, into an internationally famous movie star.

As soon as we were seated, I told Helpmann how much I had admired his dancing in *The Red Shoes.* "I especially like the bit where a newspaper swirls around and around in the wind and then turns into you, all covered in newsprint."

"That *was* rather good, wasn't it?" He smiled at me but still looked like a gaunt, long-faced man who could play a ghoul. "If you liked *The Red Shoes* so much, then you must see my latest movie, *The Tales of Hoffman.* Moira is in it, too, and it's full of magic, music, and fantasy."

"Oh, I hope *The Tales of Hoffman* is playing in Johannesburg."

"Do you live in Johannesburg?"

How easy it was to talk to Helpmann and Olivier, both of them taking an interest in me that did not seem feigned for my father's sake. He could not have heard us anyway since he and Danny Kaye were taking turns regaling their end of the table and causing explosions of laughter. Rarely had I felt so grown up and self-confident.

"Speaking of films," Olivier was saying to me, "I hope you know, Christopher, what an extraordinary actor and director your father is. He may be out of favor now—his reputation has suffered in recent years, and many people don't appreciate his style of acting or understand his films—but time will show how wrong they are. Orson is the true artist among us, and when he finishes his *Othello,* it will be a film for the ages. People will be watching it long after my Shakespearean films have been forgotten. Have you seen my *Henry V* by the way?" I nodded but before I could say anything about it, he rushed on, "Now don't tell me how much you liked it. Everyone tells me that, and it's not the point. My films may be crowd-pleasers, but they are utterly conventional, and I am the first to admit it. When it comes to making films, I don't begin to have your father's brilliance or originality."

I had been in awe of Olivier with his striking good looks and kingly bearing, and now I realized what a modest man he was, in spite of his enormous success, wealth, and fame. He was speaking to me simply, directly, and I was touched that he wanted me to know, in case I didn't, what a great creative force my father was.

After lunch the sun came out, and my father took me on a stroll through the lovely gardens, past tennis courts and greenhouses, until we found a bench under a blossoming fruit tree. "I am so proud of the way you handled yourself at lunch, Christopher," my father was saying. "Everyone's been coming up to me and complimenting me on my daughter, how self-possessed she is for her age, how intelligent and delightful. It's going to be awfully hard to send you back to Johannesburg . . ."

"Oh, please, Daddy, don't remind me!" I hadn't thought of my schoolmates in weeks, and suddenly there they were, taking up space in my mind again: all those beefy South African girls in their frog green tunics and brown stockings, stampeding up and down the hockey field while I trailed behind, feeling hopeless and inadequate.

"What we have to do is arrange the next visit with your mother so we'll both have something to look forward to. Maybe you could spend Christmas with me this year."

"Oh, yes, yes, please ask Mummy right away."

"Don't worry. I'll write to her tonight, and you must ask her, too, as soon as you get home."

So it was really ending. In less than a week I would be back in the house where my stepfather made me feel I never measured up to what was expected of me and my mother increasingly went along with his views. I would be back in boarding school where, apart from my few friends and a teacher here and there, no one found me intelligent, delightful, or worthy of notice. So, I told myself, I must remember every precious moment of these days with my father. Like treasure saved for hard times ahead, I must store them away in my mind. And the brightest jewel to gladden a dark hour would be this stupendous day at Notley Abbey, the day I had made my father proud of me—not as I had tried to do when I was younger by showing off at the piano or wheedling my way into one of his movies. No, his affirmation of me had come when I least expected it, while I was having lunch with the Oliviers, far removed from the Pringles' withering eyes—and just being myself.

ONCE I WAS back in Johannesburg, I could hardly wait for Jackie to be out of the house so I could tell my mother about my visit with my father. Fortuitously, my stepfather left early in the morning to exercise his polo ponies, continued on to his mysterious place of business, and was not seen again until afternoon tea. So I had my mother to myself while she breakfasted in bed.

It reminded me of the good old days to perch on the end of her bed and chatter away, reclaiming the child who had romped on the beach in Santa Monica. Yet my mother was no longer the beauty she had been in California. She had gained weight, lost her waistline, and the medication she took for the two slipped disks in her back made her face puffy. At thirty-five Virginia Pringle was beginning to look matronly.

Like a soft shawl hugging my shoulders, I felt wrapped in the new self-assurance I had brought back with me from London. First, in glowing detail, I told my mother about everything Daddy and I had done in Rome, every museum, church, and art gallery we had visited, and how thrilling it had been to go around Rome with him. Then I told her how in London Daddy had made history come alive for me at the Tower of London and Hampton Court, how he had introduced me to Danny Kaye and taken me to lunch at the Oliviers.

When I fell silent, there was a long pause while my mother stared off into space. Then in the crisp British voice that still sounded strange to me, she said, "I never thought I'd come off second best, but I guess that old saying is true. Familiarity does breed contempt."

"It's not true! I don't feel—"

"Oh, yes you do, Chrissie." She shoved the breakfast tray off her lap and reached for the pack of cigarettes on the bedside table. "Orson's the glamorous one in your eyes—it's obvious from the way you talk about him, as though you're in love with him, for God's sake—and I'm just an old shoe. But I'm afraid you're going to have to put up with me and Jackie, whether you like it or not!"

I was dumbfounded by her reaction. Couldn't she be even a little glad for me that I had spent such a fantastic and unforgettable time with my father? "But I thought you *wanted* me to see Daddy. I thought—"

"Of course I wanted it. Haven't I always encouraged Orson to take an interest in you? *I* was the one who arranged this visit, if you remember. *He* would never have thought of it, I can assure you."

"But he did think of it, Mummy. He called me on my birthday, remember?"

She continued as though I hadn't spoken, cold rage building in her voice. "It just never occurred to me until now, when you sit there like a stage-struck little fool, babbling your head off about Orson and Larry and Vivien and Danny, that I'd come off second best."

She's not going to spoil it for me! I flounced out of the room, leaving my mother to her novel, her nail-biting, and her cigarette, but later that day, she almost succeeded in upsetting everything.

When Jackie came home in time for afternoon tea, they held a conference in their bedroom that I overheard, in spite of the closed door. They emerged, convinced I had returned to them "with a swelled head."

So at dinner that evening, they both worked hard at "taking Chrissie down a peg." Much was made of my undistinguished academic record at Kingsmead. The only subjects in which I appeared to excel were English and music, but I should be getting good marks in all my subjects. Why wasn't I doing better, since I could hardly be accused of being stupid? It must be the lazy, self-indulgent temperament and lack of discipline I had inherited from Orson.

(*Daddy's not lazy. He works all the time!*) One of my teachers had noted in her report that I tended to daydream in class. "Well, Chrissie," Jackie continued, "if you're going to be wet behind the ears and stare out the window instead of paying attention to your teachers, then you can forget about graduating from Kingsmead or any other school. It's high time you got cracking, pulled up your bootstraps . . ." And so on.

Clinging to the last shreds of self-confidence, I managed to say, "Maybe it doesn't matter if I finish school or not because I'm going to be an actress."

"An actress!" they hooted in unison.

"What makes you think you have the talent to be an actress?" Jackie's voice conveyed that I was no more important than a bug he could crush under one of his highly polished riding boots. "Really, Chrissie, you'd better take a hard look at yourself and smarten up." He turned to my mother. "You see, Virginia, this is the result of letting Chrissie gallivant around Europe with Orson. She's obviously forgotten everything we've tried to drum into her and fallen under his influence, which, if I may say so, is hardly in her best interests . . ."

I wanted to scream at them. I wanted to throw my plate of food at them. Instead I burst into tears.

"There she goes, crying again," my mother observed to Jackie in her Queen Victoria voice. "She's *such* a little bore."

MY MOTHER WAS aware that Jackie's negative view of "Orson's influence" on me was prompted by jealousy and his own fears about coming off second best. So, happily for me, when my father wrote asking if I could spend Christmas with him in London, she agreed. As long as Orson did not try to undermine her and Jackie or interfere with their plans for me, my mother was ready to send me off at a moment's notice. "Orson's better company than anyone in the world," she told me out of Jackie's hearing, "and I'm thrilled he's finally taking an interest in you. I always hoped this would happen when you were old enough to deal with him." Either she had forgotten her earlier accusation that I overly glamorized my father and saw her as "an old shoe," or she had thought better of it. I never knew with my mother; she was as changeable as the moon.

One day while we were looking over my meager wardrobe and deciding what I should take to London, my mother suddenly snapped, "It's high time Orson began contributing to your upkeep. You desperately need a new winter coat and some smart new dresses, and this time *he's* going to pay for it and not me!" To my dismay, my mother drew up a long shopping list I was to present to my father, which made me feel like a charity case. Meanwhile, she fired off an airmail letter about the winter coat my father was to purchase ahead of my arrival.

Here is my father's bemused reply:

> 7th December 1951
>
> Dearest Virginia,
>
> Your letter regarding Christopher's coat specifies navy blue and mentions a fur collar. Is this a mistake? Have I read it wrong? Surely navy blue and a fur collar aren't a happy combination. I am not trying to save dough on the fur. Please airmail further thoughts on this subject so that I can meet our child at the airport with exactly what you think we ought to have.
>
> Much love,
> Orson

Reading the letter over my mother's shoulder, I mumbled, "I don't really need a fur collar."

"Of course you do! It will look lovely on you."

"But fur is so expensive."

"I'm not asking Orson to buy you a full-length mink, for God's sake."

In the next flurry of letters between Johannesburg and London, my father replied, "We are getting the coat including fur collar and counting the minutes till Chrissie's arrival." He asked if I might leave school a few days early in order to catch his last performance in the title role of *Othello* at Saint James's Theatre. It was closing on December 15th, after a controversial six-week run. "I expect you'll say no," he went on, "and will quite understand if you do, but can't resist asking."

Alas, she did say no, and I missed a once-in-a-lifetime opportunity to see my father's staged version of *Othello*. The British drama critic Kenneth Tynan raved, "The presentation was visually flawless," and the stage at St. James's "seemed as big as a field." (Other critics were dumbfounded by the liberties Orson took with Shakespeare's text and the cinematic elements he brought to the stage. During a midnight magic show he put on at the Coliseum, attended by Princess Elizabeth and the duke of Edinburgh, my father quipped,

"I have just come from the St. James's Theatre, where I have been murdering Desdemona — or Shakespeare, according to which newspaper you read.")

At the time, though, my mother said nothing about my father's production of *Othello,* and when I arrived in London shortly after it closed, I did not know what I had missed. In fact, I had little notion of what my father was doing during the many hours and days he could not spend with me. He seemed to be tied up with one thing or another most of the time, which was not what I had expected after our previous visit. My disappointment grew each time I was handed over to his secretary, whom I will call Phoebe since I can't remember her real name. She was a curvaceous, red-haired woman with nicotine-stained teeth and a husky smoker's laugh. She and my father seemed so easy with each other that it occurred to me Phoebe's working hours might continue late at night, in his bed — a thought I immediately swept from my mind.

Phoebe was a relaxed person, who laughed effortlessly and went with the flow — a great asset when working in any capacity for Orson Welles. She put herself out to be nice to me. Although I liked her well enough and didn't mind spending time with her, she was not the one I had flown to London to see. The morning my father told me he could not take me to the British Museum and Phoebe would take me instead, I was barely able to swallow my tears. On another outing it was Phoebe who accompanied me to the National Gallery, marveling that I was "so keen on art." She couldn't get over how many paintings I recognized from the art books I had been studying in the school library. Yet how sad and empty it felt to be impressing my father's secretary when it was my father I wanted beside me, wandering from room to room, his deep, expressive voice in my ear. I knew that if he were with me, I wouldn't be showing off. I would be standing in awe before the great works of art hanging on the walls, trying out the new pair of eyes he had given me. And later, hand in hand, we would walk along the Thames and talk and talk, and I would feel again the wonder of being treated as though I were his equal. He had lit a thousand fires in my mind that would burn as long as I lived.

"I've got a surprise for you," my father announced dramatically while we were having breakfast one morning in the living room area of our luxurious two-bedroom suite. I can't remember what hotel we were staying in, only that it was very grand. Breakfast was rolled in on a trolley by waiters who uncovered the platters of eggs and kippers, ham and sausages as though they were presenting us with the crown jewels. "Guess what? We're going to spend Christmas and New Year's in Saint Moritz." My father beamed at me with a boyish enthusiasm that made me beam back at him, even though I had no idea where Saint Moritz was or what made it so special. Over several slices of toast spread thick with marmalade, he enlightened me. We were headed for the most famous and glamorous resort town in the Swiss Alps, patronized by movie and opera stars, kings and princesses, heads of state, and everybody who was anybody. We would be staying in a hotel so magnificent that it would make our elegant London "digs" look like a shack. We would be basking in Alpine sunshine, breathing in crisp mountain air, and feasting our eyes on panoramas of frozen lakes and snow-covered peaks. "We're going to have a spectacular Christmas," he concluded, polishing off the last sausage with evident satisfaction.

"Is Phoebe coming with us, Daddy?"

"Of course. We can't possibly get along without her. Besides, I may have to go to Paris at some point, and I don't know if I'll be able to take you with me."

"Oh."

"But you'll be having such a marvelous time, you won't even know I'm gone." He laughed at my solemn face. "I can see you already, darling girl, twirling around on your ice skates and tearing down the slopes on your skis . . ."

"I'm not very good at sports, Daddy—"

"Nonsense! Who told you that?"

"—and I don't know how to ski."

"Then you'll be in the ideal place to learn. We'll find the best ski instructor in Saint Moritz. Phoebe will arrange everything." And to make sure she did, he sent her to Saint Moritz a day ahead of our arrival.

So I had my father all to myself when we flew to Zurich, then traveled by train to the city of Chur, and from there took another train guided by overhead cables that crawled up the sharp inclines like a giant caterpillar, carrying us higher and higher into the Alps. I was overwhelmed by my first sight of mountains jagged with snow whose peaks cut through the clouds. We rattled over ravines so steep I had to close my eyes until the train, shuddering and swaying on its cables, was safely across. Absorbed by the view, I was content to sit quietly by the window, leaving my father to his book and his cigar.

It was early evening when we finally arrived in Saint Moritz. To my delight, we took a horse-drawn sleigh from the station to the hotel. I felt like a

With Daddy in Saint Moritz, Switzerland, Christmas 1951.

Russian princess, snug under our fur blanket as we whooshed and glided along on streets thickly packed with snow. I could see the vast frozen lake at our feet and the village gently rising above it in layers of lighted windows, but my eyes were drawn up and up to meet the huge mountains that ringed the horizon. Meanwhile, the tinkling bells on the horse's harness inspired my father to burst into a lusty chorus of "Jingle Bells" in which I happily joined. Thus we arrived at our glitzy, mock-Gothic hotel in the center of town, singing and laughing our heads off. At such moments I was convinced that, in his heart, my father was younger than I was and always would be.

We were staying at the Palace Hotel, the first one in Europe to be called a "palace," as my father would later inform me, and the only one according to him to deserve such a name. It had opened in 1896 and attracted hordes of the rich and famous ever since. The Grand Hall—the main lounge where we would have hot chocolate and pastries in the late afternoons—soared above two black marble fireplaces and priceless antique furniture.

One of the reasons Phoebe had been sent on ahead of us was to ensure that my father got a suite of rooms overlooking the lake. He had heard the shah of Iran and his retinue were also going to be staying at the Palace. "They'll give the shah all the suites with a lake view and put us in the back, overlooking the kitchen," he had warned Phoebe in London, but he needn't have worried. Our suite was lovely. Not only could we have breakfast in full, dazzling view of the lake, but there was a gaily decorated Christmas tree in one corner of our sitting room.

Seeing the festive tree reminded me that I had not yet bought my father a Christmas present. "What do you think Daddy would like for Christmas?" I asked Phoebe during our first moment alone together.

"A windup toy," she replied, and when she saw my look of astonishment, continued, "You've seen them, I'm sure, the toy soldiers that beat their drums or the animals that dance when you wind them up. Orson adores them, especially the ones they make here in Switzerland. We'll go to a toy store in town, and on Christmas morning, he'll be thrilled."

"Are you sure, Phoebe?" I still couldn't believe that my father, a grown man after all, wanted a windup toy more than a box of hand-rolled linen handkerchiefs or a bottle of aftershave lotion that smelled like evergreens in a snowfall. I had even thought of giving him a tie so that we would no longer be stopped every time we were about to enter the Palace's dining room. "I am very sorry, Mr. Welles, but we cannot seat you without a tie," the maître d'hôtel would say, then snap his fingers to summon a lackey who somehow always managed to produce a tie for such nonchalant diners as Orson Welles. "God, how I hate these things," my father would say, as he wound it around his neck. No, opening a gift box with a tie inside would not make a hit with him on Christmas morning. Better to follow Phoebe's suggestion and buy him a fuzzy little bear banging a pair of cymbals together or a pair of mice doing a tap dance.

The toys I actually chose have faded from memory, but not my father's delight when he opened his gifts from me on Christmas Day. What a charming little boy he suddenly became as he wound up his new toys again and again, making them perform on the table and the rug, while the whole room shook with his delighted laughter. Yet it was strange to feel that, at thirteen, I had outgrown such pleasures—that my life in recent years had taken me too far away from the child who would have laughed as loudly as her daddy.

Soon after Christmas, my father left for Paris. When he hugged me goodbye, he said he would fly back to Saint Moritz as soon as he could. I hung onto this thought as one day melted into the next and there was still no sign of him. Phoebe found me a private ski instructor and we made several forays on the beginners' slopes, but I was too scared of falling down and injuring myself to enjoy it. On the other hand, I became passionate about figure skating and spent many fearless hours practicing on the hotel's private rink. The resident skating instructor, a balding, thin-lipped man who spoke English with a heavy German accent, took me in hand. I worked hard to impress him. After executing what I hoped was a perfect figure eight, I waited for the instructor to say something, then blurted out, "Wasn't that good?"

"Average, Miss Welles. Only average."

"Do you think if I practice hard every day, I'll become really good?"

"If you mean, do I think you have a natural talent, the answer is no. There are little children who skate much better than you do, Miss Welles." I was crushed but continued to skate anyway for my own enjoyment. If nothing else, it gave me something to do in my father's continuing absence.

In the late afternoon, I would finally leave the ice rink and meet Phoebe in the Grand Hall. There we would sit by one of the picture windows, Phoebe ordering tea for herself and hot chocolate for me, and I'd anticipate the delights of the pastry tray advancing in our direction. While seated there we would talk about the importance of my father's work and how nothing, not even a visit with his daughter, should be allowed to stand in his way.

"You see, Christopher, one can't expect a man like Orson, who's a genius, to behave like an ordinary father."

"Yes, Phoebe, I know." I did not tell her I had heard the same argument all my life and it didn't make me feel any less lonely or abandoned.

Daddy never did return to Saint Moritz, and finally Phoebe accompanied me to London, where I spent a few more days with my father before I had to fly back to Johannesburg. During this time I was careful to conceal how much I had missed him in Saint Moritz. That I succeeded is evident in the letter he wrote my mother shortly after I left. He told her that I

> was a huge success in Saint Moritz and was, I think, very happy there. I flatter myself it was a lucky choice for her Christmas. For the last eight or nine days I had to be away in Paris and had hoped to bring her with me but the ice skating and a constantly widening and thickening circle of contemporary friends up in the Alps made it clear that much as I would have adored being with her, the museums and theatres of a big city would have been a definite let-down. I kept hoping to get back to Switzerland but simply couldn't.

It would be nearly two years before I saw my father again.

6

Together Again

WHEN I WAS FIFTEEN, my mother and stepfather decided to send me to Pensionnat Florissant, a finishing school for young ladies in Lausanne, Switzerland. I protested that I did not want to go to a finishing school; I wanted to go to college. "Out of the question!" Jackie said. "I can't afford it, and even if I could, your grades aren't good enough." When my grandparents in Chicago and the Hills in Woodstock raised objections to Jackie's plan, he told them, "Chrissie is not college material." My grandparents, impressed by a son-in-law who counted barons and earls among his friends, went along with Jackie's assessment of me, but the Hills were shocked.

"What was wrong with Jackie? Didn't he know you'd skipped two grades in elementary school?" Granny asked me years later during one of our visits. Believing at the time that money was the issue, the Hills had generously offered to pay for my college education, but Jackie had turned down their offer. "Do you know what he wrote us? The nerve of that man! 'Dear Hortense and Skipper, It's extremely kind of you, but I'm afraid you'd be wasting your money. Chrissie is a very poor student, but Virginia and I think that with her flair for languages, she could learn shorthand and typing and become a bilingual secretary.' Our Chris not to have a college education? I was never so outraged in all my life!"

"So was Orson when he heard about it," Skipper recalled. "He'd called me from Rome or London or some damned place, and when I told him Pringle was sending our Chris to some phony Swiss school to learn French, shorthand, and typing, Orson was beside himself. 'How can you let this happen?' he yelled at me. 'You've got to talk to Virginia. She won't listen to me, but she'll listen to you.'" Skipper broke off with a rueful laugh, scratched his head, then drawled, "Well, you were in South Africa, we were in Woodstock, Orson was in Europe. Wasn't much we could do to help you, kiddo, after Pringle turned down our offer."

Years later, while I was having lunch with my father during one of his trips to New York, we were reminiscing about the school vacations I had spent with him in Europe while I was going to Pensionnat Florissant. Suddenly I blurted out, "You know, Father, I bet what it cost to send me to Florissant for two years, plus flying me back and forth from Lausanne to Johannesburg, would have paid for four years of college. Easily!"

My father eyed me carefully over his green salad. "You sound much too angry, Christopher, after all these years."

"I have every right to be angry at that bastard Jack Pringle, who screwed me out of a college education!"

"You may have every right, darling girl, but being angry won't change anything that's happened to you, you know. It will only make you miserable."

"But Daddy . . . I mean Father . . . oh, I never know what to call you!"

He treated me to the infectious sound of his laughter. Then, wiping his eyes with one edge of his napkin, "Didn't we agree on 'Father' years ago? It's what I called *my* father, you know."

"Do you know what Mother and Jackie did after telling me there was no money to send me to college and I had to support myself? At seventeen!"

"Christopher, you must get rid of your anger at them. It's a terrible poison that's eating away at you . . ."

"They moved into a larger house and built a swimming pool!"

My father considered this information for a moment, while munching delicately on what was left of his salad, then taking a sip of his sparkling mineral water. He looked me in the eyes with a complicit smile. "I was also screwed by my guardian, you know, dear old Dadda Bernstein. He stole most of my inheritance. Did you know that?" I glumly shook my head. "The grownups we love and trust when we are young are so rarely what we want them to be." He paused to light a cigar, chewing and puffing on the end of it, then blowing out a cloud of noxious smoke before he rumbled on. "What you're not taking into account is that your fate rested in the hands of an upper-class English gent. Jack Pringle was acting on his notions of what's proper for a young lady in upper-class English society, don't you see? From his point of view—and you must always try to see the *other* person's point of view, Christopher, no matter how intensely you despise it —finishing school was exactly the right place to send you before marrying you off to some English earl. If Jackie'd had his way, you'd be living in a run-down castle somewhere in Surrey and riding to hounds every morning." He was off again, laughing uproariously, and this time I joined him.

"But why a secretary, Father? You know, when I finally broke into publishing and became an editor with Encyclopaedia Britannica, Jackie was still going on about how he wanted me to take a secretarial job with a friend of his so I'd meet all the 'right people.' He and Mother didn't seem to realize I'd made it into a profession in spite of them and without a college degree."

"You just answered your own question, Christopher. Jackie wanted you to hobnob with all the 'right people' instead of those undesirable, long-haired types at Encyclopaedia Britannica. Don't you see? Nothing was more important to Jackie than meeting the 'right people.' He was boxed in by his ideas of class and the life of privilege he'd always led."

"You mean the work itself was unimportant . . ."

"Of course it was. Offices all over the United Kingdom are stuffed with the daughters of English lords who can't type or take shorthand worth a damn, but they look pretty sitting at their desks and filing their nails. They have that unmistakable air of class, which simply means they feel superior to everyone else. When they answer the phone, they sound like this." And he launched into a perfect imitation of a falsetto, upper-class British accent that had the desired effect of making me laugh—and while I was laughing, my anger began to ebb away.

IN THE SUMMER of 1953, before leaving Johannesburg to enroll in Pensionnat Florissant, I wrote my grandmother in Chicago: "You must have heard the wonderful news about my future career in Switzerland. I am so thrilled I feel like broadcasting it on the radio. Mummy and I are shopping lunatics, and I don't think anyone was ever fitted out more smartly than me. Mummy says she will write soon, but now she is on her knees all day lining a coat for me for Switzerland." (In fact, my mother sewed most of my clothes, using patterns for women twice my age and choosing fabrics in dull, somber colors. At the time I was unaware of how dowdy I looked in my homemade clothes.) After telling my grandmother there were only forty or fifty students at Florissant, I quoted from the school's brochure: "Our aim is to develop the intellectual, moral, and physical qualities of the young girls confided to us, to direct them in their studies of French and modern languages, to initiate them in their future part of mistress of the house, complete their general knowledge, in one word prepare them for life." I ended my letter, "We are taken to all the concerts, art galleries, and plays, and for the winter holidays the whole school is moved up to chalets on the mountains which sounds divine. All lessons, everything is held in French but at first I will room with an English-speaking girl (thank heaven) so I will understand something somewhere sometime."

I did not tell Grandmother how wrenching it would be to be parted from Barbara Epstein. Barbara and I promised to write each other long letters every week, leaving nothing out, and faithfully scribbling our motto on the back of every envelope— "To hell with the people and the weather"— which at our age we found hilarious.

Nor did I mention my first serious boyfriend, Alain de Courseulles, who had moved with his family into the house next door to ours. His father was an important French banker and his mother a vivacious Italian beauty. Alain was a mixture of the two, a handsome, dark-haired boy with arresting blue eyes. He had beautiful manners, a gentle nature, and was remarkably self-possessed for a boy of sixteen.

After a farewell dinner with his parents and two sisters, Alain had walked me home through the purple African dusk. When we reached my door, he told me in French that he loved me and gave me my first, tremulous kiss. We would have been wretched, clinging to each other in the doorway, had we not known that Alain and his family were being transferred to Paris. His mother had already arranged with mine that I would travel by train from Lausanne and stay with the de Courseulles during my school holidays.

PENSIONNAT FLORISSANT WAS situated at the edge of Lausanne in Ouchy, a residential area that ran parallel to Lac Léman, as the French-speaking Swiss call Lake Geneva. Prosperous and law-abiding, Ouchy did not deserve the drama of the shimmering lake surrounded by snow-capped mountains disappearing into the clouds. Its immaculate homes and gardens wore the self-satisfied air I would come to associate with the Swiss. When I went for solitary walks after classes, I was tempted to shout at the top of my lungs, and once, to the horror of a woman weeding her garden, I did. Otherwise, each day melted into the next, and the only excitement was a stray dog baying at the moon.

Although I was moved by the grandeur of the lake and the Alpine peaks sparkling in the sun, I needed more in my young life than spectacular scenery.

Why, when I had wanted so much to go to college, had I been sent to this ridiculous school? Whether German, English, Italian, or Spanish—and each nationality quickly formed its own clique—the girls at Florissant were all the same: excessively rich and spoiled with nothing on their minds but washing their hair, painting their toenails, and meeting boys. They were here not to learn shorthand, typing, or any means of supporting themselves but to acquire a smattering of French and social polish before returning to lives of wealth and privilege.

So it was a happy day for me when Marian Strauss arrived at the pensionnat. Marian was the daughter of wealthy German Jews who had fled the Holocaust and resettled in England. What drew me to her at once was her humor and wicked, uninhibited laugh, but at sixteen, Marian was already mature and possessed an unlimited store of common sense. Here was a friend on whom I could rely in all weathers and seasons, and although we didn't know it yet, we would remain friends for life.

What we did discover within days of meeting was our shared love of classical music. Soon we were playing duets on the upright piano in the dining hall when it was empty. Now I had a willing companion when we were taken to concerts in town.

Marian and I became inseparable. After lessons and homework, in the cool of the day, we would walk downhill through Florissant's tidy gardens and slip through the gate that brought us to the Quai d'Ouchy, the tree-lined lakeside promenade that led to a small harbor, bobbing with private yachts.

On balmy days we walked bare-legged and in swishing skirts, hoping to attract the stares of lone males lounging on benches or lingering over espressos at an outdoor café. Although in my heart I believed I would always be faithful to Alain, I wasn't averse to a whistle or two from any man in the vicinity and neither was Marian. We pretended not to notice, of course, tossing our hair, giggling, safe in our virginity.

I HAD THOUGHT I would be spending Christmas with Alain and his family in Paris when, with no warning, my father reappeared in my life. "After a good deal of excited telegramming and telephoning, Daddy arrived in Lausanne," I wrote my grandparents. "How wonderful it was seeing this dear father of mine again, after three years. He couldn't believe the change he saw in me . . ." (Actually, it had been two years, not three, since I had last been with my father.)

The arrival of the world-famous Orson Welles caused great excitement in our school. At thirty-eight, he was extremely handsome, tall and imposing, his dark hair slicked back, a man who might be described as heavyset but who was far from the gigantic proportions of his later years. From the moment he strode through the front door and stood towering in the lobby, girls were racing up and down the staircase or hanging over the banisters to get a good look at him. The boldest sidled up to him to beg for his autograph before Madame Favre, our elderly headmistress, shooed them away. Normally an elegant woman in complete control of herself, Madame looked as though she had flung on her clothes backward and forgotten to comb her frizzy white hair. A red spot appeared on each of her sunken cheeks as she ushered "Meester Velless" into the lounge reserved for visitors and asked him to wait there for "Christophare." No need; I was already bounding into the room behind her.

"My God!" he exclaimed, holding me at arm's length while he studied me with a mixture of wonder and delight. "How you've grown up . . . and how beautiful you've become!" There was something disquieting about the way he was staring at me. It was as though we both realized at the same moment that I was now too old to nestle in his lap. Meanwhile, Madame Favre was backing out of the room, as though leaving the presence of royalty. After she had closed the door, my father asked, his eyes sparkling, "Christophare, how would you like to spend Christmas in Paris with Meester Velless?"

"Oh, I'd love it!"

"Then that's exactly what we're going to do." And he grinned at me — his irresistible, boyish grin — as though we were two runaway kids about to hop a freight train to Paris. He was Daddy again, the Daddy of Rome, London, and Saint Moritz. "Then go and pack your things, darling girl. And make it snappy! This place gives me the creeps."

That Christmas vacation with my father in Paris was unlike any time I had spent with him before. There was no urgent work to occupy him, no secretary to whisk me away. I had my father to myself, day after day. At fifteen, I was now old enough to fully appreciate his wit and his brilliant mind. He, in turn, behaved as though being with me was a constant delight and revelation.

The details of what we did in Paris are recorded in a letter I wrote my grandparents after my return to Florissant in January of 1954.

> We went to the Louvre, the ballet, the opera, the theatre. We climbed the Eiffel Tower and went to visit Napoleon's tomb and

Versailles. We had lunch at La Tour d'Argent, one of the top restaurants in Paris, and walked for hours by the Seine. We visited
the planetarium and heard a very interesting lecture which I had
to translate for Daddy (not that I understood much myself!). We
saw an exhibition of all the paintings from the museum in São
Paulo, Brazil. Most of all we talked AND we talked. . . . I was so
happy and I feel as I always do after being with Daddy—completely changed: more confident of myself and everyone around
me and happier to be alive.

What a transforming effect he had on me in those days, my charismatic
father!

The man I still called Daddy was impressed that in a mere six months I
had learned enough French to translate a lecture at the planetarium. "And
your accent is so perfect, people think you're French, maybe not from Paris,
but somewhere in the provinces." He laughed his life-loving laugh. "But then
I remember, Christopher, how quickly you learned Italian when you were a
child living in Rome. You are obviously more adept than your father at picking
up foreign languages, but that marvelous ear of yours—for languages, music,
and doing wicked imitations of your betters—*that* you get from me!" And he
laughed triumphantly.

One afternoon while we were strolling along a boulevard on the Left Bank,
my father spotted Humphrey Bogart and Lauren Bacall having lunch in a
café. He took me inside to introduce me, and what mattered was not my brief
but friendly meeting with two of Hollywood's icons, but the unmistakable
pride in my father's voice: "This is my daughter, Christopher. My eldest. My
firstborn."

Yet along with boosting my self-confidence, my father poked gentle fun at
some of my ideas. "Why are you so set on going to college?" he asked while
we were having lunch one day at La Tour d'Argent. "Your mother never went
to college and neither did I. Only bores and mediocrities go to college," he
said with a chuckle. "Seriously, Christopher, the fastest way to ruin an original mind is to imprison it for four years in an institution of higher learning.
When I was your age, you know, I was so determined *not* to go to college
that I fled to Ireland, hired a donkey cart and traveled all over the country,
painting and sketching. And you know what I learned that summer? I wasn't
the great artist I'd thought I was." He laughed at his younger self. "Don't you

see, Christopher, I might have wasted *years* at art school if I hadn't gone to Ireland. What I'm trying to tell you is that travel is the best education. Travel and living in foreign countries. And you've had plenty of that."

Daddy doesn't want to send me to college either, I thought. But I was wrong.

AFTER THOSE TEN whirlwind days with my father in Paris, I became a lot more interested in men. Alain, barely a year older than I, seemed a mere boy to me now. Our intimate moments together had never progressed beyond the exchange of chaste kisses. I was beginning to dream of an older and more experienced lover, like the ones I was reading about in the erotic French novels I bought on the sly in a used bookstore in Lausanne.

I had also come to seen Alain through my father's eyes. He had taken the two of us to lunch in a smart bistro near Avenue Foch, where Alain lived with his family in a grand apartment. "He's a sweet boy," my father told me afterward, "and very good looking, but I'm not sure he's bright enough for you." I realized with a pang that my father was right. Yet Alain was still the brother I wished I had and my closest male friend.

On returning to Florissant in early January, I learned I had been moved up into the second French class from the top and that my mother and Jackie were delighted with my excellent marks and swift progress. As a reward, I was to resume piano lessons. My new piano teacher was aghast at my poor technique and insisted on scales, scales, scales, and endless finger exercises before I was allowed to begin a new piece. I liked her, though. She was a cheery soul who smiled often, showing the gap between her front teeth, and wore her carrot red hair in a fringe. She also had the creepy habit of wearing her dead husband's ties.

"Fringette," as I privately called her, risked losing her job when she invited me to her home on the pretext of hearing some recordings of a Beethoven sonata I was about to learn and introduced me instead to her nephew. She knew as well as I did that it was strictly forbidden for Florissant girls to meet or socialize with men from the area, yet she had obviously arranged for her nephew to drop by. "My nephew has been so anxious to meet the daughter of Orson Welles," Fringette exclaimed while he pumped my hand, a stocky, oily-haired young man in his midtwenties. I hated being introduced as "the daughter of" as much as I distrusted the instant friendliness of those who wanted to meet me for my father's sake. When Fringette suggested to her nephew that he take me "for a little drive," I did not know how to get out of it without sounding rude. So there I was, driving off with The Nephew in his sleek sports car, while Fringette called out, "This is an excellent opportunity to practice your French, Christophare."

It was a wintry but brilliantly sunny day. A few miles down the road, it dawned on me that here I was, alone in a car with a fully grown *man*. But why did he have to be so unappealing? If I were to run my hands through his hair, I would need to wash them. He looked so stodgy and old beyond his years. I could not picture him doing any of the risqué things I read about in French novels. "If anyone from Florissant sees me in your car, I'll probably be expelled," I told him in an effort to inject a hint of danger into the dullness accumulating in the car, but he looked at me as though I had said, "It's a nice day, isn't it?" Then he began asking incessant questions about Orson Welles. These I answered halfheartedly and with a growing sense of shame. Why did I know so little of what my father had been doing in Europe these past years? Until The Nephew mentioned it, I had not even known (although I pretended to) that *Othello* had won the top prize at the Cannes Festival in May of 1952, nearly two years ago. Why hadn't my father told me of this triumph himself? He was so modest in private, so reluctant to discuss — at least with me — the many projects that relentlessly occupied him.

As we drove ever deeper into the woods, I kept trying to change the subject, exclaiming over the soaring Alps or pointing out a deer that was bounding away through the bare trees. Suddenly The Nephew stopped the car and roughly pulled me toward him, but I pushed him away with equal violence. He was not going to boast to all his Swiss friends that he had made love to "the daughter of." After a brief struggle, he let me go, then drove me back to Ouchy in silence, letting me out at a discreet distance from the *pensionnat*. And that was the last I saw of him.

"DADDY DEFINITELY WANTS me to stay with him for Easter, and I am delighted. I am never happier than when I am with my charming but thoroughly irresponsible father," I wrote my grandparents a few weeks before my sixteenth birthday.

It had been drilled into me since early childhood that my father was "irresponsible," especially when it came to contributing toward my support. How many times had I heard from my mother and others that his child support payments had been woefully inadequate? How often was it pointed out that without the generosity of Charlie Lederer, who had set up a trust fund for my mother at the time of their divorce, I would not be attending Florissant? The chorus of indignant elders proclaiming Orson Welles to be a "thoroughly irresponsible father" was so loud that it drowned out any efforts I made to come to his defense. And much as I wanted to defend him, I had my own childhood memories of standing in the front hall, all dressed up and waiting to be taken to lunch by a father who did not appear.

There was no one in my life at that time to take his side, no one to point out to me that because of his difficulties in finding financial backing for his films, he was often forced to come up with the money himself. In a real sense, he was one of the first independent filmmakers who, apart from the handful of films he made in Hollywood, worked entirely outside the studio system. During his years in Europe, no matter how it might appear to my mother and others who saw him living it up in luxury hotels, he had little available cash to spend on me or himself. But when he could spare the little he had, he shared it with me.

When I joined my father in Madrid during my Easter vacation, he was in the middle of making *Mr. Arkadin*. "Daddy is working very hard on his new picture, which I think, after seeing the rushes, will be his best," I wrote the Hills. We were staying at the Ritz, a grand Old World hotel, the kind my father preferred, in the center of Madrid. "It's going to be a brilliant film," I rattled on. "The star is an unknown actor called Robert Arden. He has so much talent that Daddy has signed him for a seven-year contract." (I had a terrific crush on Bob Arden—his New York accent and his gangster good looks—whereas he was no more than polite to Orson's kid.)

The Ritz was within walking distance of the Prado museum, and here my father took me on our first morning together to see an exhibit of Goya's etchings. I noticed his face was rosy with pleasure and that he walked beside me with a buoyant step, puffing away on his cigar. He was altogether more light-hearted than he had been in Paris last Christmas. "Why are you so happy, Daddy?"

"I'm always happy when I'm with you, darling girl."

"I feel the same when I'm with you, Daddy, but you seem *particularly* happy today."

He laughed. "How observant you are, Christopher. Well, I'm finally making another movie of my own, after years of bad luck and having to earn my living on the radio or in the theater or any damned way I can." He explained the BBC had been his "bread and butter" and given him a lot of work, beginning with a half-hour radio show called *The Adventures of Harry Lime* which featured the character he had famously played in *The Third Man*. "I'm also starting to get some work in television," he went on, "but enough of all that. Right now I'm in Spain, my favorite country in the world, and taking my beautiful daughter to the Prado. It doesn't get any better than this."

Now *I* was rosy-cheeked and beaming as we walked through the majestic doors of the Prado and down to the medieval gloom of its basement. Here a rare exhibit of Goya's etchings was on display, and I will never forget seeing *Los Caprichos* for the first time with my father beside me, translating the Spanish captions, illuminating their sardonic humor, pointing out Goya's attacks on the clergy and society's brutal treatment of women in eighteenth-century Spain. "Goya had to be very careful, though, because of the Inquisition," my father explained, "and that's why he sometimes drew goblins and witches instead of real people and invented a nightmarish vision to make his point."

I was overwhelmed. Never had I seen anything so terrifying and yet so beautiful and brutally honest at the same time. "So you aren't sorry I brought you here," my father teased, clearly delighted by my response to *Los Caprichos*, "and you won't blame me if you have nightmares tonight?" I shook my head, too overcome to speak, and around the exhibit we went again, singling out those etchings that charmed us the most with their black humor.

On another afternoon, my father took me to my first bullfight. I knew how much he loved bullfighting, and I tried hard to love it also, but when the picadors came riding out in their splendid costumes, the horses half rearing as they closed in on the bull, and then the riders plunged their swords deep into the bull's back, it was too much for me. I covered my eyes. "They have to do that to lower the bull's head," my father told me a shade impatiently. "Otherwise the bull would be too dangerous." He was completely caught up in the spectacle, shouting "Olé" as loudly as our neighbors. "Did you see that?" he exclaimed after the matador executed a pass with his cape that drew another roar from the crowd. In spite of my revulsion, I could see how graceful and daring the matador was, befuddling the bull with his cape until he wore him out. At last, blood streaming down its flanks, the bull came to a standstill and stood there waiting to be killed.

"Well, what do you think of bullfighting?" my father asked after the bull's dead body had been dragged out of the arena.

"I tried hard to like it, but I felt awfully sorry for the bull."

"What about the matador? Did you feel sorry for him?"

"No. He had a sword and could defend himself."

"And what if the bull had gored him? Every time a matador steps into the ring, he's risking his life, you know, no matter how great he is. A bullfight is like a dance with death, and the spectators don't know until the end whether death will claim the bullfighter or the bull."

But that's horrible, I wanted to say. Although I would again accompany my father to the bullfights when we visited Barcelona, trying hard to see "the dance with death" through his eyes, I was never able to share his enthusiasm.

On the other hand, when my father took me one evening to a small, smoke-filled restaurant in the back streets of Madrid where after midnight the tables were pushed to the walls to make room for a spontaneous eruption of flamenco, I became an instant aficionada. A man dressed in tight black pants and an open-necked black shirt began strumming his guitar, gently at first, like a slow caress, but gradually increasing the tempo until he was lashing and pounding his instrument as though it were a war drum. Hearing such wild, imperious rhythms, it was impossible not to stamp our feet, clap our hands, and sway in our chairs. Then another man, also dressed like someone going to a funeral, began to sing. He, too, started slowly, softly, but soon his song was infused with passion; then it became a strident cry on the edge of pain and yet strangely beautiful. During a break, my father watched approvingly while I wiped my eyes. "It's all in the music," he reflected, "the knowledge of tragedy, the acceptance of death, so imbedded in the Spanish soul. That's one reason I love Spain so much and could see myself living here. They're on such intimate terms with death in this country, and it gives them a kind of nobility and depth of character you don't find anywhere else . . . Ah, here come the dancers!"

I was surprised that the female dancer was middle-aged and bulging out of her costume until she began to dance. Then the years and the pounds fell away. I saw only grace and sensuous movement, a swirl of red skirts as the dancer clicked her castanets and stamped her feet in time to the frenetic guitar. Other dancers, male and female, were wonderful to watch, but none of them moved me as much as the flamenco singer who had given me my first glimpse into the Spanish soul.

At breakfast the next morning, my father announced that he was taking me to Toledo for the day. "Are we going on location for *Mr. Arkadin?*" I asked, secretly hoping that Bob Arden might be driving to Toledo with us.

"No, we're going to see the El Grecos," my father answered. "His paintings are scattered all over the world, but his greatest work — at least I think it's his greatest — is in a church in Toledo, and I can't let you leave Spain without having seen it."

"Which work is that?"

"*The Burial of Count Orgaz.* There's also an El Greco museum — the whole of Toledo is a museum, in fact. The town's been declared a national monument, you know, which means they can't build anything new or tear down anything old. If El Greco were to return today, he might be horrified by the traffic, but he'd recognize the skyline he painted so beautifully and the town where he lived for forty years."

As I soon saw for myself, Toledo rose on a succession of hills and steep cliffs high above the Tagus River. Like every fortified hill town built in medieval Spain, it was completely surrounded by monumental walls. Its streets were narrow and cobblestoned, so narrow in places that people on opposite balconies could lean out and shake hands. Potted geraniums spilled over the wrought iron balconies, splashing the ancient stones with a profusion of pink, crimson, white, and purple blossoms. Toledo had been the capital of Spain, my father told me, until 1560, but by the time El Greco arrived, sometime in the 1570s, the capital had been transferred to Madrid. "We know very little about El Greco's life except that he came from Greece," my father continued, "and that is as it should be."

"Why?"

"What should matter the most to us is a man's art and not how he lived his life. People today scrutinize an artist's personality, crowing over his mistakes, his human failings, and don't care enough about what he produced." I couldn't help feeling that my father was talking about himself. It was also dawning on me that my father was sharing his enthusiasms and ideas in the hope of enlarging my knowledge and broadening my view of the world.

We went directly to the church of Santo Tomé to see El Greco's masterpiece. We stood a long while, admiring the scene, which covers an entire wall, of the funeral of a now forgotten Spanish nobleman. The painting is divided into two halves representing heaven and earth. In heaven Christ is surrounded by angels, saints, and saved souls in a blaze of blue sky. On earth the dead body of the handsome count, suited in armor, is being tenderly lifted by the vicar and another clergyman. Behind them stands a crowd of aristocratic onlookers in black suits with pearly white ruffs around their necks. Most are dark-haired men with long, pointed faces. They have mustaches and goatees, and all look more solemn than sad.

"It's strange. This is a funeral but nobody's weeping," I remarked to my father.

"There are no women in the picture," he observed, teasing me.

"Seriously, Daddy, the picture doesn't make you feel sad, even though it's about death."

"Ah, but it isn't about death the way you think of it, darling girl. It's about resurrection and sitting on the right hand of the Lord. The count has been saved, you see, and heaven is waiting to receive him, which is more than we can say for the rest of us." His great laugh reverberated through the hushed church as we made our way out into the mild April sunlight and went in search of a restaurant.

On the drive back to Madrid in the late afternoon, my mind was filled with vivid images of the art we had seen. "Daddy, do you think El Greco is a great artist?"

"Well, I have to confess I liked him a lot better when I was your age."

"And who do you like now?"

"Everyone except El Greco."

"Seriously!" I hated being teased.

"I've never been more serious." He lit a cigar, chuckling to himself, while I stared out the car window at barren hills spotted with patches of green and silvery groves of olive trees — all that seemed to grow in this harsh land that gasped for rain.

"Oh, look, Daddy!" Suddenly I saw windmills standing in an empty field, a magical apparition of white windmills lined up in a row, their black blades revolving in lazy circles.

"Have you read *Don Quixote*?" he asked me. I shook my head. "Then you must read it at once. It's one of the great books, and I'm going to make a movie out of it. I'll find you a copy in English before you go back to Switzerland."

Many years later, while I was watching scenes from my father's incomplete film *Don Quixote*, it all came back to me. The Goyas in the Prado. The bullfights. Flamenco. Our day in Toledo, home to Cervantes as well as El Greco. And the arresting sight of windmills in an empty field. That memory triggered yet another. I returned to Lausanne without a copy of *Don Quixote*, which I am sorry to say I have yet to read in English, Spanish, or any other language.

"Do YOU MEAN to tell me you're not *allowed* to speak to your African servants," my father thundered in disbelief.

"Only to say things like 'good morning' and 'thank you.'"

"Don't they speak English?"

"That's not the problem, Daddy. We're supposed to keep our distance because they wouldn't like it if we got too familiar . . ."

"*They* wouldn't like it," he repeated. "I can't believe what I'm hearing, Christopher." The shock on his face made me feel ashamed. It brought back the discomfort I had felt every morning when our houseboy brought me a cup of tea on a tray. "I realize you have to live in South Africa for the time being—there's nothing we can do about that," my father was saying, "but I hope you'll remember you did not *always* live in that benighted country. My God, after living with Skipper and Hortense, the prejudices of white South Africans should be abhorrent to you." He stopped, biting his lip, as though perhaps he had said too much, then continued more softly, "Even if you're forbidden to speak to the Africans working in your house, I hope you'll remember they are human beings, just like you, and always treat them with respect."

I nodded, dismayed to see my father so upset, yet feeling an urgent need to defend my mother. So I plunged into the story of how, when we first arrived in Johannesburg, my mother had fixed up the servants' quarters with rugs and curtains she made herself. She even bought the servants a radio. Soon afterward, they all disappeared in the night, taking the radio with them. "So that's why we can't be kind to them," I finished.

"Christopher, please don't tell me any more or I'm going to be ill."

"But . . ."

"Enough!"

This conversation took place on the Côte d'Azur, where I was continuing the dizzying Easter vacation that began in Madrid and would end in Barcelona. "I am the happiest girl in the world at the moment," I wrote my grandmother. "I have seen most of la Côte d'Azur, Antibes (where we actually stayed), Nice, Cannes, Vence, Saint Paul, and many other small villages. . . . I have seen a wonderful amount of my wonderful father (which makes me happiest of all)." Yet my time with my father was bittersweet because I knew it could not last. When school ended for the summer, I would be forced to return to Johannesburg and live again with my mother and Jack Pringle. In my heart, I agreed with my father's appalled reaction to apartheid, and that only made it worse.

WHEREVER WE STAYED, my father had a knack for choosing the most opulent hotel in the area. In Cap d'Antibes, we were pampered guests of the Hotel du Cap. Our suite consisted of two bedrooms, each with its own bathroom, and an adjoining sitting room. In addition, we could enjoy our breakfast on a sunny balcony while gazing at the Mediterranean. At the time, I never wondered how my father could afford such luxury. In my mind, these grand hotels with their Old World atmosphere were as much a part of Orson Welles as his laugh, his cigar, and the voluminous black cape he sometimes wore in the hope that it made him look thinner. I came to take it for granted that in every hotel, the manager would be overjoyed to see him and the staff would bow to the floor when he passed. On checking into our suite, we would find a basket of fruit or a bottle of champagne in a bucket of ice with a gilded card reading, "With the compliments and best wishes of the management" or "We are most honored to have you as our guest, Mr. Welles."

Another luxury I would always associate with my father was being driven around in a chauffeured car. He, himself, had given up driving long ago. According to my mother, he had smashed up a car soon after he got his license and that had scared him off driving forever. On one day etched in my memory, a chauffeur in cap and uniform came to collect us in the middle of the morning and drive us in style to the town of Vence. By then, my father had been up for hours, devouring newspapers in English and French, calling down to the front desk for more papers in Spanish, Italian, any language, just make it snappy, then making phone calls, notes to himself, more phone calls, then scribbling away on the shooting script for *Mr. Arkadin*, which seemed to be in a state of permanent revision. As he worked on it, the crumpled pages accumulated like popcorn balls around his feet. I, meanwhile, was out on the balcony, writing letters that went on for pages — to Barbara in South Africa, Marian in London, Alain in Paris, my grandparents in Chicago — until my hand ached. My eyes were drawn up and over the balcony and out to sea where the soft morning sun danced on the waves.

On our way to Vence, my father told the driver to stop the car at the foot of a walled village whose houses seemed to be tumbling down the hillside. This was Saint Paul, he declared, also known as Saint Paul de Vence, "the best preserved medieval village in all of Provence." As its narrow cobblestoned streets had not been built for cars, we were going to explore it on foot.

We sauntered along, my father's big warm hand in mine, letting our feet take us here and there, through curving streets, under covered passageways, past ancient walls, up one stone staircase and down the next. At last we stopped to rest in a courtyard with a bubbling stone fountain. It was so peaceful, so perfect, and suddenly I realized why. Not one person in Saint Paul had run up to Orson Welles and asked for his autograph.

We continued on to the neighboring village of Vence in order to visit the Dominican Chapel of the Rosary designed by Henri Matisse, in my father's view an even greater artist than his contemporary Pablo Picasso. We entered the whitewashed building and immediately found ourselves in an airy, joyous space flooded by colored light from the stained glass windows. The white tile walls, the white marble floor, the altar covered with a simple white cloth, all added to the feeling of serenity and well-being. I was especially drawn to the stained glass windows that rose from floor to ceiling, revealing a childlike pattern of leaves, the kind that might have grown in the Garden of Eden.

"Well, what do you think?" asked my father, eyeing me in that way he had when he was waiting for me to say something clever.

"This place feels too happy to be a church."

"And why shouldn't people be happy in a church?"

"What I mean is, most churches are dark and gloomy and make you feel you should kneel and ask forgiveness for your sins, and this place . . . well . . . it makes you feel good just to be standing here."

"You're right." He squeezed my hand. "Matisse felt we should bear our burdens with a light heart. He calls this chapel his masterpiece, you know. He says it's the result of his entire life as an artist." (Matisse was still alive on that day we stood in his chapel.)

"Daddy," I whispered, even though we had the chapel to ourselves, "do you think there really is a God up in heaven who cares what happens to us?"

"Now, Christopher, that's two separate questions. Is there a God? Question one, and question two. Does he give a damn?"

"At moments I want to believe in God, like now," I went on, still whispering, "but I suspect people made up the idea of God a long time ago because it was too scary to imagine a world without him . . ."

"The God of the Old Testament is *terrifying*! Haven't you read your Bible?"

"Seriously, Daddy . . ."

"On the subject of God, one can't be too serious."

"Does that mean you believe in him?"

"One minute you sound like an atheist and the next like the Grand Inquisitor."

"I'm sorry."

"No, no, it's just that at moments you frighten me and I wish—now don't misunderstand me—I wish you were less intelligent. A lot of men will be scared to death of you, you know, even though you're so beautiful. But to answer your question, I can't go as far as you do and say I *don't* believe in God. I want to allow for the possibility that there might be a God, somewhere, in some mysterious form. So I guess that makes me an agnostic."

He smiled down at me and took my arm, leading me out of the chapel and into the sunshine.

WE TRAVELED BY train from the Côte d'Azur to Barcelona, and it took us something like eighteen hours. The train, carrying livestock as well as passengers, made every stop along the way, and at each station the wait was interminable while crates of chickens were unloaded or a cow was led lumbering down a ramp. To pass the time, I told my father that I had begun studying French dramatists at Florissant, progressing from the classical plays of Corneille, Racine, and Molière to such contemporary dramas as Jean Anouilh's *Antigone*. "I gave a dramatic recitation before the entire school—I played Antigone—and afterward Madame Favre praised me to the skies, which she very rarely does. She said that if I want to become an actress—"

"Which I hope to God you don't!"

"—I definitely have the talent." I stopped, remembering another conversation that seemed to have taken place in another life when my father had been none too pleased by my success in Todd School's talent show. Then I had been ten years old, but now I was old enough to have it out with him. "Why don't you want me to become an actress?"

"Because it will make you miserable." He had said as much when I was ten.

"But I love doing it. I don't feel a bit nervous when I'm up on a stage. In fact, it feels like home, and Madame Favre says—"

"You mustn't listen to what people say, Christopher. They don't always know what's best for you, but I believe I do. It isn't a question of whether you have the talent to become an actress. Of course, you do—you get that from me, unfortunately—but that isn't enough, you see, because you don't have the temperament for it. In that way, you are very like your mother."

"I'm not like my mother at all!"

He laughed. "We won't go into that." The train lurched forward and began chugging out of the station, having left a few bewildered hogs on the platform.

"Why don't I have the temperament for it?" I could feel tears tickling the back of my throat.

"You don't want to be in the limelight. How you'd hate it if you ever became famous! I've seen you scowling at all those poor people who ask for my autograph—don't think I haven't noticed! No, you hide in a corner, like your mother, not wanting to draw attention to yourself, but all the time, you're listening, listening, not missing a thing, and making endless notes in that busy brain of yours . . ."

"No, I'm not!" But even as I protested, I knew he spoke the truth.

"And while I haven't seen you on a stage, I'd wager you can't project, like your mother, because you are an *interior* person and too private. An actor has to be something of a damned fool, you know, and a grand exhibitionist, ready to strip off his clothes and stand naked on the stage. He has to turn himself inside out to find whatever warts and moles the part calls for. Your mother couldn't do that. She was such a lady that she couldn't be anything else."

"Stop comparing me to my mother!"

"But why? I thought you and your mother were close."

"I don't want to talk about my mother!" I began to cry but softly.

"Good God in heaven, what have I done!" He patted my hand, suddenly awkward and flustered while he fumbled for the linen handkerchief poking out of the breast pocket of his black shirt. "All I want for you is to be happy, and I don't think you will be if you become an actress. There now, dry your eyes and stop making me feel like a cad."

I mopped my eyes while we sat in silence, staring out of the grimy windows at the countryside passing before us. We had crossed the Spanish border at last and how different the land looked from the south of France. Little grew here except gnarled olive trees and low-lying scrub.

"There's another reason why a life in the theater wouldn't suit you," my father resumed. "You are too damned intelligent. Most actors are children, you know, not very bright or original, and if you had to spend every day of your life with them, you'd be profoundly bored."

"Are you bored by most of the theater people you know?"

"God, yes! But don't tell anyone." He gave me a conspiratorial wink and looked relieved when I smiled. "No, darling girl, the thing for you to do is to marry a *very* smart banker, lawyer, or stockbroker who'll make pots of money and take excellent care of you. Then you can settle down in a lovely home somewhere in the suburbs and have lots of kids. That will not only make *you* happy, it will make me a grandfather!" He laughed his fulsome belly laugh and lit another big, fat cigar as the train crept through the drab outskirts of Barcelona.

Is that the only future Daddy sees for me? I looked away to hide my disappointment. Perhaps he was right and I should not pursue a career in the theater. Yet I wanted to do far more with my life than make Orson Welles a grandfather.

7

The Phone Call

I FELT IMMEDIATELY AT home in Barcelona, a city that welcomed strollers and pleasure-seekers, staying up all night to accommodate them. Well past midnight, throngs of people still paraded up and down the spacious, tree-lined boulevards. Restaurants, bars, and cafés were packed. Children bowled hoops or ran shrieking along walkways reserved for pedestrians, followed by Spanish Civil War veterans hobbling along on crutches and hunched-over grandmothers pushing squalling infants in carriages. It seemed no one in Barcelona went to bed before dawn.

Like a homing pigeon, my father had booked us into Barcelona's Hotel Ritz. It had first opened its doors in 1919 and still stood on the Gran Via like an imperious dowager wearing the family jewels. The lobby was magnificent with tiled marble floors and archways reminiscent of a Moorish palace. The Ritz had been built, my father informed me, at the height of Barcelona's *modernista* movement, the Catalan equivalent of Art Nouveau, which began in the late nineteenth century and continued to be fashionable into the 1920s. It was an exuberant style that blended Arabic, Moorish, Gothic, and many other influences.

"Wait until you see Gaudí's houses," he told me, smiling broadly, as we rode the elevator to our suite on the top floor.

"Who?"

"Antoni Gaudí. The most inventive *modernista* of them all. He was original to the point of madness, and what's really incredible is that he got away with it." A mighty gust of laughter shook the elevator. "The Catalans let this madman turn his fantasies into houses and start to build a cathedral that looks like mounds of melting chocolate and stands unfinished to this day.

George Orson Welles, ten years old.

Virginia Nicolson Welles with her newborn daughter, Christopher (1938).

Orson sported a
beard when he first
arrived in Hollywood
in 1939.

Orson's drawing of the building
at 319 West Fourteenth Street in
Manhattan where he lived with
Virginia in the 1930s.

Watching Daddy paint
a hand puppet.

Applying stage makeup.

Orson directing the dancing girls in a scene from *Citizen Kane* (1941).

Orson sharing a joke with his good friend Joseph Cotten on the set of *Journey Into Fear* (1943).

Looking through the lens.

With his assistant Dick Wilson standing by, Welles talks to actor Richard Bennett on the set of *The Magnificent Ambersons* (1942).

Welles practicing a card trick for his magic act (1944).

Welles and Gary Cooper celebrate their birthdays, which are one day apart, shortly before Welles appears in *Tomorrow Is Forever* (1946).

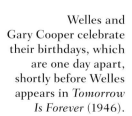

Welles and Oja Kodar in his essay film *F for Fake* (1974).

Orson with Oja Kodar at an exhibit of her paintings.

Now the whole world flocks to see these creations and the name of Gaudí is inseparable from the name of Barcelona. I'll take you to see his houses tomorrow."

Yet when morning came, clear and invigorating, my father decided we should first explore the Ramblas, Barcelona's most famous promenade for strollers, vendors, and street entertainers. The Ramblas stretched for blocks between two busy streets lined with houses that desperately needed a coat of paint and ended just shy of the port. We began in the northern end, picking our way through the flower market: so many lovely blossoms, all kinds and colors, still wet with dew, bunched and waiting in pails of water to be taken home in armfuls. Soon the flower stalls gave way to vendors of caged birds, but we did not linger here, not liking the sight of hundreds of exotic songbirds in captivity. Farther on we stopped to watch a flamenco dancer from Andalusia, a pathetic old woman in garish makeup, make a valiant attempt to entertain us. My father gave her a few coins.

"Daddy, does Ramblas mean 'rambling' in English?"

"No, it comes from an Arabic word, *ramla,* which means 'dry river bed.'"

It never failed to amaze me how much he knew about everything. "Daddy, didn't you ever go to college?"

"No, as I've already told you, I went to Ireland at the age of sixteen precisely to *avoid* being sent to college."

"But later on, after Ireland, didn't you—"

"After Ireland, I eloped with your mother and started the Mercury Theatre."

"Don't you ever wish you'd gone to college?"

"Never. I've taught myself everything I need to know."

"But how?" I waited impatiently while he stopped to give money to a blind man grinding away on a hurdy-gurdy.

"Mostly by reading every book I can get my hands on, but also by listening to people who know more than I do. If you're curious by nature and willing to admit how little you know about anything, you'll spend your entire life educating yourself and do a far better job of it than any university."

We had come to the end of the Ramblas and stood on the waterfront, facing a statue of Christopher Columbus. My father had me notice that the statue's lifted arm was pointing in the direction of North Africa and not, as it should have been, toward the New World. After sailing west to discover the land he thought was India, my father continued, Columbus arrived back in Barcelona with several "Indians" in tow and got a royal welcome from Ferdinand and Isabella.

"Why didn't they receive Columbus in Madrid?" I wanted to know.

"Because, in 1493, the capital of Spain was Barcelona."

As we retraced our steps to the hotel, it occurred to me that if I could spend one full year in my father's company, I would never need to go to college.

EARLY ONE MORNING I accompanied my father in a chauffeured car that took us north of Barcelona and around the rugged coastline of the Costa Brava. At that time there were no hotels or high-rises standing shoulder to shoulder on a super highway. There were only private villas built into the cliffs and well hidden from the road, including the one my father was considering as a location for *Mr. Arkadin*. When we arrived at our destination, a splendid villa with gardens overlooking the sea, our Catalan hosts gave us lunch on the terrace. Then they withdrew, leaving my father to explore the house and grounds with me trudging along at his side.

Suddenly, he turned to me, his voice warm with concern. "What's the matter, darling girl? You don't look as happy today as you usually do."

"I don't want to go back to Florissant."

"Why not?"

"I don't want to be a secretary, Daddy."

"Come." He took me by the hand and led me to a stone bench shaded by a trellis thick with grapevines. His hand felt so gentle over mine, so warm and comforting. "If you could be anything in the world," he asked, looking deep into my eyes, "what would you choose to be?"

I'd be just like you, I wanted to say. "I don't know," I hesitated. "I mean, I wanted to be an actress, but you don't think I'd be any good at it . . ."

"That's not what I said, Christopher. You *would* be good at it—you'd be good at just about anything you wanted to do—but I'd like to see you do something that uses your mind. It would be terrible to waste a mind like yours on *acting*."

"And what about my becoming a secretary?"

He was silent for a moment. Then, gazing out to sea, he continued, "Whatever you do in life, it's not forever, you know. Even if you started out as a secretary, in a few years, you could be doing something entirely different, something you can't even imagine now."

"Do you know what I want more than anything in the world, Daddy? I want to go to college." There. I had finally come out with it. "I know *you* didn't go to college and you don't really believe in it, but that doesn't mean I shouldn't go. I'm sure I'd get a lot out of it. There are so many holes in my education, and I don't see how I'm ever going to amount to anything if all I can do is speak French and take shorthand and type letters."

"You're right. Instead of that finishing school, you should be going to the Sorbonne in Paris. Well, if that's what you really want, I can arrange it."

"You can? You mean it?"

"Of course, I can. They love me in France. Leave everything to me."

"You're wonderful! " I threw my arms around him and hugged him so hard that we almost fell off the bench.

THAT EVENING, I sat at the desk in my hotel room, describing the Costa Brava in a letter to Grandmother. "It has a savage and natural beauty that I have not seen elsewhere," I wrote her. "Whereas the Côte d'Azur's charm lies in cultivated beauty which everyone can enjoy without any discomfort, the Costa Brava's charm lies in the impression one has of being the first person to stand on those rocky cliffs and gaze at the lashing waves."

I did not tell Grandmother that I would soon be leaving Florissant and attending the Sorbonne. Nor did I tell her that while I was rhapsodizing about the Costa Brava, I was also eavesdropping on a telephone conversation my father was having in the adjoining room. It was clear from his solicitous tone, his fervent assurances, that he was speaking to someone important to him. How could she think he had forgotten her when every day, every hour, he thought of her and missed her terribly? He had *wanted* to call, but he had been so occupied with Christopher . . . but *of course* he still loved her, he was besotted with her, how could she think for a moment . . . In a few days Christopher would be back in Switzerland.

I clapped my hands over my ears to shut out this unknown woman. Why, when I knew nothing about her, did I feel so sure she would take my father away from me? Moments later, my father stuck his head around the door and asked if I was ready to go out for dinner. "Who were you talking to?" I asked him.

"Oh, that was Paola." He gave me his Harry Lime smile. "You don't realize it, but you've already met her."

"I have?"

"Yes, you saw her in the rushes I showed you the other day. She plays Raina, Mr. Arkadin's daughter. Remember?"

I called up the image of a tall brunette with black, magnetic eyes. In fact, her eyes—heavily lashed and framed by thick, black eyebrows—were the most striking thing about her. "She's very beautiful."

"She certainly is. She's also a genuine Italian countess, you know. The Countess di Girfalco . . . but she lets us commoners call her Paola Mori." He laughed with delight, but for once I didn't join him.

"Am I going to meet her in person?"

"Not here in Barcelona, but you will when you come to Paris. Paola and I are planning to live there after we finish the picture, and then you'll have a place to stay while you're going to college."

"But won't Paola mind? I mean, maybe she doesn't want me staying with you."

"Christopher, you worry too much about everything, just like your mother. Paola is the most warmhearted, loving, mothering kind of woman you'll ever have the good fortune to meet. She's a lot like Hortense Hill, you know, except that she's incredibly beautiful and only twenty-three."

Only seven years older than me, I thought. Why couldn't she be old? Old and ugly with hairs growing out of her chin. Well, I consoled myself, perhaps like all the other women in my father's life, she wouldn't last long.

SOON AFTER MY return to Florissant, I wrote my mother about my vacation with my father, describing in detail what we had seen and done in Madrid, the south of France, and Barcelona. "And now for the most fantastic news of all," I exulted. "Daddy is going to send me to the Sorbonne!" Wasn't this the best plan for my future now that my French was so fluent? I had been moved up to the most advanced class the *pensionnat* had to offer, but in truth, I had outgrown Florissant. I was eager to move on to a university where I could study in depth the subjects that most interested me: French literature and art history.

My letter went on to spell out the details of my father's plans. He was going to rent an apartment for the two of us (I decided to leave Paola Mori out of our ménage for the time being). When he had to be out of Paris, I could stay either with the de Courseulles or with friends of his. Through Alain, I had already met a large number of boys and girls my age. In fact, it was amazing how many people I knew in Paris . . .

In a matter of days I had my mother's cold reply. "I can live with your dislike of me and poor Jackie who has tried so hard to be your friend," she began. "I can survive your ingratitude in spite of all we have done for you; I can even brush aside your disloyalty to us as the by-product of your pathetic schoolgirl crush on Orson (for which I am partly to blame), but the one thing I cannot tolerate is having a daughter who is a bloody fool."

I was so shocked by her reaction that several moments passed before I was able to read on. "You are worse than a fool if you really believe Orson will set you up in an apartment in Paris and pay your tuition at the Sorbonne. He will promise you the moon and the stars — he is very good at that — and then leave you high and dry. You are much too young, at sixteen, to be left anywhere on your own. So if you join your father in Paris, you can forget about seeing me ever again. I'll cut you off just like that!"

I was so taken aback that I had to stop reading her letter and take a few deep breaths before I could continue. Then came the final blow. "On the other hand, if you still want a relationship with me, you must stop seeing Orson or having anything to do with him. There will be no more visits, letters, or phone calls from now on. Jackie and I will not tolerate Orson's interference in our plans for your future."

Sobbing, I fell on my bed. I was six again and terrified of the mother who had turned inexplicably into a witch who was lunging at me, foulmouthed, hitting any part of my body she could grab, hitting to hurt with closed fists. Even then her fury had struck me as out of proportion to my "crime." Now she was just as angry with me, just as out of control, and I was as helpless at sixteen as I had been at six.

Time passed, making room for other memories. The afternoon I fell off the swings in the school playground, landing on my hands and breaking both wrists. Then my mother rushing to school, driving me to the hospital at breakneck speed, and making such a scene that I was attended to at once. It had always been my mother who made sure I was fed, clothed, cared for. Buying me a mountain of presents at Christmas. Celebrating my birthday with an elaborate party — would I ever forget the one where she had a circus tent erected in the backyard, complete with clowns, acrobats, and pony rides? She had never vanished in smoke, as my father had done, for years at a time. No one had needed to send *her* five letters to five different addresses with an appeal for money for my tuition or school uniforms, only to have them all returned and stamped *Moved. No Forwarding Address.*

When at last I stopped sobbing, I realized I could not join my father in Paris if it meant losing my mother. (Knowing her, I took her threat to cut me off "just like that" very seriously.) Maybe at eighteen or nineteen I could have done it, but not at sixteen.

The days that followed were the most distressing of my life. My friends at the *pensionnat* kept taking me aside and asking what was wrong. Was I ill? Had there been a death in my family? I forced myself to smile and pretend everything was fine. Meanwhile, Jack Pringle was communicating from Johannesburg with Madame Favre. In a copy of his letter, which fell into my hands a good forty years after it was written, he wrote, "We were pleased to receive your letter . . . regarding Christopher's development. Her last visit with her father was, we fear, rather unsettling. Chrissie has written us several letters with which we are not altogether pleased. They exhibit an unattractive conceit, and a tendency to forget the reasons why she was sent to Florissant. This has led us to reply in a somewhat sharp manner. You may find that she is somewhat upset in the next weeks, and it could well be that it is our letters which have upset her. We fully realize that our letters may have this effect, and I would ask you not to intervene if you notice that she is unhappy."

In spite of my stepfather's directive, Madame Favre invited me to have tea with her one afternoon in her private apartment. I was no longer intimidated by this gaunt, white-haired woman with piercing blue eyes. She had put herself out to be kind to me ever since, at the behest of Jack Pringle, she had given me a bad report. My stepfather claimed that if I got a good report, I would turn into "a slacker," whereas a bad report would make me work harder.

It happened like this. The entire school was assembled in the lounge and Madame began reading our reports aloud, one by one. When she got to mine, my immediate reaction was that there had to be some mistake. Everyone knew I was the best student in the school, the only one, in fact, who took her classes seriously. So it was ludicrous to say that I was "not applying" myself or "not progressing rapidly enough." The gross unfairness of my report turned my cheeks a flaming red.

Barely able to suppress my indignation, I waited until Madame Favre had finished and then asked if I might speak to her in private. She immediately confessed that the "bad" report had not been her idea but my stepfather's, and that I deserved not only a good report but an excellent one. From that moment on, Madame Favre was my friend.

"Now tell me, Christophare," she began while pouring our tea in her pleasant living room, "why are you so unhappy these days?" I burst into tears and told her everything. When I had finished, she kept stirring her tea, twirling the spoon around and around in her cup while she gazed out the windows at Lac Léman and the towering Alps beyond. What would it be like, I wondered, to have such a view every day of one's life? I mopped my eyes, determined to lift myself out of my misery. At last Madame said in a quiet voice, "I think your mother is very frightened."

"Frightened?" *Furious, hysterical*—those were the adjectives that sprang to my mind.

"Yes, she is afraid of losing you, don't you see? And so she threatens you in this way to make you stay with her. She is also afraid of what might happen if you go to Paris to be with your father. I think she is trying to protect you from him, Christophare, and that is why she does not want you to see him."

"But Madame, Daddy is the kindest, most generous, most wonderful . . ." My voice broke, and I buried my face in my hands. She leaned over and patted my shoulder.

"Now Christophare, I am going to say something that perhaps I shouldn't, but somebody needs to say it to you. The feelings you have for your father are not natural. You do not feel about him the way a daughter normally feels about her father."

"What do you mean?" I did not intend to address her so sharply, but I suddenly felt under attack.

"I mean that when you are expecting to see your father or stay with him—and I have observed this several times since you have been with us at Florissant—you get much too excited and overwrought, as though you were going off to see a lover." She gave a little laugh. "Then, when you return from these visits, you are much too dejected, again as though you have been parted from a lover. Don't you see, Christophare? To feel this way about your father is not natural or desirable. If I were your mother, I would also be thinking about limiting your visits with him."

"But, Madame, my mother wants to *end* my visits for good."

"That is what she says now, of course, but I do not think she means forever."

That gave me some hope. Perhaps if I gave my mother time to calm down, she would come around. As Madame Favre had suggested, she may have been overreacting out of her fear of losing me.

Although I managed to say "Au revoir" to Madame and thank her for the tea, I left more troubled and confused than I had been before our tête-à-tête. If what Madame had said about me and my father were true—and I suspected it was—what was so wrong about it? How was I supposed to feel about him, a man who, quite apart from being my biological father, was an extraordinary human being and a great creative force? Hadn't my mother always said Orson Welles was not to be judged by normal standards? "Orson is a genius, Chrissie, and you can't expect a genius to behave like an ordinary father." Always my mother had been my father's champion, explaining away the long lapses when I didn't hear from him. Always she had encouraged me to think well of him, no matter what he failed to do. How often she had told me I would never have a better companion in the world than my father . . . how often, until now.

STUNNED BY A blistering letter he received from my mother, my father turned to his staunch allies, Hortense and Roger Hill, in the firm hope that they would come to his defense. (I knew nothing of this until years later when Skipper gave me the correspondence.) First my father appealed to Granny, writing, "I sent a very happy and loving Christopher back to school this Spring. We exchanged letters . . . and she begged me to keep a week free for her before school this fall. Then she went to South Africa, and after that silence." He told Granny that, not understanding why he was no longer hearing from me, he had wired my mother repeatedly and finally received "a communication" bursting with "hysterical anger." "[Virginia] seems to have the idea that I have been poisoning Christopher against her," he wrote to Granny. "This charge is utterly false . . . I have never spoken anything but warmly of Virginia to anyone . . . and certainly it would be unlike me to begin with Chrissie." He went on to explain that although he had discussed my future with me on several occasions, he and I had talked "only in general terms as I should think any father or even friend would have the right to with a young lady of sixteen." He assured Granny that his conversations with me had always been qualified by his "pointing out to Christopher that she must talk these things over with her mother as a point of final authority" (which is not how I remembered it). He concluded, underlining words for emphasis, "Now Virginia writes (and I quote exactly), 'If I could prevent your seeing Chrissie until she is of age I should do so. The Hills agree with me. I am in constant touch with them.'" He signed it "in great haste and unhappiness" with a huge, dashing capital O.

Granny promptly replied with a letter my father read as a scolding lecture on his failure as a parent. Although he had been reluctant to involve Skipper in this matter, he now sent him a heartrending appeal. "Virginia wants me to stop seeing Christopher," he began,

> and she quotes "The Hills" as agreeing with her. I wrote Hortense asking her to deny — or at least hoping she'd deny this astonishing claim of my ex-wife's. Her answer frankly horrified me. She states that it is "hard" for Chrissie to have a "part-time" father, that the "wonderful times" she had with me last Christmas and spring only made my absences more difficult. This is obviously nonsense. I am not responsible for the child having spent her summer holidays in South Africa, and I don't suppose Hortense would say that I should have made an attempt to keep Christopher from seeing her mother. She — Hortense — then goes on to quote Christopher as saying "wistfully" that she "doesn't know how to reach me." This is more nonsense. The same business address which Christopher has had for almost two years will forward my mail, when I'm not in Paris, within a matter of days.

My father urges Skipper to read the letter he wrote to Hortense "and then see if you, too, feel that 'it would be better if I didn't see Christopher at all.'"

Under the heading Supplementary Information Dept., he enumerates the points in his defense. First, he has paid in full my school tuition and other expenses. Second, he has written "many more letters to Christopher than she has written to me. There is honestly no question of neglect on that matter." (Nor was there any truth in his claims to have paid for my schooling and showered me with letters.) Third and fourth, he has never uttered a word of criticism against my mother or the way she has brought me up — quite the reverse — nor has he shown the slightest disapproval of my Swiss school or any other school. "My only conversations with Christopher regarding education have had to do with the necessary limitations of all schools."

He goes on to tell Skipper that after appealing to Hortense, she "has only seen fit to send me little lessons on how to be a good parent." While he fully grants her the right to do this, he also recognizes that Hortense thinks men are usually in the wrong. "Well, God knows, I'm wrong a lot more times than I'm right—but this time there really is some justice on my side," my father concludes.

> Christopher and I have been getting along so marvelously to-gether . . . Well, anyway, I do think that this is a moment when "The Hills" ought to be flocking around my banner without any prior attempt to judge me, and if there are to be attempts to keep me away from my daughter, I hope "The Hills" will make it pretty strongly clear that they're not part of the plot.

Although she had not hesitated to chide my father for not meeting his responsibilities to me and would continue to do so as long as she was alive, Granny did not feel she could come between him and my mother. "It wasn't any of our business," she told me years later.

"That's right," Skipper agreed, "and besides we hadn't seen Virginia in years, and we didn't even know that English gent she'd married . . . major somebody or other."

"Jack Pringle," I put in.

"Right. Well, this Pringle guy was making all the decisions where you were concerned, Chris—"

"Like deciding you weren't 'college material,'" Granny huffed.

"—and Virginia was going along with whatever this Pringle guy said, and we didn't feel we could stick our oar in."

While I understood the Hills' position, it hurt my father deeply at the time. He saw their refusal to come to his defense as their lack of faith in him as a parent. He had been counting on them to put matters right with my mother because, as he had confessed in his letter to Skipper, "I'm in no condition for this Christopher business." He was going through "fairly hysterical times" with "millions of troubles and so little dough that I'm actually facing a winter without an overcoat."

A CHILLY RECEPTION was waiting for me in Johannesburg when I returned that summer of 1954. Although Jackie could not dispute the excellent report he had received from Madame Favre, he found constant fault with my behavior, being determined to snuff out the "unattractive conceit" he thought he had detected in my letters home. Whether we were having our afternoon tea on the veranda or were gathered around the dinner table, I could not open my mouth without being told my ideas were "half-baked," I was "wet behind the ears," and that at my age it was "unattractive" to put forward my opinions. What could I possibly contribute to the conversation that would be of the slightest interest or importance? I would do better to drink my tea, eat my dinner, and listen attentively to those who were older, wiser, and better informed.

Yet learning to keep my thoughts to myself did not win approval either. "Chrissie hasn't said a word all evening," my mother observed to Jackie one night during dinner, speaking as though I were not in the room. "Do you think she's sulking about something? What a bore it is having to live with a moody adolescent!"

"Why are you so sullen, Chrissie?" Jackie demanded, staring me down across the table. "Why are you being so tiresome, and upsetting your mother?"

Not knowing what to answer, I burst into tears.

"There she goes, crying again," my mother complained. "What *is* the matter with her, Jackie? I really can't take too much more of this. It isn't good for my nerves."

"Either you stop crying this instant, Chrissie, or go to your room!" my stepfather commanded. Then, turning to my mother with his most charming smile, "Perhaps in the future, Virginia, we should have dinner by ourselves."

Later that evening my mother came to my room, where I was lying face-down on my bed but no longer crying. She perched on the edge of the bed, one tentative hand smoothing my back. "I know Jackie's being hard on you," she began, "but it's for your own good, darling. You're much too full of yourself after you've been with Orson, and that's why Jackie has to take you down a peg, don't you see?"

"Yes, Mummy," I lied.

Where inside this puffy-faced, dowdy British matron was the slim, glamorous American mother who had been married to Orson Welles and Charlie Lederer? Yet what upset me more than the loss of her looks was the change in her personality. There was a new hardness about her, a suspicion of everyone's motives and particularly those of Orson Welles. Whenever I mentioned my father, which I was careful to do out of Jackie's hearing, my mother glared at me as though I had defected to the enemy.

I waited for a morning when my mother seemed in a better mood than usual and Jackie was safely out of the house, exercising his polo ponies. The African houseboy in his crisp, white uniform had brought us our "elevenses" on a silver tray. It seemed as good a time as any to open up the subject that had been tormenting me. "Mummy, you've always encouraged my visits with Daddy and told me how wonderful he is, and now, all of a sudden, you don't want me to see him anymore. If I stay in Florissant and complete the secretarial course —"

"What do you mean 'if.' You will do what Jackie and I think is best for you with no ifs, ands, or buts."

I waited for her to stop frowning. "What I meant was that after I finish business school and get a job as a secretary, couldn't I see Daddy then?"

Now she was glaring at me and barely able to control her exasperation. "Once you're out on your own and supporting yourself, you can do anything you like, and I won't be able to stop you, will I?" She stabbed out one cigarette while reaching for another. We sat in silence for a while, my mother drawing the smoke of her freshly lit cigarette deep into her lungs as though it were life-giving oxygen. When she spoke again, it was in the firm voice of one who has arrived at a difficult decision. "Since you *will* be on your own in the next year or so, I think it's time I told you a thing or two about Orson. You're old enough now to hear this father you adore has some serious faults. You should know who you're dealing with, and I don't think you do yet. That's why I'm ending your visits with Orson for now, until you get your head on straight about him. Do you understand what I'm saying, Chrissie, or does that awful look on your face mean you hate me?"

I could be just as tough as she was. "What is it about Daddy that you think I don't see?"

"Well, for one thing, you believe he really cares about you when the truth is, and I honestly don't want to hurt you, Chrissie, but the truth is . . ."

"He *does* love me. I know he does!"

"No one knows better than I how seductive Orson can be," my mother went on as though I hadn't spoken. "He can make you believe you're the most important person in the world to him and he can't live without you. Then the next thing you know, he's fallen in love with somebody else."

"But he's not *in love* with me," I protested. "I'm his daughter."

"The trouble is that Orson has no idea how to be your father. Does he behave like a father when you're with him?"

"Well . . ." I hesitated. "Daddy treats me like an equal, but I can't say he always behaves like a father."

"At least you see that much." The houseboy stood hovering in the doorway, and with an impatient wave of her hand, my mother signaled that he was to remove the tea tray. He moved so softly that I could hear the whisper of his starched white uniform as he bore the teacups away. "I think that's enough truth for one morning," my mother remarked after he had left. "I'll just say this for now: As long as you think you really matter to Orson, you're in for a lot of heartache and disappointment. I'd hoped to get through to you, but I see I haven't been very successful, and you'll have to find out the hard way, like I did."

"What do you mean?"

"I'll tell you some other time."

"Please tell me now."

"I said. Some other time."

ONE EVENING, AFTER my mother had gone to bed early complaining of a headache, I sat with Jackie in our spacious living room. Each of us occupied a comfortable armchair before the fireplace. A recording of Beethoven piano sonatas played in the background. At such moments, I was seduced by the seeming coziness of "home." Even Jackie sounded friendly when he asked, "What's that book you're reading, Chrissie?"

I showed him my copy of Anouilh's play *Antigone,* and then went on to tell him I had given a dramatic recitation before the whole of Florissant, playing Antigone, and everyone, including Madame Favre, had thought I was wonderful. Then, before I could stop myself, "I want to be an actress more than anything."

"Do you?" It was not a question but a mocking statement. "I suppose this is Orson's doing."

"No, Daddy's tried to discourage me."

"Quite right, too. What on earth gave you the idea that you could be an actress?"

"Well . . ."

"So you're ready to go on the stage, are you? Do you already see your name up in lights, Chrissie? How extraordinary!" The contempt in his laughter made my skin prickle. "I'm sorry I can't agree with Madame Favre and your friends at Florissant, but I think I know you better than they do. After all, I've known you since you were a little girl of eleven, and in all that time, Chrissie, you haven't shown the slightest talent for acting or anything else." He paused to make sure his words were having their intended effect, but I guess I wasn't looking crestfallen enough because he added, "You are a very ordinary person, and the sooner you accept that, the better off you will be."

There were furious questions to hurl at the suave man sitting opposite me, smoothing down his mustache with one finger, but I fought them down. Nothing was going to change Jack Pringle's low opinion of me or his relentless need to put me down. The silence lengthened and deepened in a room that had lost any trace of coziness.

"I'VE ARRANGED TO have you spend this Christmas in Paris with the de Courseulles," my mother announced one morning while we were having our eleven o'clock tea. In less than a week, I would be flying back to Switzerland for my second and final year at Florissant. "Orson wanted you to be with him for Christmas, but that's out of the question."

"Then you've heard from Daddy? Where is he now?"

"As a matter of fact, he's living in Paris with some Italian countess or other."

"Then couldn't I see him?"

"No."

"Not even once?"

"Don't be so tiresome, Chrissie. I've made it very plain why you are not to see your father, and if I find out you *have* seen him in Paris or anywhere else . . ." She left the threat hanging in the air.

"But how am I going to tell Daddy?"

"Tell him what?"

"Why I can't see him. He won't understand why I'm in Paris, and he isn't hearing from me."

"He'll understand all right. Don't you worry about that! I've written him a stinging letter and told him exactly what I think of him. I'm one of the few people in Orson's life who's never been afraid to stand up to him."

"But I have to call him at least once, I have to, so I can explain to him."

"And what are you going to *explain* to him, pray tell?" Her jaw was clenched.

"That you don't want me to see him—"

"That's right. Blame me! Blame me for everything!"

"But—"

"If you want to go on seeing Orson and let him ruin your life, I guess that's what you'll do, and no one is going to stop you, me least of all, apparently." She gave her little laugh, the one that meant life was a cruel, cosmic joke beyond her control. "But there's something you should know first."

All at once I began to dread that I was about to hear what she had *not* told me several days ago when she had said, "Some other time." She reached for a cigarette, lighting it, inhaling, languorously blowing out the smoke. She was making me wait. Deliberately.

"I swore I'd never tell you this," she began, "but you're so pigheaded about Orson, you leave me no choice. I was seven months pregnant with you, and we were living in Sneden's Landing." She was referring to the rambling farmhouse with a garden and swimming pool that she and my father-to-be had rented in a wooded enclave not far from Manhattan. Then she fell silent, bending her head over her sewing. The South African sun streamed into the alcove where we were sitting.

"What happened at Sneden's Landing, Mummy?" I prompted her.

She looked up with a smile. "I'll get to that in a moment. I was just remembering the summer I found out I was pregnant with you. It was one of the happiest times in our marriage. The theater season was over, and we were safely tucked away in Sneden's Landing where none of the people clamoring for Orson could get at him, especially all those shameless women waiting at the stage door who literally *threw* themselves at him. You had to see it to believe it, Chrissie, how those hussies ran after him down the street, grabbing at his clothes. Of course, there was no way Orson could hide out with me indefinitely. He was already too famous and the offers were pouring in from radio stations and even Hollywood studios, although Hollywood didn't interest him yet, thank God." Her voice trailed off and she was bent over her sewing again, smiling to herself, while I sighed and fidgeted. After a few moments, she continued, "Orson devoted himself to me that summer. Every day we swam in the pool and lazed in the garden. We paid no attention to Doctor when he wrote us from Chicago, 'I hear you have a lovely house with four spare bedrooms.'" She laughed, sounding girlish. "We didn't need any company except each other and Budget." Budget was the cocker spaniel they had named in honor of their early days of thrift.

The idyll lasted, she went on, until Orson's partner arrived unannounced one sultry August evening and stayed for dinner. Known to his friends as

Jack, John Houseman had teamed up with my father when he was becoming a big radio star but was still eager to work in the theater. Their first smash hit was a production of *Macbeth* with an all black cast. "Orson and Jack started reminiscing about the sensation they'd caused in Harlem and on Broadway, and how the two of them had made theater history more than once, and suddenly Orson leaned forward and asked Jack, 'Why don't we start our own theater?' And that's how the Mercury got started, the idea of it anyway. They took the name from an old magazine I fished out of the fireplace . . ."

Why was she telling me all this, I wondered? When were we going to get to the terrible thing my father had done?

"Orson and Jack found a dilapidated theater on Forty-first and Broadway," she continued. "They fixed it up in no time and renamed it the Mercury Theatre." They planned to open their first season with Shakespeare's *Julius Caesar.* "Now Orson told me he needed to go off by himself for ten weeks so he could work on adapting *Julius Caesar* without any distractions. Ten weeks! I could hardly bear the thought of being without him all that time and

rattling around that big house on my own—I was still having morning sickness, thanks to you—but what could I say? I told him that of course he must go and not to worry about me. I'd be fine." She gave me the plucky smile she must have given him.

"The night before Orson left for his mountain retreat in New Hampshire, I asked him if he'd write in a part for me in *Julius Caesar.* I didn't care how small it was, I told him. Well, he stared at me as though I'd lost my mind. How could I *dream* of staying up all night in the theater when I was going to have his child? I had to swear on his mother's grave that I'd stay home every night, drink my milk, and be in

The first Mrs. Orson Welles.

bed by ten o'clock." She laughed. "He was *so* concerned that I take proper care of myself and our unborn child and yet he was leaving me alone for ten weeks . . . and there you have Orson in a nutshell." She paused, studying my face. "Shall I go on? I'm not sure I should, really."

I was feeling sick with anxiety, but I nodded. "Please go on, Mummy."

"All right. It's high time you got the stars out of your eyes and realized what it's really like to live with Orson."

Once Orson began rehearsing *Julius Caesar,* she told me, he was hardly ever home. In addition to spending anywhere from sixteen to twenty hours a day in the theater, he was also doing his regular radio shows. "When I begged him to cut back on his radio work, he reminded me that if it weren't for the big bucks he was making in radio, we couldn't afford to live in Sneden's Landing or to start a family." Not only that but his lucrative earnings also paid for the motorboat he used to ferry himself back and forth across the Hudson when he did manage a trip home. "That was becoming such a rare event that I told him he might as well give up the boat and swim across. I meant it as a joke, but he didn't find it funny."

"Weren't you awfully lonely with Daddy away most of the time?"

"Yes, I missed Orson like mad, but I read a great deal and took Budget for walks in the woods. I've always been able to amuse myself, but it helped a lot when Chubby and Whitford came to see me." She was referring to the actors Hiram "Chubby" Sherman and his partner, Whitford Kane, who were members of the Mercury Theatre company. "They were such dears. They brought me the latest gossip and what Chubby called 'tales of Orson.'" She laughed. "I can laugh about it now, Chrissie, but it wasn't funny then."

"What did Chubby mean?"

"I'm getting to it." She poured herself another cup of tea, then sat drinking it in a reverie. "Being married to Orson was the hardest thing I've ever done in my life, but it was also the most thrilling," she finally resumed. "I was just remembering how I came out of seclusion and went to the opening of *Julius Caesar.* You have no idea what a novel idea it was then to put on that play, or any play, in modern dress. Now it's been done so often, it's become a theatrical cliché, but then it was electrifying and people talked of nothing else for weeks."

Why was she taking so long to "get to it"? Surely the fact that my father worked day and night and rarely came home was not the reason she had decided to end my visits with him.

Sneden's Landing
N.Y.

We hope you are well. Virginia's self-portrait (above)
may give you some notion of how we are doing in case you
didn't know. In the meantime, Merry Christmas to you
from Budget, Orson, Virginia and ....

The Christmas card Orson drew when Virginia was pregnant with Chris, December 1937.

"On New Year's Eve," she continued, "Orson and I went dancing at the Waldorf, and many of our friends couldn't get over how light-footed I was for a woman six months pregnant. It was one of our few times together that Christmas. Orson was working such long hours that he'd begun checking into a hotel for the night. He worried that he was leaving me on my own too much. So he sent Geraldine to keep me company."

"You mean Geraldine Fitzgerald?"

"Yes, she'd just arrived from the Gate Theatre in Dublin where Orson had made his stage debut when he was sixteen. Well, Orson hired her on the spot. Geraldine was marvelous-looking in those days with her red hair and her green eyes. Orson decided she'd be perfect as the ingenue in *Heartbreak House,* the next play on his list, but before rehearsals began, he sent her to Sneden's Landing to cheer me up."

I had always assumed my mother and Geraldine became friends during the years we lived in Hollywood. "I never knew this . . ."

"There's so much you've never known. Anyway, I loved having Geraldine stay with me—she was such good company—but I was still fed up with seeing so little of Orson. So one night I decided to go to the Algonquin Hotel, where I knew he was staying. It was a very cold night in January, and I was in my seventh month."

Yet she remembered setting out in high spirits, thinking how surprised my father would be when he came back to his hotel room late that night and found her in his bed. "When I got to the Algonquin, I swore everyone at the front desk to secrecy and went up to wait in Orson's room. I was so sure he'd come back eventually to shower or change, but it got later and later, and still no sign of him. I called down to the desk a couple of times, but there was no message, of course. Why should there be? He wasn't expecting me. What a silly goose I was in those days!"

My mother gave her husky laugh and reached for a cigarette. "Hand me the lighter over there, will you, darling?" While she went through the ritual of lighting up, I peered through the screen of smoke, trying to imagine my matronly mother in her slim twenties, seven months pregnant with me.

"Well, the sun came up and there was still no sign of Orson," she continued. "I decided there was little point in waiting any longer, but before going home, I wanted to leave a love note on his pillow. That's when I opened a desk drawer, looking for some notepaper, and found his love letters from other women." She laughed again, this time with an undercurrent of sadness in her voice. "At first, I thought they were fan mail—I was *so* naive in those days—but, of course, that made the shock more terrible, you see, my being so innocent and trusting. It seemed every ballerina in New York had written to him, and there were also letters from my good friend Geraldine. I couldn't believe it at first, that Orson would actually send Geraldine to stay with me when he'd been having an affair with her." She smashed out her cigarette in the ashtray with a force that made me shudder.

I didn't know which revelation upset me more—my father two-timing my mother with Geraldine or my mother and Geraldine remaining close friends. "But once you knew Geraldine had betrayed you, how could you want to have anything to do with her?"

"I couldn't hold it against her, you see, because in those days, you simply fell into bed with anyone who asked you to, especially if you were an actress trying to get ahead, although how Orson found the time to be unfaithful to me with Geraldine or anyone else, I will never understand." She had collected herself, sounding as cool and controlled as though she were giving an interview on being the first Mrs. Orson Welles. "I suppose it was because we were both so young and inexperienced when we married that we were never very good at sex. Your father was a virgin when he met me, whatever nonsense he tells his biographers these days . . . but I never dreamed he would go looking for plea-sure with other women. Until I found those letters I honestly thought he was as devoted to me as I was to him." A few moments passed in silence while I felt the unwelcome weight of all she had told me. But more was still to come.

"Well, Chrissie, you won't believe what I did next." She paused, her eyes on my face, and now I knew she was going to tell me what she had sworn she never would. "I tried to throw myself out the window—and you, too, of course, although you weren't born yet—but I couldn't get the window open. God knows I tried. I pulled with all my strength, but it was sealed shut, one of those hotel windows that aren't supposed to open. Oh, Chrissie, I wish you could see the shock on your face!"

I was seeing my pregnant mother falling like a rag doll from an open win-dow, then hitting the sidewalk, lying limp and still, both of us lost in a widen-ing pool of blood.

AFTER I RETURNED to Florissant, I began going for long walks by the lake, needing time alone to reflect on what my mother had told me. Now that she was far away in Johannesburg, I could hardly believe what she had revealed, but I was unable to sweep it from my mind. So, at the end of the day, when the light was blue and the Alps were mirrored in the lake, I wandered along the quay, the beauty around me only adding to my misery. Why had my mother told me she had tried to kill herself before I was born? Had she told me so I would understand why she was incapable of loving me? Or had her purpose been to make me feel sorry for her? I could see how devastating it must have been for her—innocent, trusting, still aglow from her happiest summer with my father—to come upon the love letters in his hotel room, especially the ones from Geraldine. But did she stop for a moment to consider how devastating it would be for me to hear she had wanted to kill us both?

She could have made a case against my father without telling me that. As it was, her arguments and predictions made so little sense that I had to conclude she was semihysterical. Obviously she felt my father had ruined *her* life, but that didn't mean he would ruin mine. How did his inability to be a faithful husband have any bearing on his relationship with me? Nor did it matter in the same way if he stayed home every night with me or was away half the time. I was going to be occupied with my studies at the Sorbonne, and when my father was out of town, I had Alain and plenty of other friends my age to keep me company.

So the worst that could happen was that I would get to Paris and discover my father had done one of his vanishing acts. Then—my mother was right—I would be stranded. But had she been a loving mother, she would have given me the option of returning home to her if things did not work out in Paris. She would never have threatened to cut me off "just like that" and put me in this agonizing position of having to choose between her and the father I adored.

THE DE COURSEULLES were wonderful to me when I spent Christmas with them in Paris, but all I remember about that holiday is the phone call I made to my father and the terrible hours of indecision that led up to it. I kept looking for a way to avoid it, knowing there was none, going around and around in my cage like a trapped animal. Nothing in my life thus far had been as bad as this.

On my next to last day in Paris, I turned to Alain, who walked with me for hours in the dismal rain, his sympathetic hand in mine. We crossed to the Left Bank and wandered along the Seine to Notre Dame, our favorite spot, but the sight of the green angels climbing the spires did not lift my heart that afternoon. Nothing could distract me from the dilemma I spelled out again and again to Alain, who patiently listened and wisely said nothing.

When we were too tired and chilled to walk any farther, we went into a café, where Alain ordered two cups of hot chocolate at the bar and I eyed the pay phone in a corner. I couldn't put it off any longer. I rummaged in my pocket for the crumpled piece of paper on which I had scribbled my father's phone number in Paris. I walked to the phone, slowly, then dialed his number with a shaking hand. I prayed my father—not Paola—would answer.

"Hello." It was my father.

"Daddy?"

"Yes?"

"It's me, Christopher."

"Yes?" He sounded guarded, when I had expected to hear him say, as he nearly always did, "Is that my darling girl?"

"Mummy's very angry . . ."

"I know. She wrote me . . ."

"Daddy, I think it would be better if we didn't see each other for a while and gave Mummy time to calm down . . ."

"So you want to end our visits, too?"

"Just for the time being. I think it would be best."

"All right, Christopher, if that's what you want."

But it wasn't. It wasn't.

8

In His Absence

AFTER COMPLETING MY SECOND year at Florissant and obtaining a secretarial diploma in French and English, I returned to Johannesburg, where I was not to remain for long. Although I was willing to get a job and move out of the Pringle household, my mother felt I was still too young to live on my own. She also saw South Africa as "a backwater country" in which I did not have much of a future. "You'll be far better off living in the United States," she told me, and I had to agree. So it was decided that for the next several years I would live with my grandparents in Chicago.

While I didn't want to spend the rest of my life in South Africa, it was not easy to leave my mother, not knowing when I would see her again. Now that she had banished my father, she was the only parent I had left. As cold and mean as she could sometimes be, I believed that in her own imperfect way she really did care about me.

Yet the years of being belittled by my mother and stepfather had had their effect. I had grown painfully shy and unsure of myself, bearing little resemblance to the high-spirited child I had once been, the child who had wheedled her way into her father's movies. Until recently I had been able to count on visits with my father to restore my self-esteem, but now that I would be living with my grandparents, who heartily disapproved of Orson Welles, there was not much hope of seeing him again. Not for a long time.

During the first weeks I stayed with my grandparents in their elegant apartment half a block down from the Drake Hotel and around the corner from Lake Michigan, I couldn't believe how kind they were to me and how they accepted me just as I was, without criticisms or reservations. At least once a day they told me I was their "pride and joy" and that my very existence "made up for everything else that's happened in this family." This was as close as

Christopher's last summer with the Pringles in Johannesburg, South Africa (from left to right: Jack Pringle, Angie, Simon, Virginia, Chris).

they came to expressing their disappointment in my mother and Aunt Caryl, neither of whom had stayed in the fold and married old money in Lake Forest. But now that I was nearly eighteen, Grandmother saw in me a new chance to break into the social register.

Although my grandparents were careful not to criticize my mother and stepfather, they made it clear they did not approve of the way I had been treated in Johannesburg. "It isn't right to give a child an inferiority complex," Grandmother said more than once, naming no names and pursing her lips in that prim way she had.

"Hell, Chrissie is as smart as they come," Grandfather exclaimed from the easy chair where he spent his evenings, highball in hand. "Look at how she beats the pants off me every time we play Scrabble."

Nearing sixty, white-haired and heavyset, his complexion ruddy from alcohol, Leo Nicolson was still a handsome man. While we played our endless games of Scrabble, the apartment was so hushed that I could hear the tick-tock of the antique clock in the entrance hall and the tinkle of melting ice cubes in my grandfather's scotch and soda. Then, as though thinking aloud, my grandmother looked up from the novel she was reading and murmured,

"Chrissie's had such a hard life, and look how well she's turned out in spite of it."

"She's a great gal all right," my grandfather muttered, "but hell, I wish just once she'd lose at Scrabble! This is getting monotonous . . ."

Eager to show me off to society, my grandmother gave a lavish reception at the exclusive Fortnightly Club. That my "debut" became a news item in the gossip columns owed something to my grandparents' social standing in Chicago but far more to my connection with Orson Welles. In the accompanying photo, I am wearing a formal cocktail dress, too much makeup, and a strained smile. At the reception reporters came up to me, asking questions about my father: Where is he? What is he doing? Is he coming to Chicago to see me? To my embarrassment, I didn't know the answers. Seeing my confusion, my grandmother led me firmly away by the elbow, saying under her breath, "Don't *ever* talk to reporters about Orson. They're bound to pester you the moment they know who you are, but tell them, very sweetly, that you don't want to be interviewed."

It was the first time reporters had cornered me, demanding information about my father. It would not be the last time, I realized. My grandmother was right. The moment they knew I was the daughter of Orson Welles, they would descend like buzzing flies. There was no escaping my father's fame and the intense interest his name evoked. Even in his absence, his long shadow fell across my life.

WHENEVER ANYONE MENTIONED Orson Welles, my grandmother would sniff and press her lips together as though one had said something in bad taste. My grandfather would begin his diatribe about the emotional unreliability of "theater folk." He was convinced they were all "pansies." You couldn't count on a "damned fool actor" for anything, he liked to say, and if you did, you were "a damned fool yourself." He had told my mother the same thing years ago, when she was my age and all starry-eyed about Orson. Well, he hoped to God his granddaughter had more sense than her mother. "You know, Chrissie, I offered your dad a job on the stock exchange, a good solid job that would have put meat on the table when he and your mother were practically starving in New York—"

"That *dreadful* apartment in the basement where Virginia told me they slept in the bathtub," Grandmother sniffed.

"—and Orson told me he couldn't be a stockbroker, because he was

Chris's maternal grandmother,
Lillian Wayman Nicolson, at age thirty.

already an actor. The fact that he was an out-of-work actor when he could have been an employed stockbroker didn't enter into his thinking, of course. And he was so damned polite about telling me to go to hell with my job on the stock exchange."

"When I *think* of what poor Virginia went through, having to pawn all her pretty dresses and her jewelry just to pay the rent on that *dreadful* . . ."

It saddened me that my grandparents saw my father in such a negative light and that they were so narrow-minded in general. Now that I was seeing the Nicolsons at closer range, I understood why my mother had rebelled against them and eloped at eighteen with Orson Welles. "I was her ticket out of town," my father had told me once, as though the main reason Virginia Nicolson had run off with him was to escape from her family. She had been at constant odds with her social-climbing mother, whom she still referred to as "that silly woman," and although she had been her father's favorite and, by her own admission, "thoroughly spoiled" by him, she had recoiled from his racist and ultraconservative views.

Now that I had come to take my mother's place, I saw how maddening Grandmother could be. Although she had a good mind and was a gifted pianist—"her one and only accomplishment in life," my mother liked to say with a scornful laugh—she was obsessed with trivia and social niceties. She was the only person I knew who kept a meticulous list of every menu she had served at every dinner party to assure that no guest would eat the same dish twice. Yet I did not lose sight of her virtues: She was thoughtful, generous, a woman of elegance and exquisite taste. We shared a love of classical music and went to many splendid concerts together. And because I knew my grandmother really loved me and would do anything she could for me, no amount of fundamental disagreement could diminish the special closeness between us.

I also loved my grandfather in spite of his prejudices. An earthy, self-made man of shrewd intelligence, he had not lost touch with his humble beginnings as a farm boy in Alma, Kansas—unlike my grandmother, who could barely bring herself to tell me about her Quaker parents, dismissing them as "simple nobodies" with an airy wave of her hand. On the surface my grandfather seemed more charming and easygoing than my grandmother until, after a few too many highballs, he began spewing poisonous remarks about blacks, Jews, Democrats,

Chris's maternal grandfather, Leo Malcolm Nicolson.

"pansies," and "theater people." At such moments I intensely missed my father. Until I came to live with my grandparents, I had not realized how much I had modeled myself on my father's freedom from prejudice.

Although Leo Nicolson had friendly dealings with Jews in his industrial real estate business, he would never dream of inviting them to his home. "You must always keep your business life separate from your personal life," he advised me during the many evenings he spent coaching me on how to conduct myself in the business world. I noticed that he drank steadily from the time he came home from the office until he lumbered off to bed, but I did not think anything of it. Then, one night, I was awakened by his incoherent shouting and my grandmother screaming, "No, Leo, no!" There was a scuffle in the hall outside my door. I sat up in bed, terrified that my grandfather was going to burst into my room in a drunken rage, but somehow my grandmother stopped him. The next morning she had a black eye—the result, she said, of "banging into a door." I knew she was lying, and she knew that I knew. It was understood between us that I had been given this haven only until I could afford a place of my own—and the sooner that happened, the better.

WHILE I WAS living in Chicago, I often visited Granny and Skipper Hill, who had remained a vital link between me and my father. Grandmother disapproved of my having anything to do with the Hills. She had never forgiven them for encouraging the romance between young Orson and Virginia, but what really bothered her were the Hills' lifestyle and values, which stood in direct opposition to her own.

The Hills were still living in their rambling farmhouse outside Woodstock, Illinois. It felt like coming home to sit once more in their cozy living room paneled in knotty pine, or to curl up in the window seat, gazing out at fields of alfalfa tossing in the wind, remembering how I had romped in them as a child, pretending the wind was the sound of ocean waves. Of course, everything had shrunk in the intervening years, but how comforting it was to sit again at the harvest table covered with a red-checked cloth in Granny's kitchen, watching her bustle around the stove and waiting for the cuckoo clock to sound the hour.

On one of these visits I learned my father had married Paola Mori in London two days after his fortieth birthday. Skipper showed me some recent photographs of my new stepmother, whom I had first seen when my father showed me the rushes of *Mr. Arkadin*. She had been striking in the role of Raina, with her huge, expressive eyes, heavy brows, and short, curly hair, but now she was a full-blown beauty, soft and womanly. Her hair was long and sleek, swept up in a French twist. She had a lovely smile and looked warm-hearted. Would I ever get to meet her, I wondered, and if I did, would she like me?

Skipper reminded me that Paola Mori was a stage name. She was really the Countess di Girfalco and came from a distinguished Italian family. When her parents learned Orson had made her pregnant, they were horrified and insisted he marry her. "It was a shotgun wedding all right," Skipper chuckled.

"What a thing to say!" Granny objected. "Why, you know how devoted Paola is to Orson and how much she's helped him cut back on his drinking. Why, she worships him and there's nothing she wouldn't do—"

"That may all be true, Horty, but I doubt Orson would have married her if she hadn't gotten herself pregnant and her family hadn't made him feel he had to do the honorable thing."

"I don't see how you can say that, Skipper."

"I just did!" He laughed like a mischievous schoolboy.

Six months after my father married Paola, my half sister Beatrice was born in New York, and once again it was the Hills who gave me this news. Although my father could have easily called me up in Chicago and told me I had a new sister, he did not. Was he turning his back on me, or had he forgotten all about me?

I could not bear to think my father had erased me from his life when he was so present in mine. Even if he hadn't been in the news, there were always people meeting me for the first time and exclaiming, "Are you really Orson Welles's daughter?" Yes, I really was, but now it was becoming a source of shame and humiliation. I felt the whole world knew he had abandoned me.

MY MOTHER'S SISTER Caryl came to Chicago to visit for a few days. My father had once told me that when he first met Caryl, he found her better looking than Virginia and that Caryl had been blessed, he felt, "with a sweeter nature." Tall, blond, and extremely attractive, my aunt certainly wore her years better than my mother; but at the moment, she told us, she was "totally exhausted and fed up to the gills with Orson." Her latest encounter with my father had been a financial disaster for New York's City Center and a professional embarrassment to her.

Caryl worked in public relations as a fund-raiser and was friendly with Jean Dalrymple, director of the City Center on West Fifty-fifth Street. "I talked Jean into putting on Orson's adaptation of *King Lear*," Caryl told us, "and after she agreed to do it and we raised the horrendous amount of money Orson said he needed, he injured both his feet. It was bad enough that he broke one foot and had to hobble around with a cane on opening night, but then he tripped over a prop on his way off the stage and sprained his other ankle. I never knew anyone as clumsy and just plain self-destructive as Orson."

"But Aunt Caryl," I chimed in, "could he really help it? I mean, anyone can have an accident, and my father's always had weak ankles."

"Listen to this child. Defending the father who hasn't lifted a finger for her." Caryl turned her lovely blue-gray eyes on me, the same color as my mother's but with more warmth and laughter behind them.

"But it was such bad luck that he hurt himself twice."

"Luck had nothing to do with it. What's the matter with you, Chrissie? You're a smart girl. Don't you see Orson's a fuckup?"

"Caryl, watch your language," my grandfather said disapprovingly, but my aunt just shrugged. She lived in New York City now.

"Seriously, Chrissie," Caryl went on, "what's Orson ever done for you?"

I looked down at my hands on my lap, not knowing how to explain that it wasn't what my father had done or not done but who he was and what he believed in: being tolerant of others, for instance, and being kind and considerate while living a life in which the making of art was supreme. There wasn't a mean bone in him; if he hurt people along the way, it was always unintentional. How could I persuade my grandparents and Aunt Caryl that the Orson Welles I knew was not "irresponsible" and "self-destructive"?

"Orson ended up having to perform *King Lear* by himself in a wheelchair," my aunt was telling us with exasperation. "We lost oodles of money, and I don't think Jean Dalrymple will ever speak to me again. That's the last time I'm going out on a limb for Orson." (As my father would tell me years later, Caryl was not appeased by the fact that her ex-brother-in-law had tried to put on a good show for the sold-out performances, even if he was confined to a wheelchair. He recited lengthy passages from *King Lear* and told his most amusing anecdotes, a bravura performance which he repeated for twenty-one nights, but that was not long enough for City Center to recoup its investment in Orson Welles.)

After my aunt's visit, it was a relief to spend another weekend with the Hills, and it was on this visit that I finally broached the subject that had been causing me such distress. Why hadn't I heard from my father in over a year? My question hung in the air. After a long, uncomfortable silence, Skipper sprang out of his chair and began his restless pacing. "Well," he drawled, "we weren't going to tell you, Chrissie, but since you brought it up . . ." He stopped short and looked at Granny for guidance.

"It was that time you called Orson in Paris and told him you couldn't see him anymore," Granny explained. "Paola was with him when you called, and she said she'd never seen Orson so upset."

"He reacted like a wounded King Lear," Skipper observed.

"You mean overreacted," Granny added tartly.

"Well, now Orson's got this idea in his head about Chrissie being 'a thankless child,' and you know how he is, Horty, once he feels betrayed."

So that was it. In my father's mind, I had become the embodiment of the lines from *King Lear,* "How sharper than a serpent's tooth it is / To have a thankless child."

"That's all nonsense, Skipper, and you know it," Granny snapped. "If anybody's put ideas about Chrissie into Orson's head, it's Paola."

"Now, Horty, you don't know that for a fact."

"I *do* know it's all Paola can do to get Orson to pay attention to little Beatrice, and the last thing she wants is competition from our Chrissie."

I stopped listening. It had nothing to do with Paola or Beatrice and everything to do with my father's reaction to that fatal phone call. Why hadn't he understood I was acting against my will and under my mother's threats to disown me? Didn't my father understand what it had cost me to be in Paris, a short Metro ride away, and prevented from seeing him? Apparently not. Instead he saw me as the "thankless child" who had rejected him, wounding his heart beyond any hope of forgiveness.

"I always trust people with all my heart and think the best of them," he had told me once, this child-man who was my father, "until they give me a reason not to."

From his point of view, I had given him a reason. Knowing this, I could not go ahead with my plan: to ask Skipper to call my father and then, after a brief exchange of pleasantries, put me on the phone. I could not be sure what kind of reception I would get from the father who now believed I had cast him aside, but I feared it might be a cold one, and that would have hurt far more than his continuing absence.

I BEGAN TO be afraid that no one in Chicago would give me a job, without which I could not afford to live on my own. In interview after interview, I was turned away because I did not have a high school certificate, let alone a college degree. My knowledge of languages and ability to take shorthand in French were of no use to me in Chicago. So much for Jack Pringle's plans for my "future."

To improve my chances of being hired, my grandfather enrolled me in a business school in Chicago's Loop. A certificate from such a school, he reasoned, would count more with a prospective employer than all my foreign languages and exotic travels. Yet the exact opposite turned out to be the case.

One of the companies where I sought employment was Container Corporation of America. The personnel director there, a pleasant woman who immediately put me at ease, spent our entire interview asking me about living in Rome and Johannesburg, going to school in Lausanne and traveling all over Europe. "What a fascinating life you've had," she exclaimed, "but I guess that's no surprise since you're Orson Welles's daughter." Once again "Orson's kid" was stamped on my forehead, but this time I didn't mind. Paying no attention to the holes in my education, the personnel director gave me my first job: junior secretary in the advertising department.

That I survived even a week I owe entirely to the amazing patience of my boss, Mr. Doughty, the short, sandy-haired director of advertising. Every letter of his that I took down in rapid shorthand and typed up at the furious speed of 120 words per minute had to be corrected and retyped—two, three, sometimes four times. My main problem was that I confused the spellings of similar English and French words and used British spellings, such as substituting *colour* for *color*. To avoid having Mr. Doughty summon me yet again into his office, peer wearily over his horn-rimmed glasses, and then hand back the letter in which my errors had been circled, I kept an American dictionary at my elbow. Weeks passed, my spelling improved, and to my astonishment I was still on the payroll.

Another stride toward independence came after my grandfather had a serious heart attack and needed absolute quiet at home. We were all agreed that it was time for me to move out, but my grandparents felt I was still too young to be living on my own. So my grandmother found the perfect solution: the Three Arts Club. This attractive residence for young women in the arts—singers, dancers, actors, artists, musicians—was housed in a stately mansion on North Dearborn Parkway, a stroll away from Lincoln Park and the lakefront with its spectacular view of Chicago's skyline winding into the distance. (My grandmother would not have been pleased to learn that Hugh Hefner lived up the block in his *Playboy* palace.) Offering room and board at reasonable rates, the Three Arts Club was designed for students on scholarships or young artists who came from families of modest means, but I was accepted thanks to my grandmother, who was on the board of directors and presented me as a budding pianist.

I had a large, pleasant room to myself on the second floor. It was handsomely furnished with everything I needed, including an upright piano, which I diligently played as soon as I got home from work and for hours on weekends. The Three Arts Club could not have been too different from a college dorm or sorority house, and, for the first time since arriving in Chicago, I was making friends my own age who were bright, cultivated, and who shared my passions for music and art. After dinner, which was served on the main floor in the communal dining room, we hung out in each other's rooms, sharing favorite recordings of classical music. At last I had someone besides my grandmother, someone as young and enthusiastic as myself, to accompany me to Orchestra Hall and sit in the cheap seats, clapping and cheering after we heard Bruno Walter conduct Mahler's symphonies, or the incomparable Artur Rubinstein interpret Chopin.

It was a giddy time of feeling young and free to do what I wanted. I could go out with any man I fancied, and, at the end of the evening, I would not find my grandmother sitting up in the front hall like a guard dog waiting to pounce. I knew it distressed her that I was drawn to Jewish men, and to one in particular who had aspirations to be a painter but eventually became a prominent art dealer. Grandmother had made every effort to introduce me to the "suitable" young men of her acquaintance, but I had found them extremely dull. I could not imagine myself married to one of them, yawning my life away in the wealthy suburb of Lake Forest.

Yet when I allowed myself to look more than a few weeks ahead, I felt confused and not a little apprehensive about the direction my life should take. Should I go to New York and become an actress, as any number of theater people who had known me since childhood were urging me to do? I felt a strong pull toward the stage, yet at the same time it terrified me. Even in my most confident moments, I knew it was madness to try to beat my father at his own game. Instead, I was hungry to accomplish something on my own, something that owed nothing to Orson Welles—except the gift of his exceptional genes. I hadn't any idea what this great accomplishment might be, but it hovered in the air like a deceptive mirage.

SEVERAL MONTHS HAD passed and I had not thought once of my father. Now that I had a job, a place to live, and friends my own age, I was forming a life that owed nothing to Orson Welles. Just when I felt I was beginning to walk free of my father's shadow, I got a call from my godfather, Chubby Sherman. Chubby had been my father's close friend and an actor in his Mercury Theatre company. Now he was passing through Chicago and wanted to take me to lunch at the Drake Hotel. If hearing from Chubby had not reminded me of my famous parent, then meeting him at the Drake certainly would have. It was the kind of grand hotel with an Old World atmosphere that my father loved.

The last time I had seen my godfather, I had been eleven years old and visiting my mother in New York, so he could not get over the change in me. "How old are you now, Chrissie?" he exclaimed. "Are you really eighteen?

I just don't believe it, that's all!" He, on the other hand, looked exactly the same, a round-faced man of medium height and build whose main characteristic was his affability. Shortly after I was born, he had appointed himself my godfather, blithely ignoring the fact that I was never going to be christened. "Any child of Orson's needs a godfather," he liked to say.

"Now tell me about your dear mother," Chubby began as soon as we were seated in the Drake's elegant dining room. "Does she like living in South Africa? Is she happy with her new husband?" After I had assured him that she was, he went on in his amiable way, "I'm very glad for her. The poor dear was so miserable when she was married to Orson."

"But weren't my parents happy together before I was born?"

Chubby considered this for a moment. "I suppose they were, dear, but their happiness didn't last long. It never does with Orson. When it comes to women, he's worse than an ally cat . . ." He bit his lip. "Oh dear, I shouldn't have said that."

"I know about the ballerinas," I said evenly. "My mother told me."

"She did?" For a moment, he let his affable mask slip. "Well, *I* thought it was the pink limit, Orson running around with all those hussies and leaving your poor mother to fend for herself. It got to the point where I couldn't *stand* to hear about another of Orson's ballerinas."

"Then you knew?"

"We all did, dear." He recalled the time when my father had been four and a half hours late for a rehearsal at the Mercury. "None of us believed Orson's preposterous story about flying to Boston in a snowstorm and having to take over the plane and land it himself after the pilot passed out. Everyone knew Orson had spent the night in Chicago with his latest lady love." Chubby clucked his tongue. "So Virginia found out he was cheating on her. I hoped she never would. What a sweet thing she was in those days. So pretty, too." He looked at me closely. "You know, Chrissie, you look a little like your mother did at your age, although you have Orson's eyes and his dark coloring."

We smiled at each other, and I thought how lucky I was that this kind man had adopted me. For a while we concentrated on our food. Then Chubby asked, "Are you in touch with Orson these days?" I told him what had happened in Paris. "And you haven't heard from him since then?" I shook my head. "That's so typical of him. You know, of course, that Orson and I were the best of friends until the day he decided I'd done him wrong."

Hiram "Chubby" Sherman (third from left), Joseph Cotten
(center), and other cast members in *The Shoemaker's Holiday*
(1938), Welles's Mercury Theatre hit that made Sherman a star.

"Tell me about it, Chubby."

He studied me thoughtfully. "I guess you're old enough to hear what
happened."

Chubby told me he had joined the Mercury believing that my father and
Jack Houseman were forming a repertory theater, but it began to unravel
when their first production, *Julius Caesar,* became a smash hit. "I argued with
Orson and Jack about moving *Julius Caesar* from our theater into a larger
one—that defeated the whole idea of repertory—and I also protested when
our next runaway hit was taken off the boards early to make room for *Heartbreak House.*" He was referring to Thomas Dekker's restoration comedy *The
Shoemaker's Holiday,* which had made Chubby a Broadway star. In the Mercury's last offering, George Bernard Shaw's "very talky" *Heartbreak House,*
Chubby had not been given a part. "That convinced me we weren't going to
be a repertory company after all but a one-man show. Orson's show."

He paused while the waitress cleared away our dishes. After ordering coffee, he continued, "Believe me, there was plenty of grumbling backstage about
Orson getting all the credit. What about the rest of us who'd contributed to
the success of our theater?" Chubby mentioned the article in *Time* magazine
that had featured my father but made no mention of Jack Houseman. "Without Jack, we'd never have made it through the first *week,* let alone a whole

season, and Orson was starting to treat him like a tiresome old uncle. Orson was becoming impossible. All that fame was going to his head."

"But why did Jack Houseman let my father hog the publicity?"

"Because he knew perfectly well that if he didn't, he'd be out on his ear." Chubby laughed, but it had a bitter edge. "Orson has to have it all, dear. *All* the credit. *All* the fame. He doesn't understand about sharing. A lot of the actors who started out with him didn't become famous until after they'd left him. Did you ever think of that? Who cares anymore that your Aunt Geraldine was in Orson's staged production of *Heartbreak House.* She'll be remembered for her role in *Wuthering Heights* and other movies Orson had nothing to do with."

"But isn't that the nature of the theater? When the curtain comes down—"

"Oh, you know perfectly well what I mean!" My godfather had never shown me the slightest irritation until now, when we were discussing his theater days with my father.

"So did you leave the Mercury because you felt my father was taking too much credit for everything?"

"Partly. But I'd also reached the point where I couldn't go on. Dear God, I couldn't face another one of those all-night rehearsals!" He rolled his eyes and threw up his hands in mock despair. "And Orson had changed—for the worse, I'm sorry to say. He was no longer sweet or considerate, bringing food to rehearsals or setting up cots in the aisles when we worked until dawn. Oh no. Now he was yelling his head off, drinking a quart of whiskey a day, and cheating on your poor dear mother with all those ballerinas. The whole thing was making me ill. Literally." He smiled at me sadly. "You know, Chrissie, if I hadn't left when I did, I'd have had a nervous breakdown. But Orson didn't understand that, and he's never forgiven me."

I thought this over while we drank our coffee. "I hope he forgives *me.* Do you think he will, Chubby?"

My godfather patted my hand. "Maybe you're better off not seeing much of Orson. Did you ever think of it that way, dear?"

THE ADVERTISING DEPARTMENT at Container Corporation of America was in an open area adjacent to the art department. Several times a day, the assistant art director loped past my desk, his mood as buoyant as his step, his infectious laugh ringing to the far end of the hall. It was impossible not to look up from my typewriter and smile at his handsome face shining with good humor. Curiously, I had never been drawn to a tall, blond, blue-eyed man who looked like a Viking, but I found something very attractive about the assistant art director's exuberance and, above all, his breezy self-confidence.

Whispered conversations with the other secretaries revealed that the Viking's name was Norman DeHaan. He was thirty years old and still unattached, although he was dating a woman as tall and blond as he was. So he wasn't available, I thought, putting him out of mind until the day he stopped at my desk and asked me to go out to dinner with him. "Well?" He gave me a broad grin as I continued to stare up at him. "Or if you prefer, we can walk over to the Art Institute and have lunch."

I opted for the Art Institute, where we were to have many lunches in the exhilarating weeks that followed, often skipping the meal in favor of wandering the galleries, hand in hand. Norman opened my eyes to contemporary artists I had been unable to appreciate before, and he also pointed out art treasures from Japan, China, India, and Southeast Asia that were a revelation to me. Much as I enjoyed these outings, I felt shy and unsure of myself, but Norman did not seem to notice. He covered my long silences by talking about himself.

He had grown up on Chicago's south side, he told me, in a rough immigrant neighborhood where a boy who preferred books to sports and wanted to be an architect when he grew up was not appreciated. Although Norman had been sent to a vocational high school, he refused to give up his dream of becoming an architect. At fifteen, he took some courses given by Ludwig Mies van der Rohe, the innovative German architect from the Bauhaus school of design. After winning a scholarship, Norman continued his studies at the Illinois Institute of Technology.

The next defining experience in his life was the Korean War. He spent eighteen months in Korea, working with the Army Corps of Engineers, and during that time, he told me, "I fell in love with Korea and all things Korean." So after the war, he stayed on and served as architectural advisor to South Korea's first president, Rhee Syngman. It was Norman who built the Bando, Seoul's first Western-style hotel. He was twenty-five years old at the time. "After the Bando opened, I became a kind of hero in Seoul." Wistfully he added, "I'd give anything to live there again."

Soon after this conversation Norman invited me to his apartment in Old Town, where he unveiled his fantastic collection of Korean art, which included hanging scrolls, bronze funerary urns, and celadon bowls. Yet I was even more impressed by the collector with the taste and refinement to acquire such treasures. Who would suspect that this sophisticated, cultivated man had begun life on the grim south side? Norman Richard DeHaan was his own creation, I realized, and that struck me as more remarkable than any of his other achievements.

I SHOULD HAVE anticipated Norman's next move, but it came as a complete shock to me. We were spending the weekend with friends of his in their country house by the lake. It was a chilly evening in late August, the air crisp with a premonition of fall, when Norman suggested the two of us go for a walk on the shore. We had not gone far when a storm blew up and it started to pour. Before I could run back to the house, Norman had swept me up in his arms and kissed me hard on the mouth. Then he blurted out that he wanted to marry me.

"C-c-could we be engaged first?" I asked him. I was shaking so hard it felt like malaria. Now the rain was coming down in sheets, but Norman did not release me from his arms.

"Engaged for how long?"

"At least a y-y-year."

"A year!" He sounded terribly hurt.

Once back at the house, wrapped in blankets but still shivering, I told Norman as gently as I could that I didn't see how I could marry him until I got to know him better. "There isn't that much to know about me," he said, and laughed in his hearty way, "but if it makes you feel better to be engaged for a while . . ." I assured him that it made me feel a lot better.

The next day I was rushed to the hospital with pneumonia complicated by a severe attack of asthma. This put me under an oxygen tent where I lay for days, grateful for every breath and trying to wrap my mind around the idea that the tall, good-looking man arriving daily with armfuls of flowers, books, and magazines was the same man I had promised to marry in a year.

It seemed unreal until the day my grandparents burst into my hospital room, demanding to know who this "Norman person" was. He had telephoned them in Nantucket, where it was their custom to spend the summer, and broken the "shocking news" that I was going to marry him once I got out of an oxygen tent.

"What kind of name is DeHaan?" my grandfather barked, not appeased when I explained between wheezes that it meant "the rooster" in Dutch.

"We don't know a thing about his people," my grandmother wailed. "How could you do this to us, Chrissie? How could you be so selfish and thoughtless? You must break off your engagement to this Norman person at once!"

"I'm not going to do that, Grandmother!"

The more I told Grandmother about Norman's "people," the more appalled she looked at the inevitability of having to be in the same room with them. As soon as she heard Norman's father worked the locks on the Chicago River, she sniffed that he must be "common as dirt," the type who ate dinner in his undershirt. Norman would do the same, she predicted with a sour little laugh. With my newfound serenity, I replied that when he was home, Norman did not eat dinner in his undershirt, but he would certainly look splendid if he did.

Would I have married Norman if my grandparents had not rejected him out of hand? It was more than an act of rebellion against the Nicolsons — the same determination never to be like them that had propelled my mother to elope with my father. By marrying Norman, I resolved the immediate dilemma of whether I should go to college, as the Hills were urging me to do, or move to New York and start a life in the theater.

Through family friends who had known my father in his Mercury Theatre days, I had been offered a job as an assistant to a well-known director who was creating a new dramatic series for television. It was not the prospect of moving to New York that made me hesitate: I was used to picking myself up and starting over again. It was the director's reaction to my stammering confession during our informal interview on a long-distance phone call that I had no qualifications or experience for the job. "Hey, you're Orson's kid," he responded. "What other qualifications do you need? I bet you're loaded with talent and just don't know it." He went on to tell me how in awe he was of Orson Welles and what a privilege it would be to work with his "kid."

But that wasn't how I wanted to get ahead in the world. Whatever I achieved in my life had to be on my own merits and in a field that had no connection with Orson Welles. As I told Norman one evening, "I don't want anyone whispering, 'She made it because she's the daughter of Orson Welles.'"

"So you don't want to be another Jane Fonda," Norman said, planting a fond kiss on my cheek. "Good for you!"

WHILE STILL LIVING at the Three Arts Club, I was in the habit of going to a neighborhood movie theater that showed art films and foreign imports. It was there that I saw for the first time such masterpieces as Fellini's *La Strada* and Bergman's *Wild Strawberries*. It was a raw, windy Saturday and raining hard, I remember, when I ducked into the theater to see my father's *Citizen Kane*. Although I had been hearing about this movie all my life, I had never actually seen it until that wet afternoon.

Nothing I had ever seen before on a movie screen prepared me for the overwhelming impact of *Kane*. It felt as though I had boarded a runaway train and was hurtling into a dark tunnel where the mounting sense of doom was close to unbearable. At times the actors talked over one another so that it was impossible to understand what they were saying. Yet it didn't seem to matter. The black-and-white images were so compelling—the gigantic close-up of Kane's lips as he lies on his deathbed, murmuring "Rosebud," or the flashback to Kane as a boy, joyously riding his sled down a snow bank. The boy is seen through the window of a shadowy room where his elders plot his future. In that one shot, my father captured youth and age, innocence and corruption, darkness and light. It all moved so fast that I felt swept from one arresting shot to the next, barely able to grasp what was happening.

When the lights came on, I realized that what I had seen was so extraordinary that I had to watch the entire movie again. This time, less dazzled by the movie's visual effects and unusual camera angles, I was better able to appreciate my father's superb performance as Charles Foster Kane. His portrayal of Kane as an old man was very moving, especially in the scene where, after his mistress leaves him, he destroys her bedroom in a cold rage. It reminded me of what my father had said after we watched *The Third Man* together: If a picture is to work, the villain has to evoke sympathy from the audience.

When the lights came on again, I was crying. Even though he had been wearing a false nose, the young Kane had looked like the Daddy I had last seen in Europe. It broke my heart to think I might never see him again.

SOON AFTER WE became engaged, Norman had to make a business trip to Los Angeles, where my father and Paola had been living for almost a year and a half. "It's time to break the ice," declared Norman. He intended to present himself to Orson Welles as his future son-in-law, but he did not get the chance. Paola received him alone in a living room Norman later described as "very large and very Hollywood," the stuffed sofa and chairs upholstered in flowery chintz and the closed lid of the grand piano covered with photographs in heavy silver frames. Orson, she explained, was tied up in meetings with studio executives. "Paola said Orson would be so sorry he'd missed the chance to meet me," Norman told me on his return, "and I said I hoped they'd both come to our wedding, and he could meet me then."

The truth, not revealed until years later, was that my father had plunged into a depression after he lost artistic control of the last movie he would ever make in Hollywood, *Touch of Evil*. He had hoped this movie would be his comeback, permitting him to settle in tinsel town, the prodigal son welcomed back, forgiven and allowed to make more "ribbons of dreams," as he called the movies, but *Touch of Evil* was the final debacle. My father may well have been home when Norman came to call on him, but in no mood to meet his "future son-in-law."

Yet Norman's visit had not been entirely in vain because it established a connection with Paola. They spent several hours together and seemed to enjoy each other's company. It was strange to realize that my husband-to-be was two years older than my stepmother.

"What's she like?" I asked Norman.

"Absolutely gorgeous, a real stunner, and very charming. I know you're going to like her."

Somehow I wasn't so sure.

Our yearlong engagement went up in smoke after Norman was offered a prestigious job that would take him back to South Korea. He was to head up a team of industrial designers. The project, jointly sponsored by the U.S. government and the Rhee regime, involved establishing a design center in Seoul that would be used to work with local artisans, developing handicrafts and other articles for export. Norman had to leave in early January and wanted me to accompany him as his wife. There was no longer any doubt in my mind that where Norman went, I would follow. That left less than three months to plan our wedding and squeeze in a honeymoon.

In *Touch of Evil* (1958), good guy Mike Vargas (Charlton Heston) confronts bad guy Hank Quinlan (Welles with a false nose).

Orson and Virginia Welles on their second
wedding day, December 23, 1934.

MY MOTHER FLEW from Johannesburg to attend our wedding. (I did not mind at all that Jackie stayed home.) When I told her I was planning to wear the same wedding dress she had worn when she married my father, she exclaimed, "But that old thing must be full of moth holes by now!" I assured her it was in perfect condition; Grandmother had kept it in tissue paper all these years. The close-fitting white satin gown in a classic Grecian style fit me as though it had been custom-made, and I loved the idea of being married in my mother's wedding dress.

"But, Chrissie, I didn't wear that dress when Orson and I were really married at city hall soon after we got to New York. I wore it months later at our phony second wedding. You know, the one at Aunt Adelaide's house in New Jersey to make everything look respectable."

Adelaide Gay was Lillian Nicolson's oldest friend and my mother's godmother. A woman of enormous wealth and generosity, Mrs. Gay offered her spacious mansion in West Orange to the runaway pair, who had braved the wrath of the Nicolsons and eloped to New York in a rattletrap car they borrowed from the Hills. The "phony" wedding took place on Sunday, December 23, 1934. The bride was eighteen and the bridegroom nineteen.

"It meant nothing to Orson and me, but we went through with it to please Mother and Daddy, who were still furious with us," my mother continued with a wicked laugh. "Mother insisted Orson wear a cutaway. She was *such* a bore, and poor Orson didn't own one and couldn't afford to buy one, but his actor friend, George Macready, came to the rescue and lent him his. The pants were too short on Orson but I don't think anyone noticed, except Mother, of course. In any case, Chrissie, I can't think why you want to wear that old wedding dress of mine. It will probably bring you bad luck."

In "the bad luck wedding dress," the same dress that her mother wore, Chris marries Norman DeHaan in Chicago, 1957.

When my mother met Norman, she was none too thrilled with him, treating him with icy politeness and a British accent thicker than marmalade. On the other hand, she was delighted to see her old theater friends from New York, Chubby Sherman and Paula Laurence. My Aunt Caryl also flew to Chicago for our wedding, but my father and Paola did not. They did send us an elegant set of matching luggage, though, an appropriate gift for a couple destined to travel around the world, but I suspected it was Paola and not my father who had chosen it. Orson Welles was known to travel with cheap cardboard luggage tied with rope on the theory that no one would be tempted to steal such worthless bags, for what could they contain of value? Only his unsold scripts, his scribbled notes, his charming drawings, his genius.

Undeterred by my mother, I wore the "bad luck" wedding dress on December 14, 1957, when, at the age of nineteen, I became Norman's wife. We were married in the lovely chapel of the Fourth Presbyterian Church on Michigan Avenue in a small ceremony attended by family and a few friends. I did not want anything to mar my wedding day, but as I walked down the aisle on my grandfather's arm, keeping my eyes on the Viking who stood waiting for me with a radiant smile, the question nagged with every step: Where was the father who should have been here to give me away?

As he would tell me years later, he was writing a memorandum that ran fifty-eight pages in which he pleaded with the moguls at Universal Studios to keep his directorial vision of *Touch of Evil*. Yet even as he wrote, he knew with a heavy heart that they wouldn't listen. He had been locked out of the editing room and lost artistic control. Already so many changes had been made to his picture that he no longer felt it was his. Still he wrote the memo, for himself if no one else, and then, in January of 1958, he gathered up his little family, which he could no longer support in Hollywood, and returned to Italy. While Norman and I were beginning our married life in Seoul, South Korea, the Orson Welles family was settling in Fregene, outside Rome.

The chance that my father and I might find ourselves in the same city at the same moment in time seemed more remote than ever.

9

Reunion in Hong Kong

BEFORE ARRIVING IN SEOUL in January of 1958, I had never seen a city devastated by war. In the weeks that followed, I was numb with shock. For every reconstructed building Norman pointed out to me, I saw block after block of bombed-out skeletons. The poorest of the poor camped in these ruins, finding what food they could. The first time I saw a cluster of refugees roasting a mangy dog on a spit over an open fire, I didn't know whether to cry or vomit. In those days it was impossible to imagine that Seoul would become the thriving metropolis that it is today. In 1958, most of the downtown area was a morass of unpaved streets swarming with army jeeps, rickety bicycles, and the occasional sleek sedan of a foreign dignitary. Plodding down the middle of the muddy road were farmers hauling their wares on A-frames strapped to their backs.

It was heartbreaking to see so many filthy, ragged children playing in the gutters. Norman explained they were mixed-blood orphans, the offspring of American soldiers and Korean prostitutes, forced to live in the streets because no self-respecting Korean family would adopt them. We couldn't walk more than a few steps without being surrounded by these children shouting *Mikook! Mikook!* (American! American!), then running after us, tugging on our clothes, pleading to shine our shoes for a few miserable *hwan*. Norman kept his pockets filled with coins to give these children while I resolved to do volunteer work for the orphanages.

Norman was tied up in meetings with government officials most days, leaving me to fill the hours as best I could. Anxious to get out of our hotel room, which was overrun with cockroaches and stank of sewage backing up in the drains, I began to explore the surrounding streets. I found a dress-maker's shop where a perfect copy of a Christian Dior evening dress could be made in exquisite silk for a mere seven dollars. I spent hours browsing in the art and antique shops that offered Korean folding screens, hanging scrolls, black lacquered boxes inlaid with mother-of-pearl, and ancient funerary urns in bronze turned powdery green. What appealed to me most of all were the delicate, sea green celadon bowls.

One afternoon I walked past a movie theater, and there on the marquee was the title of my father's film *Othello* written in Korean Han-Keul characters and a handsome blowup of Orson Welles playing the Moor. Until that moment, it had not occurred to me that my father's fame could reach as far as South Korea—or that I might wish it hadn't. I had been hoping I had found a remote corner of the world where no one had heard of Orson Welles. At the same time, it filled me with pride that my father's haunting rendition of Shakespeare's *Othello* was playing in Seoul with Korean subtitles. We went to see it several times, and Norman took photographs of the theater marquee, which we mailed to my father and Paola in Fregene.

I would have liked to hide my connection with Orson Welles, but almost everyone I met in Seoul, whether Korean, American, or European, already knew who my father was. This was obvious from the feverish excitement they showed, grinning at me and pumping my hand when we were introduced at the diplomatic functions we were required to attend. It had been happening all my life, of course, but now it bothered me in a way it never had before. In a few months I would be twenty, and I was determined to be accepted on my own merits.

Newly arrived, I was obliged to pay "courtesy calls" on the wives of the American ambassador and the economic coordinator for South Korea. Being unfamiliar with diplomatic protocol, I found it ridiculous that I had to have calling cards printed up before I could show my face at the American embassy. Nonetheless, invited for midmorning coffee, I dropped my calling card on a silver platter in the entrance hall. Then I was ushered through double doors into a sitting room so typically American that for a moment I thought I was in Washington, D.C. There was not one folding screen or celadon bowl to remind us of the splendid art and culture that had flourished in Korea for thousands of years.

I sat on the edge of the deep sofa, a coffee cup trembling in my hand, waiting for the inevitable questions—*Where's your father now? What's he doing these days?*—and the embarrassment that flooded through me because I had no idea. I could not even be sure he was still living in Fregene as he had not responded to my letters or Norman's photographs. So I talked instead about the unique experience of seeing *Othello* in a Korean movie theater, suggesting to the roomful of women that they might also want to see it while it was playing downtown. They stared at me, open-mouthed. Did I really walk around in downtown Seoul on my own? I assured them that I did. Didn't I mind the beggars, the filth, the "slicky boys," as thieving urchins were called? I *had* minded in the beginning, I admitted, but now I was used to it. Relieved to have moved the topic away from my father, I went on to describe the lovely music one could hear in tearooms and the pleasure of browsing in antique stores. But it was clear my listeners did not comprehend why I would want to go to such places. They were not likely to venture out of their foreign compounds or shop in any place except the post exchange or PX, as we called it, on the Eighth U.S. Army base.

Would I find even one American or European woman in Seoul who shared my interests and was close to my age? Failing that, would I be able to cross the cultural barrier and find friends among Koreans? Those I had met so far seemed open and welcoming. As I wrote a friend back in Chicago, "Whenever Norman and I are invited to a Korean home, we can't help feeling that we have been admitted into a more evolved civilization. In all my life, I have never felt such warmth and respect for a people as a whole."

DUE TO A mix-up in our government contract, Norman and I had to spend our first six months living in hotels. We began at the Bando, where my husband was welcomed with great fanfare, only to discover that his beloved hotel was going to seed—hence the cockroaches and smell of sewage in our otherwise comfortable room. It also became apparent that the Bando was too expensive for our housing allowance. So we moved a few blocks to the much cheaper Dong A House. Here we were absurdly happy in a small room where the bed was lumpy, the bathroom window overlooked the bed, and the toilet was mounted on a high platform so that your legs dangled when you sat on it. But at least it was a Western-style flush toilet, still a luxury in Seoul. The entire bathroom got wet when you took a shower, and so did the bed if you had forgotten to close the bathroom window. As we could not drink the tap water at the Dong A, we had to lug our tin water cans over to the Chosun, a U.S. Army hotel several blocks away, where the kind manager allowed us to fill them as often as needed. I was learning to cook on a hot plate. When the power failed in the middle of making dinner, I was learning to shrug my shoulders and get out the candles. Or else we walked over to the Chosun. "Last night," I exulted in one of my letters, "we had a filet mignon dinner with wine, potatoes, vegetables, salad, apple pie, and coffee for a GRAND TOTAL of $2.90!!!" That was dirt cheap even in 1958.

THE NEWS GOT around that Orson Welles's eldest daughter had arrived in Seoul and was living in a Korean hotel. The Dong A House had a pleasant garden, and it was here that an amiable young Korean reporter came to interview me for his newspaper. I had agreed to the interview hoping that a touch of celebrity might help Norman untangle the red tape that was not only keeping us in hotels but threatening to strangle his project before it got off the ground.

This was my first interview on the subject of my father, and to my surprise, I found much to say about his films, having seen all the ones he had made to date, but my interviewer soon interrupted me. "What is it like to have Orson Welles for a father?" I fell silent. How could I put into a few words the joys and heartache, confusion and certainties that assail the child of fame? "How do you feel about your father?" the reporter persisted with the directness I had come to recognize as a Korean trait.

"I don't know. How do you feel about *your* father?"

He laughed and scribbled away on his pad. (He would include my lame attempt to evade his question in his published article.)

Almost every week brought a fresh reminder of my father. The manager of the Chosun, whose many kindnesses to us included the loan of a fan when the temperature in our hotel room soared past 104 degrees Fahrenheit, now asked if I could possibly get him a recording of my father's *War of the Worlds* radio broadcast. I relayed his request to Granny and Skipper, confessing in a letter, "I don't have Daddy's latest address (it's so hard to keep up with him). I got a postcard from Paola months back from Italy and wrote them there but never got an answer . . . Also, I'm afraid if I wrote them about the record-ing that Daddy wouldn't do anything about it." Skipper promptly mailed us the recording, as I knew he would, and our benefactor at the Chosun was thrilled.

To ward off loneliness, I often spent the entire morning writing letters to my mother in Johannesburg, my grandparents in Chicago, or the Hills in Woodstock, Illinois. Filled with cheerful attempts to make light of such ex-periences as finding a rat in our hotel room, bed bugs in our bed, and having to take "the worm cure" at the U.S. Army dispensary, my typed, single-spaced letters often ran as long as ten pages.

My special confidant was Granny Hill, the only person to whom I could write about my father, because I knew that no matter how much she criticized him, forever nagging him to pay more attention to me, she truly loved him. One passage from my voluminous letters to her catches the person I was struggling to become. "Norman has given me so much confidence—you can't imagine. I feel I am now on the brink of doing something creative, but I can't decide what it is right now, but one of these days I shall do something worth noticing. I'm sure of it. I should so like my father to be proud of me one of these days instead of feeling his daughter is a bourgeois vegetable."

I still believed I had to do something extraordinary before my father would sit up and notice me—that it was all up to me. It was also getting harder to deny that, while the world would not let me forget Orson Welles, he had surely forgotten me.

LIVING IN SEOUL during a crucial period of its reconstruction gave me opportunities I could never have had in Chicago. For example, I began giving private lessons in English and French to Korean businessmen. I also went several times a week to Changdeok Palace where I taught English to Princess Yi, the widowed sister of the last Korean emperor. What would my father think, I wondered, about my teaching English to one of the last surviving members of the Yi dynasty?

In addition to teaching, I put on an evening of theater with a group of American teenagers during their summer vacation. I proposed to them that we stage a play to raise money for an orphanage of mixed-blood children. Thrilled at the prospect of leaving their dull compounds and venturing into downtown Seoul, they agreed at once.

I swung into action with my customary zeal and chose two one-act plays whose titles I no longer remember. What I do recall is the fun I had working with these young people who had never acted before, and showing them how good they could be. In the end, our amateur show was a huge success, and we raised over three hundred dollars for the orphanage.

After the show, the man who ran the American missionary school came up to congratulate me. How would I like to teach dramatics at his school? I thanked him for the offer but said no. How could I possibly teach dramatics, I wondered to myself? And would he have offered me the job if my father had been John Smith instead of Orson Welles? Once people knew who my father was, they seemed to expect impossible things of me. Yet it was I who expected the impossible of myself.

MY FATHER HAD not written, called or made any attempt to contact me in four years. He had left it up to Paola to send us a wedding present and an occasional postcard. Then, in early December as our first anniversary was approaching, Granny Hill wrote that Orson, Paola, and Beatrice were going to be in Hong Kong, where Orson was starring in a British film. Norman and I had been debating where to celebrate the fact that we had been married a whole year — Tokyo or Hong Kong? Granny's letter decided our destination.

Compared to Seoul, being in Hong Kong was almost like being back in London or Paris. This sophisticated British colony boasted luxurious hotels, smart shops, gourmet restaurants, and nightclubs . . . except that beneath its layers of European influence, it had remained Cantonese. The square sails of Chinese junks dipped and swayed in Victoria Harbor alongside yachts, motorboats, and passenger ferries crossing back and forth between the island city of Hong Kong and Kowloon on the mainland. For every French and Italian eatery, there was one where the menu, if it existed at all, was in Cantonese, and we had to order by pointing to mouthwatering dishes being consumed at a nearby table.

We were staying in Kowloon in a small but well-appointed hotel that we learned had been built by the eccentric Chinese multimillionaire who lived next door and whose hobby was raising orchids. Late at night, we were told, he slipped into the hotel and painted yet another orchid on the walls of the downstairs public rooms.

Every morning at breakfast, we scoured the newspapers to find out if Orson Welles and family had arrived yet. The Hills had not been sure of the exact date, but they had alerted my father that our stay in Hong Kong would coincide with his. "I don't want Daddy dropping dead of shock at the sight of me," I had written Granny and Skipper, trying to make a joke of it. Finally, when we had been in Hong Kong almost a week and ordered enough tailor-made clothes to last us the rest of our lives, Norman spotted the news item we had been waiting for: Orson Welles was arriving the following day and would be staying at the Peninsula Hotel. As luck would have it, the grand old Peninsula was within walking distance of our small hotel.

The article went on to say that Mr. Welles was playing the part of the skipper of a ferryboat in the British movie *Ferry to Hong Kong,* being filmed on location in the colony and in Portuguese Macao. It was rumored that Mr. Welles had agreed to be in the picture only after the director allowed him to write his own dialogue. This led to a falling-out with his costar, the German actor Curt Jurgens, who had objected to having *his* lines rewritten by Welles in their scenes together, to which Welles had retorted, "I hate all actors — stupid, empty-headed creatures."

"Do you think your dad really said that?" Norman asked me.

"No, or if he did, he didn't mean it." Perhaps he had blurted it out in a moment of disgust, now he was down on his luck and had to take any work he could get. I reminded Norman of the loyalty and devotion my father evoked in actors who had worked under his direction. Marlene Dietrich, for instance, had agreed to her cameo role in *Touch of Evil* for no other reason than she loved him as a friend and esteemed him as a director.

Around noon the next day Norman and I went to the Peninsula Hotel, and there was my father, a monument of flesh in loose black clothing, making the lobby reverberate with the magnificence of his voice while he reminded the flustered desk clerk that his suite should have been ready hours ago. I hung back, shocked at the sheer size of him. *He must weigh close to three hundred pounds,* I thought, trying to remember the Daddy who had squired me all over Rome in search of paintings and sculptures by Michelangelo. And there was Paola, tall and long-limbed with limpid eyes, her dark hair falling to her shoulders. Why did the realization that Paola was so stunning in person make me feel hopelessly inadequate? She had secured a table among the palm fronds and was ordering from a gilt-edged menu. Meanwhile, three-year-old Beatrice was skipping among the tables and white-coated waiters, and to my astonishment, my old nanny, Marie Cunningham, was swooping down on her. I hadn't known she was now in charge of my half sister and had to repress a pang of jealousy. Older and grayer, Marie had shrunk until she barely came up to my shoulder. Yet I would have known her anywhere from the weary look on her lined face and the stoic patience she exuded.

Tentatively, I approached my father, fighting an impulse to flee through the doors of the Peninsula, never to be seen again. "Daddy?"

He turned, his face lighting up. "Christopher? Can this be you, all grown up and so beautiful? Hortense told me you were going to be in Hong Kong, and I still don't believe it — but here you are!"

He folded me in his arms and for one happy moment, it was as though the four years of silence and separation had never happened. Yet the man I was hugging wasn't Daddy anymore—not the Daddy I had known in London, Paris, Rome, Madrid, and Saint Moritz. Now he held me at arm's length as though I were some exotic creature who had fallen from the sky, and I realized with a shiver what strangers we had become.

"You are so beautiful," he was exclaiming and beaming down at me while I blushed, "and what's more, you look *exactly* like your mother. For a moment, you know, when I first saw you, I thought Virginia had come back to haunt me." He laughed uproariously, his whole body shaking, and I did not want to spoil the moment by pointing out that my mother was a petite, blue-eyed blond, while I, on the other hand, was a brunette with hazel eyes, the same color as his. "Come, Christopher, you must meet Paola and Beatrice."

"And you must meet Norman."

"Norman? Ah yes, how do you do." He shook my husband's hand distractedly.

Paola and Norman greeted one another like old friends, while Marie and I were so overcome at seeing each other again that we shed a few tears. Beatrice was dancing around the circle of adults, shrieking to get our attention. After all the hellos and the hugs, the hotel manager came scurrying up to inform Mr. Welles that his suite was ready at last. His moon face glistening with embarrassment, the manager had begun to apologize profusely for the delay when my father interrupted him with a lordly wave of his hand. "Never mind the apologies, my good man. Just send up a magnum of champagne."

"Oh, Orson, not so early in the day!" Paola sounded more dismayed than shocked. I suddenly remembered Granny Hill telling me Paola had been trying very hard to help my father control his drinking. Was she succeeding, I wondered, now that I noticed his ruddy face and bloodshot eyes?

"Just kidding, my love. Just kidding." He put one jovial arm around her. "But we do have a lot to celebrate, you know, seeing Christopher again and meeting . . . uh . . ."

"Norman," I supplied.

"Ah yes, Norman." He turned away from our little group, looking for the elevators. "You must tell me all about yourselves, but right now, if you'll excuse me, I need to go up to our suite and make an urgent phone call." I wanted to put a restraining hand on his arm but did not feel I had the right to keep him away from the telephone. Then Norman asked the question on my mind.

"When will we see you again, Orson?" I marveled at my husband's easy familiarity.

"Whenever you like." Orson treated us to his most captivating smile. "Talk to Paola—she knows my schedule—and arrange it with her."

As I watched him walk away—and how gracefully he moved for a man carrying close to three hundred pounds—I wondered what I should call him now that *Daddy* was out of date. *Dad* struck me as too familiar, and I could hardly call him *Mr. Welles.*

ALTHOUGH I SAW a great deal of my father during the rest of our two-week stay in Hong Kong, I could not shake off the feeling that he was keeping me at an amiable distance. That did not mean he was not affectionate toward me, booming "Here's Christopher!" the moment I appeared and enveloping me in a bear hug. But we were not connecting the way we had years before. For the first time, I was finding it difficult to reach him, as though he had erected a barricade of preoccupations and sorrows between himself and everyone else. Even Paola, who clearly adored him and would have done anything in her power to make him happy, could not distract him from the gloom that descended when he was alone with us in their lavish suite at the Peninsula. Which was worse for him, I wondered: mulling over in private the lost opportunities, the criminal waste of his talents, or having to play "Orson Welles" in public, besieged for his autograph, his photograph, his handshake, while fielding such questions as, "Why'd you leave Hollywood, Orson?" (It infuriated me when strangers appropriated his first name as though it were their right.) As for Beatrice, he treated her like an adorable nuisance to be led away by Marie and not seen again until bedtime, when she made a brief appearance in pajamas, to be hugged, kissed, and promptly dispatched to oblivion.

If my father had asked, I would have told him about our life in Seoul. I was eager to boast about the enormous success Norman had made of his design center in a very short time, and how the economic coordinator for South Korea made sure to show it off to every visiting U.S. senator . . . but my father did not ask. When he talked to me, which he did in his better moments, he was like a man roused from a troubled sleep who suddenly remembers he has a visitor. Then he talked about himself as a schoolboy at Todd or about the Hills and his parents. These monologues took place in the intimacy of his suite where he sat in a free-flowing caftan, the inevitable cigar clamped between his teeth. After a while I felt that, although I happened to be the one sitting across from him, another being could have slipped into my skin and it wouldn't have made any difference. This was not the father I had been missing so acutely but a world-famous personality who had graciously consented to spend a few moments with me, recounting the same witty anecdotes he had told only weeks before on British television. Did he really expect me to believe that my grandmother Beatrice Ives Welles had been a crack shot with a rifle or that my grandfather Dick Welles had broken the bank at Monte Carlo? Maybe he was keeping me at a distance because he knew he wasn't fooling me. Did he see in me that irritating member of his audience who refuses to believe in magic and wants to know how the trick is done? Or perhaps he feared that if he let me get too close, I might pull back the curtains, as Dorothy had done in *The Wizard of Oz,* and expose him for the lovable illusionist that he was.

Of course, I could hardly blurt out, "What were my grandparents *really* like?" No, my role was to listen, laugh, applaud, and discreetly disappear into the next room when the phone rang. Or I could hang around and watch him work. He would scribble away on a yellow pad, pause to stare glumly out of the window, then attack once more the script spread out on his expansive lap.

When I got up the nerve to ask him about *Ferry to Hong Kong,* he sighed and said it was a terrible movie, he hated his part, and he had agreed to it only because he was desperate for money.

"And all the lovely money Orson is making from this terrible movie is paying for this suite," Paola wailed.

"Not *all,* my love. Let's not exaggerate."

"It costs much too much to stay here, Orson. You know it does! I can't bear giving away all that money to the Peninsula Hotel!"

"We're not giving it away and getting nothing in return," my father said with a laugh, gesturing at their well-appointed rooms that overlooked Victoria Harbor with its cheerful procession of boats. "You're staying in the best suite in one of the world's top hotels."

"But it's so impractical, Orson. Why can't we move to a small, inexpensive hotel, like the one where Christopher and Norman are staying? I'd be perfectly happy in a place like that."

"No, you wouldn't, my love. There'd be no photographers to catch you making a grand entrance down the staircase or wearing your latest outfit for afternoon tea in the lobby."

"Do be serious, Orson." I could tell from the way Paola's lovely dark eyes were flashing that she didn't like being teased by my father any more than I did. "I'm ready to move to a cheaper hotel right now!"

"But I'm *not* moving, my sweet." It was said with quiet finality, the way a parent says no to a child, and Paola found a pretext to flounce out of the room. "I do have an image to maintain," he muttered to Norman and me, "such as it is."

For a moment I was able to put aside my own neediness and empathize with my father's dilemma: how humiliating and depressing it must be for a genius like him to have to appear in a potboiler like *Ferry to Hong Kong*. Perhaps the only thing that made it tolerable was staying in "one of the world's top hotels," which had always been his preference, even if he had to pay for it himself.

The following morning, I went up to the suite without Norman, hoping to have a private moment with my father. I found myself alone with Paola instead. "Orson's going to be shooting all day today," she explained, then patted the sofa cushion beside her. "Come sit down next to me." She smiled engagingly. "I've been wanting to have a talk with you."

"Oh? What about?" Something in her voice put me on my guard.

"That time you called up your father in Paris and told him you couldn't see him anymore . . ."

"But that isn't what I—"

"He was so hurt! He couldn't believe you'd turn against him like that."

"But I—"

"I was with him when you called, and I saw his reaction with my own eyes." She paused, studying me, no longer smiling. "So many people in Orson's life—people he loved and trusted—have betrayed him in the end, and so you can imagine how bitter it was for him when you, his own daughter—"

"But I *didn't* betray him, Paola! It was my mother who—"

"Orson said you turned away from him because you didn't trust him. That is a betrayal, not to trust your own father!"

There was so much I could have said in my defense, but I saw it would do no good. To break the escalating tension, Paola called up room service and ordered coffee for us both. Then, turning back to me, she continued on a note of wonder: "I don't understand how you could do such a thing. It would never happen in an Italian family. The only way I can explain it, as I told Orson, is that you must be very close to your mother."

"Actually, we're not that close. My mother doesn't like me very much."

"She doesn't? I can't imagine a mother who doesn't love her own child."

"Then you should meet mine some day."

"You say that so coldly, Christopher. I have had many ideas about you and what you are really like, but I never imagined any daughter of Orson's could have a cold heart."

I got up and walked over to the window so that Paola would not see my eyes filling with tears. Behind me I heard a discreet knock on the door. Our coffee had arrived on a gleaming silver tray. "Do you take sugar?" asked the stepmother who saw me as unfeeling and capable of wounding her beloved Orson.

"No, thank you." I glanced at my watch. "Oh, I didn't realize it was so late. I'm supposed to meet Norman at the tailor's." I rushed off without saying goodbye.

STILL HOPING TO see my father on his own, I went to his suite the following morning and found him at work in his usual armchair by the window. "Paola's out having her hair done," he told me distractedly, then went back to his scribbling. I sat down on the couch and waited. Time passed and I was beginning to think I should leave him to his work, when he looked up at me, scowling, as though my presence had brought back unwelcome memories. To my surprise, he suddenly asked, "Do you ever see Chubby Sherman?"

"Yes, I do. As a matter of fact, he came to our wedding." *And you didn't.*

"I suppose he's given you an earful about me."

"Well . . ."

"Just as I thought." He chomped on his cigar, but he was no longer scowling. "He did the most terrible thing to me, you know."

"You mean when he left your Mercury Theatre company?"

"I mean the *way* he left me. If he'd reached the point where he couldn't take it anymore, he should have come to me and talked to me, man to man. This was my dear old friend from Chicago, you know, the actor I believed in long before anyone had heard of him. This was the man who had eaten at my table, befriended my wife and child . . ." He paused, his eyes misting. "And he didn't have the decency or even the professional courtesy to let me know he was leaving me. Not a phone call. Or even a note if he was too embarrassed to talk to me. That's what I can't forgive, Christopher. Our ship wasn't sinking, far from it, when our dear Mr. Sherman turned into a rat."

"The first rat in history to leave a ship that wasn't sinking."

"That's good," he muttered, but he didn't laugh. After relighting his cigar, he went on, "We'd planned our entire second season with Chubby in mind, and when he left us at the last minute, there was no time to recoup. I knew we were finished as a repertory company, and I couldn't believe Chubby had done this to me. I lay in bed for days, trying to believe it . . ."

His voice trailed off as he revisited the scene of his first betrayal by a good friend and colleague. The first of many.

IN THE DAYS that followed, I found it awkward whenever the four of us got together, which we did almost every evening. Yet I seemed to be the only one feeling the strain. Paola put herself out to be charming, and my father regaled us with witty anecdotes. Norman's buoyant laugh rang out in the right places, and any onlooker would have assumed we were all having the time of our lives. I envied Norman his easy capacity to enjoy himself. He seemed oblivious to the undercurrents that were bothering me, and he plunged into the conversation whenever there was an opening, which was not often. Unless my father or Paola asked me a direct question, I said very little. Periodically my father would exclaim to Paola in his most velvety voice, "Isn't my daughter beautiful?"

"Especially when she's blushing," Paola would reply with her vivacious laugh.

I wanted to ask my father if that was all he saw when he looked at me with his penetrating eyes—a beautiful young woman who happened, amazingly, to be his daughter. Now that we had spent some time together again, was there really nothing else about me that awakened his admiration? Why couldn't he observe to Paola, "Isn't my daughter clever?" Better yet, "Isn't it wonderful to have Christopher with us?"

My shyness was hardly helping the situation, nor were my mixed feelings about Paola. I could see her good qualities and wanted to like her, but that was difficult now that I knew how she felt about me. Then the girlish, flirtatious way she behaved with my father made me uncomfortable, even jealous, as though my lovely, young stepmother had displaced me in my father's affections. We were too close in age to behave like a stepmother and stepdaughter. Now that I had met Paola, I realized Granny Hill had been right about her. Paola was so determined to make Orson behave like a father to Beatrice—a feat she had not yet achieved—that she would do everything to put Beatrice forward at the expense of me and my half sister Rebecca.

My father with his third wife, Paola Mori, and their daughter Beatrice.

One night my father took us to a well-known "floating restaurant," as the boats converted into restaurants were called in the fishing colony of Aberdeen. At the entrance, we ordered the fish we wanted for dinner while they were still swimming or scuttling around in a huge tank. "Now that's what I call fresh," my father laughed while ordering several lobsters. We were then ushered ceremoniously to our table.

During the superb meal, Paola began to boast about her cooking. "When you come to visit us in Fregene," she told us, "I will make you a *pasta d'amore* that will be more delicious than all the fishes in the sea."

"What you mean, my love, is that you will go out to the kitchen while our cook is making dinner and sniff the pots and lick the spoon she used to stir the sauce."

"How can you say that, Orson? You know what a good cook I am!"

"It's true you're very good at tasting the sauce after someone else has made it. In fact, there is no one better."

"Oh, you're impossible! Why won't you take me seriously?"

My father began to laugh in his inimitable way, while my stepmother pouted and Norman tactfully changed the subject.

After dinner we boarded a junk my father had hired to take us for a moonlit sail up and down Victoria Harbor. For my father and Paola, kissing and murmuring endearments to each other, it was a moment of high romance, but for me it was as embarrassing as if I had come upon them naked in the act of love. Even my gregarious Norman found nothing to say, nothing to dispel our growing discomfort as we rode the choppy waters, the junk rocking under our feet, its red sail creaking in the wind. The two of us retreated to the other end of the boat where Norman put a comforting arm around my shoulders. I fixed my eyes on the gentle hills of Hong Kong rising and falling as though they were breathing — the hills wearing diamond necklaces of lights.

MY FATHER HAD to spend an entire day on location in Macao, and I was delighted when he invited Norman and me to accompany him. (Paola, Beatrice, and Marie were staying behind in Hong Kong.) At last I had a chance to spend considerable time with my father on his own. I was up half the night, going over in my mind what I might say or do to reestablish myself in his eyes as a loyal, loving daughter. My memories of our times together in Europe, before the Fatal Phone Call, gave me hope. Surely, the relaxed, fun-loving Daddy I had known as a schoolgirl had not entirely disappeared into the polite father who talked to me as though he were being interviewed on television.

We left Hong Kong at six in the morning, traveling with the cast and crew on the same ferryboat being used in *Ferry to Hong Kong*. Standing at the railing beside my father, watching the churning waters below, I realized I could not make any of the impassioned speeches that had held off sleep the night before. "I was so impressed with the way you handled that drunk in the elevator the other night," I told him instead. Clearly, he had no idea what I was talking about. "The drunken man who wanted your autograph and was so rude about it?"

"Oh, that."

"And you were so polite and gracious to him."

"Well, I'm glad I've done something to impress you, Christopher." Yet how low in spirits he sounded.

"Oh, Daddy, you know . . . I mean . . . oh, I don't know what to call you these days."

"What's wrong with Daddy?"

"I'm not a little girl anymore."

"That is true."

"Would you . . . would you mind if I called you Father?"

"Not at all. In fact, that's what I called *my* father, you know. *Father*. Yes, it has a nice biblical ring to it." He laughed delightedly, and I wanted to bury my head on his massive chest and say how sorry I was, and ask was it true what Paola had said about the phone call, because I had never meant to hurt him, never, and I would do anything to make it right between us again . . . but at that moment, the director's assistant came up and spirited him away.

After the ferry docked in Macao, everyone went to work on the day's shoot, everyone except Norman and me, idling on the sidelines and succumbing to the boredom that pervades a movie set. During one long wait between takes, my father sauntered over to us and confided in a stage whisper, "I don't know how many times I've told them that the only way this picture is going to work is if we turn it into a comedy." It did not look to Norman and me as though the picture would "work" under any circumstances, and as the hours dragged on, we became convinced that possibly the worst movie in cinema history was unrolling before our eyes. For the first time in my life, I felt something new and uncomfortable: pity for my father.

A sudden commotion jolted Norman and me out of our stupor. I heard a voice calling my name, and there on the pier below, waving and struggling to board the ferry, insisting she knew me, was a slim, olive-skinned young woman I recognized: a former schoolmate from Pensionnat Florissant, Didi Jorges. "Didi!" I screamed, rushing down the gangplank. "It's okay," I told the men who were restraining her. "She can come on board. She's my friend." We were giddy young girls again, laughing and assuring each other that we looked exactly the same, as though five years had collapsed into a few hours.

"But what are you doing in Macao?" I asked her.

"I live here. Don't you remember?"

Then it came back to me. Of course, Didi was Portuguese and her family had settled years ago in the Portuguese colony of Macao. Although she and I had liked each other at school, we had failed to keep in touch later on, which made me feel a little ashamed now that I saw how glad Didi was to see me again.

Once Didi was on board, I introduced her to Norman and my father. Then, to our surprise, she proposed that we all come to her house for lunch. My father demurred. Wouldn't we be putting her to a great deal of trouble at the last minute? Didi insisted that nothing would give her or her family greater pleasure than to have us share their midday meal. Her eyes sparkled when we accepted, and I realized that, as pleased as she was to see me again, nothing could beat the thrill of having Orson Welles to lunch.

How sweet and genuinely himself my father was as we sat around the dining room table with Didi and her family. We were treated to an elaborate five-course lunch, and as each delicacy was set before him, my father exclaimed that this was the best Portuguese food he had ever eaten. Shyly at first, Didi's mother and other family members asked him a few discreet questions about himself, which he answered with such endearing modesty that everyone around the table visibly relaxed. Soon they were all laughing and talking as though having a world-famous actor and director to lunch was nothing out of the ordinary.

After lunch Didi brought out some photo albums that commemorated our schoolgirl days in Pensionnat Florissant. She was eager to share her memories of our adventures in Lausanne and on the ski slopes of Crans-sur-Sierre, whereas I felt embarrassed. Didi recalled the name of every girl in every photo, while I, at best, dimly recognized a face here and there.

After saying our goodbyes to the Jorges family and on our way back to the ferry, my father took me to task. "I felt awfully sorry for your poor friend Mimi—"

"Didi."

"—trotting out her photo albums, which she was so anxious to share with you, and then you just sat there in a trance." He frowned at me. "How is it possible, Christopher, that you remember so little about your days in finishing school?"

"I don't know. Maybe it will come back to me one day."

"Maybe it will come back to you? What in God's name is the matter with you *now*?" Although he laughed, I could tell he found my lapse of memory disquieting. "It isn't as though you went to that fancy school in Lausanne fifty years ago, you know."

But I remember everything you ever told me, I wanted to tell him. *Everything we ever did together. Every moment with you. Everything.*

"YOU CAN'T LEAVE Hong Kong until you've had Sunday brunch at the Repulse Bay Hotel," my father declared. "It's a grand old tradition at one of the world's grandest hotels." So, on our last Sunday, my father hired a limousine, and we made the scenic trip to Repulse Bay. In this tranquil spot, a British colonial hotel even more imposing than the Peninsula stood overlooking the bay and miles of beach. Here we enjoyed the famous brunch.

When we had finished eating, my father suggested a stroll on the beach, but Paola preferred to sit in the hotel garden, and Norman stayed behind to keep her company. I had given up hope of having more time alone with my father but now here we were, sauntering down to the beach, with no Paola, Norman, Marie, or Beatrice trailing behind us.

I had been waiting for such a moment to tell my father something close to my heart. Now I came out with it. "You know, while I was living in Chicago, I saw *Citizen Kane* several times, and I thought it was the most extraordinary movie I'd ever—"

"*Citizen Kane*! Good Christ, that's all I ever hear about. You'd think I'd never done anything else in my life."

I was dumbfounded by his reaction, but then I realized he didn't seem to be talking to me. He was thundering away instead at a huge, invisible audience gathered around us. "This one picture I made in my hot youth, when I didn't know any better and used every trick shot in the book just to prove I could do it, this is the picture they rave about. This is the one they hold up to me like the gold standard so that every other picture I've made falls short of the mark. And now my own *daughter* comes prattling to me about *Citizen Kane*. I'm not to be spared even that!"

He walked on, propelled by his demons, while I hung back, still wanting to tell him what a revelation *Citizen Kane* had been to me. Until I saw it, I had never imagined a movie could also be a work of art. And while I was sitting in that movie theater in Chicago, thrilled by his handiwork up there on the screen, he had seemed close to me again, as though we were back in Europe, wandering through an art gallery, and he was taking me by the hand. Opening my eyes to greatness.

It was our last day in Hong Kong before flying back to Seoul. I was about to go into the Peninsula Hotel to say my goodbyes when I saw my father getting into a chauffeured car parked out front. "Daddy!" I called out without thinking. He turned, smiled, and held the door open for me.

"I'm on my way to our location for today. Want to come along?" I scrambled into the backseat beside him. "After the driver drops me off, he can take you back to your hotel or wherever you want to go, but at least this way we'll have a few moments together." As we drove along, I was transported back to childhood when I had driven with my father to the studio every morning during the frantic filming of *Macbeth* . . . but the illusion crumbled when I heard him say in a low, caressing voice, "You're so beautiful. I just can't get over it, how beautiful you are." He was gazing at me in a way that I found intensely embarrassing.

"It's been wonderful to see you again, Father."

"It's been wonderful for me, too."

"And I'm so glad you finally got to meet Norman. Isn't he terrific?"

"Yes . . ." It was said with a hesitation that took me by surprise.

"He's been awfully good for me," I rushed on. "I used to be horribly shy. Well, I still am, but Norman has helped me enormously with my self-confidence."

"Has he? I don't remember your being that shy or unsure of yourself when you were a little girl, or a teenager for that matter, so this must be something new."

We've spent days together, I thought, *and yet we've shared so little of ourselves.* My father was warmly affectionate with me — he had always been that — but the closeness between us was gone. And now, to complicate matters, there was Paola, who no matter what she said would never invite me to sample her cooking in the many homes she would occupy with my father. I could not ask my father if he had distanced himself from me because he felt, as Paola claimed, that I had turned against him. Nor could I assure him that I had always taken his side and refused to join the chorus shouting that he was unfit to be my father.

How do you see me, Father? What do you really think of me? My worst fear, as I had written Granny Hill, was being "a bourgeois vegetable" in his eyes. If he had revised his view of me in Hong Kong, I had merely become a beautiful bourgeois vegetable, which was still insufficient to hold his interest.

"Norman thinks I have a talent for writing," I suddenly blurted out.

"I'm sure you do." It was said smoothly, easily.

"He says all I have to do is to start believing in myself."

"Is that all?" My father laughed softly. "I would think doing a *lot* of writing would be essential, and I mean writing every day, until it becomes a habit you can't do without . . ." His voice trailed off. Now he was gazing intently out the window, no longer listening.

I wanted to tell him — if only we had more time! — that living in South Korea had been a transforming experience for me. It had expanded my ideas of landscapes, art, architecture, and interior decor. For the rest of my life, I would feel a special connection with Chinese, Korean, and Japanese art.

We were nearing our destination. Too late to rattle on about Norman, who had taught me how to cook and now claimed I had far surpassed him. Sometimes we had as many as forty people to dinner, I might have mentioned. And if I was dressing more stylishly these days, it was also thanks to Norman, who had spent a fortune on my wardrobe while we were here in Hong Kong.

The car stopped. There was just time for me to say, "Norman's the best thing that ever happened to me."

"Well, that's good. I'm glad you're so happy with him." The driver was holding the car door open.

"Don't you think he's wonderful, Daddy . . . I mean, Father?" *Please say that he is.*

"He's very nice and very good-looking, and I gather he's good at whatever it is he does, but I'm afraid . . ." Half in, half out of the car, my father paused, carefully choosing his words. When he spoke again, there was a hint of sadness in his voice. "I'm afraid you'll find out he's not enough of a man for you."

There was no time to ask him to elaborate. In the next moment he was gone.

Reconnecting with My Father

I DID NOT SEE my father again for eight years. In the interim, his prediction about Norman turned out to be correct, and with much heartache on both sides, we were divorced a year after our return to Chicago. It was also in Chicago that I began a career in educational publishing, first getting my foot in the door as a secretary and then working my way up to assistant editor and, finally, a full-fledged editor for Encyclopaedia Britannica. My work took me to Vienna and Los Angeles for long periods, and I also spent about a year in Rome.

What my father had been doing all this time was not clear to me, as we were not often in touch. Although I wrote him letters, which I mailed to his constantly changing addresses, I rarely received a reply. He preferred to make telephone calls or send telegrams, and I usually heard from him at Christmas, provided he knew where to reach me. It was not easy to track me down during that peripatetic stage of my life, when I might be spending Christmas in Vienna or Rome, or perhaps in Lisbon, where my mother and stepfather had moved from Johannesburg. Nor was it any easier to keep up with my father in his gypsy wanderings across Europe with Paola, Beatrice, and their caravan of luggage trailing after him.

At least our meeting in Hong Kong had broken the painful silence between us. I no longer became upset at the mention of his name, nor did tears spill down my cheeks whenever I sat alone in a darkened movie theater, watching him on the screen. What I felt instead was an incurable longing to see him, talk to him, spend time with him, and be invited to his home—along with a stubborn refusal to accept that the little he gave me of himself was all he had to give. No matter how hard I kept trying, he was not going to enfold me into his personal life. He would remain the affable figure who once announced himself on the long-distance phone in that full-bodied voice of his: "Hello, Christopher? This is your errant father speaking."

When my father and I did talk on the phone, much of our conversation was wasted on protestations. "But I *did* write to you, Christopher," he would say in the aggrieved tone of one falsely accused of paternal neglect. "Many, many times. Do you mean to tell me you didn't get *any* of my letters? Then you must have moved *again* and not told me." As for why he had not received any of my letters, the only explanation he could offer was that I had sent them to the wrong address unless, in a momentary aberration, I had forgotten to apply the necessary postage. We would then meticulously record each other's addresses, repeating them several times to be sure we had written them down correctly, and my father would invariably add the address and phone number of his current secretary, whom he portrayed as the most reliable being on earth. She knew where to track him down at any hour of the day or night and would forward his mail to the North Pole if necessary. So there was absolutely no reason in the world why any letter I wrote to him should not reach him. While we were on the subject of writing letters, he wished I would communicate now and then with my little sister Beatrice. "It might help her believe in you," he said, sounding plaintive. "She thinks I made you up."

"She doesn't remember meeting me in Hong Kong?"

"She was only three years old, you know. You can't expect . . ."

These conversations would leave me fuming. I didn't believe in the mythical letters he claimed to have written to my "vanishing addresses" as he called them, any more than I believed stamps had fallen off my letters. And why should I write Beatrice, as much of a stranger to me as I was to her? Besides, if my father was really so anxious for Beatrice to get to know me, all he had to do was invite me to his home. During the six months I had lived in Vienna, working on a special project for Encyclopaedia Britannica, I could have spent a weekend with the Orson Welles family in London, and later, when I was living in Rome, I could have visited them in Madrid. It rankled that Paola had invited my half sister Rebecca several times to stay with them and "get to know Beatrice." And I was still waiting like the wallflower at a dance.

NEW YORK! I had been circling the globe all my life and never staying in one place long enough to put down roots. Then, in the spring of 1967, I returned to the city of my birth. I had not been living in Manhattan more than a few months when I got an unexpected call from my father, who was staying at the Plaza Hotel. He began, as usual, by saying how difficult it had been to track me down, since the last he had heard I was living in Rome, but "the indefatigable Hills" had come through as always and given him my New York phone number. "I'm in town for a few days," he went on, "taping my first appearance on the Dean Martin television show."

"The Dean Martin show?" I hoped I didn't sound too shocked, but I couldn't picture my father on a variety show hosted by a pop singer whose public persona was that of a handsome drunk.

"Never mind that. Will you have lunch with me tomorrow?"

I accepted with a mixture of joy, hope, and anxiety. The office where I was working for Encyclopaedia Britannica was within a few blocks of the Plaza, and as long as we editors got our work done, we were not reprimanded for taking long lunch hours. So on a lovely Indian summer day, I set out to meet my father. I felt like an aspiring actress on her way to an audition, desperate to please, determined to be chosen. Geraldine Fitzgerald had once said to me, "Orson will be anything you want him to be," and now it was the same for me. I was ready to play the role of Eldest Daughter any way he wanted until the show folded.

Arriving at the Plaza ahead of time, I roamed around the lobby, trying to calm myself amid the marble columns, ornamented archways, plush chairs, and gilded elevator doors. Here, I thought, was the Old World opulence that my father loved. And here was the Palm Court where paying a fortune for a cup of tea and a tiny plate of petit fours was a New York institution. I was reminded that not long ago I'd had afternoon tea in the Palm Court with my grandmother visiting from Chicago. In the midst of leafy potted palms, shiny marble floors, sparkling mirrored doorways, and clinking tea cups, she had delivered an irate message from Jack Pringle: He was at a loss to understand why I insisted on working for Encyclopaedia Britannica and had turned down an offer to be a secretary to a business friend of his who would have introduced me to "all the right people" in New York. My grandmother had taken the Pringles' side, dismissing my hard-won "career" as an editor with an airy wave of her hand. All that mattered, she insisted, was to find a suitable husband and take my place in society, which was not going to happen until I stopped being so stubborn, quit my job at Britannica—that hotbed of Jews, Democrats, and homosexuals—and began socializing with "the right people."

Marking time in the ladies' room and nervously preening before the gilded mirror, I reflected that my father was the only person in my immediate family who would support my decision to remain with Britannica and meet people of every color and persuasion. Always it had given me strength to know where my father stood, a man without prejudice of any kind. The mirror returned my smile.

When I felt calm enough, I approached the front desk and asked the suave man standing behind it to let Mr. Orson Welles know that his daughter Christopher was waiting for him in the lobby. "Oh, Mr. Welles left a message for you," the desk clerk replied without looking up. "He wants you to meet him outside the Oak Room."

I heard Mr. Welles before I saw him. "Do you mean to tell me my daughter can't eat with me in the Oak Room?" he was asking at the top of his voice. "What kind of an establishment won't let a father take his daughter to lunch?"

"I'm very sorry, Mr. Welles, but we have a men-only policy at lunchtime," explained the flustered maître d'.

"Your policy is medieval and should be banned at once!" Then with a sigh, "Since I can't take my daughter here, what do you suggest?"

"The main dining room, sir, but I'm afraid you will need to wear a tie." Obligingly, the maître d' whipped one out of his pocket and handed it to my father who carelessly flung it around his neck.

"Everywhere I go in this hotel, they lie in wait for me with their neckties," my father grumbled, giving me a bear hug. "Come along, Christopher, we're not wanted here." I smelled liquor on his breath during our embrace and couldn't help wondering how many drinks he'd had while I was pacing off my nerves in the lobby. Could *he* be anxious about seeing *me* again?

My father ambled down the hall with the innate grace I remembered from Hong Kong, a man carrying so much height, bulk, and charisma that people turned to stare, whether or not they knew he was Orson Welles. I hung back for a moment to get a quick look at the Oak Room. It reminded me of a sedate London pub with its oak-paneled walls, its booths and tables packed with men in expensive business suits, smoking and drinking in the semidark, speaking in the lowered voices of those entrusted with wealth, power, and weighty decisions. I was glad we would be eating lunch instead in the airy dining room with its chandeliers and enormous windows overlooking Central Park.

"So," my father began after we had been ceremoniously seated in a quiet corner. "I'm curious why you left Rome and decided to live in New York."

"Well, I'm not sure how long I'll stay here," I began.

"You're as bad as I am," he laughed, "moving from one place to the next. How do you expect your aging father to keep up with you?" As a matter of fact, I had been struck by how much he had aged, quickly calculating that he was now fifty-two, although the weight made him look older. The years had streaked his dark hair with gunmetal gray, and carved lines around his expressive eyes and sensuous mouth. Yet his round face with its button nose still had the innocent look of a baby's. Not for the first time I thought, *There isn't a mean bone in him.*

I started to tell him I had chosen New York because I knew I could stay with a girlfriend here until I found a place of my own. "You've barely arrived in town and already you sound like a New Yorker," he said, interrupting me. "It's that marvelous ear of yours, which you get from me." And he laughed so heartily that all heads turned in our direction.

"I also came to New York because I knew I could get work right away with Encyclopaedia Britannica."

"Work is crucial," he agreed. "That's the only reason I'm going to be on Dean's show, you know. To pay the rent."

"Tell me about it. What are you—"

"I'd rather not. What I have to do these days to keep my name alive won't make you proud of me."

"But I *am* proud of you, Daddy. Very proud of you!" The "Daddy" had slipped out before I could stop it.

"That's my darling girl!" His eyes twinkled at me across the table, and for a moment it was like old times. "Let's not talk about me," he went on. "I'd much rather hear about you."

So I told him we editors were compiling an international edition of the encyclopedia that would be sold in Europe and Japan. I had been assigned the articles on theater and motion pictures. "In fact, I'm going to be editing an article on you," I told him.

"Really?" He looked astonished. "And just how are you going to edit me?"

"Well, what I mainly do is make sure everything in the article is accurate and up-to-date, and take out parts that are repetitive or too opinionated."

"That's right! We can't have opinions in an encyclopedia."

"You wouldn't believe how long-winded and biased some of the original articles are."

"Does the article on me mention *Chimes at Midnight*?"

"I think so, but I haven't looked at it closely yet. I just know I'm going to be—"

"Then you make sure it does, Christopher, because I believe it's the best work I've ever done. I can't tell you how sick I am of people raving about *Citizen Kane* and not saying anything positive about the film I consider my true masterpiece."

"I will. I promise."

"Have you seen it, by the way?"

"Oh yes, I saw it in Rome, several times. I thought it was fantastic. The battle scene moves like a ballet. It's one of the most poetic—"

"Thank you. But you haven't told me yet why you left Rome."

"Well, I was involved with an Italian man, and we lived together for almost a year, but it didn't work out. I wrote you about it."

"Italians make the best wives in the world and the worst husbands," he pronounced. I took note of the compliment to Paola. "Italian women are also among the most beautiful in the world. Except for their ankles."

I stared at him. "What's wrong with their ankles?"

"They have a certain thickness around the ankle which is unattractive."

"Really?"

"They also have thick and pudgy wrists."

"Are you teasing me?" His eyes were twinkling at me again.

"I'm dead serious. But how could you live in Rome for a whole year and not notice these things?" I watched him polish off the bottle of wine and then down several brandies with his coffee. "By the way, while we're on the subject of the men in your life, whatever happened to that husband of yours I met in Hong Kong?"

"You mean Norman."

"Yes. Unless there's another husband I don't know about."

I told him Norman was living in Chicago where he had started his own architectural firm. After our divorce, he began living openly with another man. Then, tentatively, "You knew he was homosexual before I did, didn't you, Father, and you were trying to warn me."

"I suppose I was trying to hint at it, hoping to soften the blow, because these things always come out in the end. I could see you were very much in love with him—"

"Oh, I was!"

"—so it must have hurt you tremendously when you found out."

"It did."

"I'm so sorry." He laid a sympathetic hand over mine. "But now you're looking marvelous! More beautiful than ever!"

"Yes, I've gotten over it. Although after Norman and my recent fiasco in Rome, and some other disastrous love affairs I'd rather not tell you about, I doubt that I'll marry again."

"Nonsense!"

"Do you know what my mother said about me?"

"I'm not sure I want to know."

He got slowly to his feet and suggested we continue on to Toots Shor's, the celebrity hangout that was more of a saloon than a restaurant on West Fifty-first Street. "Toots is a friend of mine," he was saying as he squired me out of the Plaza. "We can talk there as long as we want, undisturbed." While we stood waiting for the doorman to hail a cab, I was tempted to tell him my mother had predicted I would be a success in my work and a miserable failure in my love life. I would have enjoyed hearing another, thundering "Nonsense!"

What I did tell him in the cab was how very sorry I was about what had happened in Paris years ago, when I had called him up and told him I couldn't see him for a while. "I never meant to end our visits forever," I explained, tears springing to my eyes, "just until my mother came to her senses. She was threatening to throw me out of the house if I went on seeing you. I was only sixteen and I didn't really have a choice. I hope you see that now and don't hold it against me."

"But I *always* saw it," he said. "I knew it was your mother's doing and not your fault. I was furious with Virginia, but never with you. You were my darling girl."

And I'm not anymore? While the cab inched forward in midtown traffic, I had an impulse to fling myself on his chest, crying, *Daddy, Daddy, take me back!* It was the old yearning to be in his life every day and turn him into the Daddy he couldn't be. Wasn't it time to lock these feelings away with my childhood toys? Well, at least I had been forgiven for my transgression at sixteen. A wave of relief swept over me. Now my father and I could start afresh.

I SPENT HOURS with my father that day, and he was more forthcoming than he had been in Hong Kong, but he said nothing about having left

Paola to live with the captivating woman he had met in Zagreb in 1962. Part of Tito's communist Yugoslavia, Zagreb was a magnet for European filmmakers who needed to cut costs, and while it had drawn the ever-impoverished Orson Welles for that reason, the communist-built housing developments on the city's outskirts also provided him with the stark, impersonal locales he needed to make *The Trial,* his extraordinary movie based on Franz Kafka's novel. Although my father was strongly attracted to the lovely young Croatian casually introduced by his cameraman, he did not pursue the relationship until a few years later, when he was working in Paris and heard she was studying at the Ecole des Beaux-Arts. Soon afterward, they began the passionate relationship that would last for the rest of my father's life.

However, not once, during all the lunches and dinners I was to have with my father in elegant New York hotels, not to mention our numerous long-distance phone calls, did he ever speak to me about his Croatian companion, Oja Kodar. Nor did he ever make it clear that he and Paola were living apart, their marriage reduced to a fiction they both kept alive, presumably for the sake of Beatrice.

When my father moved back to the United States, he first lived with Paola and Beatrice in Sedona, Arizona. This amazed me. Why Arizona, I asked him? It was Paola's idea, he explained. She felt the climate would be beneficial for his asthma, and she wanted to create an oasis far from Hollywood where he could come home and not be disturbed. As it turned out, his work took him so frequently to Los Angeles that he needed a home there as well. Since Paola hated Hollywood even more than he did, she and Beatrice moved to Las Vegas to make it easier for him to commute back and forth. What my father did not tell me was that he and Oja were living together in Los Angeles and he rarely put in an appearance at his home on Montecito Drive in Las Vegas.

I first learned of Oja's existence from Granny and Skipper Hill. In August of 1968, almost a year after I had seen my father at the Plaza and a few years before his return to the United States, I was visiting the Hills in their retirement home in Coral Gables, Florida. Skipper had met Oja earlier that year and could not say enough about her. Yet even he did not know her name was invented and the story behind it. That I would hear in time from Oja herself.

Born Olga Palinkas, her baby sister, Nina, who was unable to say Olga, called her Oja (pronounced "Oy-ya") and the nickname stuck. The invention of Kodar as Oja's surname came about years later when she and my father were living in her house in Orvilliers near Paris. A visiting Croatian friend asked Orson how he saw Oja and what she meant to him. "She's a present to me from God," Orson answered, which Oja translated for her friend. In Croatian, *kodar* means "as a present," and the moment he heard that word, Orson cried, "Well, that's what you should be called: Oja as a present."

During my visit with the Hills, Skipper showed me snapshots he had taken of Oja, revealing a black-haired beauty in her midtwenties, her hair pulled straight back in a style that would have been too severe on almost anyone else but accentuated her high Slavic cheekbones and her dark eyes tilting up at the corners. She was tall, slender, and her scanty bathing suit revealed a body of classic proportions.

"Gorgeous, isn't she?" Skipper drawled, taking back the snapshots. "But it wasn't just her looks that got Orson interested in her. He can't get over how smart she is, and how talented. Why, at one point, he took me aside and told me in that stage whisper of his, 'At last I've met a truly intelligent woman!'"

"What about Virginia?" Granny asked, no doubt for my benefit. "She's no fool."

"You're right, Horty," Skipper agreed, "Virginia's a bright gal all right, but even she couldn't keep up with Orson, and he got bored with her in the end — sorry, Chris, to say that about your mother, but it's true."

"Rita's as sweet as they come, but I have to admit she's no whiz kid," Granny observed with a fond laugh. She had always felt warm and mothering toward Rita Hayworth.

"Let's face it, none of the women who came after Virginia knew how to keep Orson interested and faithful."

"And when I think of how many women he's had . . ." Granny muttered, sounding disgusted.

"All of them gorgeous, too, but the point I'm trying to make is that Oja is different. He's never going to get tired of her."

"Why not, Skipper?" I asked him.

"Oh, I don't know, honey. It's just a feeling I have about her. And the way the two of them are when they're together."

"Well," Granny said, sighing, "this much is clear anyway. Now Orson's with Oja, there's no hope for our Chris."

"What do you mean, Granny?" I asked her.

"Why, she's even younger than you are, dear."

"But Granny . . ." I began to protest that a daughter is a daughter and a lover, a lover, but I stopped myself. Better not to wander into that dark territory where one might be mistaken for the other.

Skipper stopped his pacing long enough to give me one of his penetrating looks. Then he began: "There's something I should tell you now you're in touch with Orson again. With a man like your dad, you've got to concentrate more on what he's achieved and less on who he is or isn't. Do you understand what I'm saying?"

"Yes." *But I'm not sure I can do it.*

"Good. And another thing, kid. Orson may not be the father you've always been looking for, but in his own way, he cares about you. As much as he can, that is."

Then the conversation turned to Skipper's involvement in the film my father had begun shooting the year before in Yugoslavia. First called *Dead Reckoning* and later renamed *The Deep,* it told a lurid tale borrowed from a British thriller. A honeymoon couple (Oja Kodar and Michael Bryant) have been blissfully cruising on their yacht until one stormy day they pull a man out of the sea (Laurence Harvey), not realizing they have rescued a psychopath who will lead them into a nightmare of kidnapping and attempted murder. The two other characters on a second boat were played by my father and his old friend, Jeanne Moreau, who had recently starred in *The Immortal Story,* his first movie made in color. *The Deep* was also shot in color, but in my father's mind it had one purpose only. "My hope is that it won't be an art house movie," he told an interviewer after filming began off the Dalmatian coast near Primosten, the small village where Oja lived, and on the island of Hvar. "I felt it was high time to show the world I could make some money." It was a hopeless quest that he had pursued since the days of *The Lady from Shanghai,* also intended to be a box office success. It would be like asking Leo Tolstoy to write pulp fiction.

Skipper had been "suckered into Orson's folly," as he put it with a mock grimace, because of his lifelong knowledge of boats and sailing. "We started getting telegrams pages long and transatlantic phone calls at all hours of the day and night," he grumbled, "picking my brain about this and that. Of course, Orson's up all night anyway—he's had insomnia ever since I could remember—and in his urgency to ask me something, he'd forget that ten in the morning in Yugoslavia is three or four a.m. here in Miami. Well, Horty and I were getting pretty tired of being waked up in the middle of the night, so I told him to just send me the shooting script with his questions written in the margins and I'd take care of it pronto." Skipper spent considerable time going over the script, making corrections and suggestions. "I worked like a dog, and then Orson paid no attention to anything I said. After a while, I felt he was playing a game of one-upmanship with me. He'd sought me out in the first place because he sees me as the Old Man of the Sea and the world authority on sailing, but then he had to prove he knew more than I did!"

Skipper gave a wry laugh, shaking his head. "I thought that was the end of it, and I was well out of it. Then I get a frantic call from Orson, another crisis, another catastrophe, and before Horty can stop me, I'm off and running again, this time to the Bahamas." Skipper agreed to meet Orson and Oja with a yacht, cameraman, and deep-sea divers willing to double for the characters played by Orson and Laurence Harvey, who fight an underwater battle among the sharks. After the sequence was shot, happily without the sharks, it had to be scrapped because the fake blood came out green instead of red. It was another mishap in the unending stream that had plagued the production of *The Deep* since its inception.

Skipper was left complaining about the canisters of film that he was storing in his freezer while awaiting instructions from Orson. "I don't know what the heck I'm supposed to do with it or if Orson even remembers I've got it." I felt sure my father remembered every frame and was only waiting for the money to materialize so that he could go forward. I was equally convinced that no matter how much Skipper grumbled about the film taking up room in his freezer, he would do it all again in a minute. What could match the excitement of the phone ringing before dawn, telegrams arriving daily, and then a week of mayhem in the Bahamas?

Before I left Coral Gables, Granny put her arm around me. "Skipper and I are so proud of you, Chris. We feel you've become what you are almost single-handedly, and we hope you see that about yourself."

"That's right, kid," Skipper put in. "You've made it on your own with no help from Orson or Virginia."

"And now you're a grown woman with your own life," Granny went on, "you don't need Orson the way you once did. I hope you see that."

I knew Granny was right, and yet I didn't feel free of my famous parent. The shadow of Orson Welles still fell across my life—and probably it always would.

ALTHOUGH I NEVER revealed my father's identity to my co-workers, more often than not they already knew. Such was the case the first time I walked through the door of Encyclopaedia Britannica's New York office. Everyone from the man in the mailroom to the director in charge of our project knew that my father was Orson Welles. That included Irwin Feder, the attractive senior editor who would be supervising my work. Had it not been so, would Irwin have assigned me the articles in the encyclopedia that pertained to motion pictures? Despite my father and my Hollywood childhood, I was far from being an expert on the movies. Yet I loved editing this section and making sure, when I got to the article on Orson Welles, that his masterwork, *Chimes at Midnight,* was given its due.

I worked desk to desk with Irwin and four other editors in a large, pleasant room we called "the library." As we were a congenial group, we usually went out for lunch together. Yet, in spite of being thrown together day after day, Irwin and I managed to ignore each other for several months. Working at such close quarters and with only one telephone in the room, it was impossible not to eavesdrop on everyone's calls. I gathered from the number of women calling Irwin every day that he was not available. I also learned from chance remarks that he was still married, although separated from his wife, an American artist who was living in Paris with their two children. Whenever I felt myself becoming attracted to Irwin, I had to remind myself, *He's married, forty-four, and too old for me.*

Then one day, to my astonishment, Irwin suggested dinner after work and a popular British film, *A Man for All Seasons.* While I accepted his invitation at once, the fact that he had chosen a movie in which my father played a cameo role put me on my guard. Was Irwin taking me to *A Man for All Seasons* so that he could boast to his friends he had seen Orson Welles in this movie in the company of Orson's daughter? This had been happening to me all my life, but I sensed that Irwin was different from most people. He was not impressed by celebrity.

I knew Irwin was a man who spoke his mind. Nonetheless, I was unprepared for his opening remark at dinner. "I've been meaning to tell you for some time, Chris, that you're much too nice and polite to everyone. You're almost *too* well bred. Nobody can be *that* nice and *that* much of a lady. Why don't you just relax and be more the person you really are?" Rather than being annoyed by his remarks, I found myself intrigued. No one had ever suggested to me before that I fling off my mask and show my warts and moles.

Orson as the corrupt Cardinal Wolsey in *A Man for All Seasons* (1966).

We both enjoyed *A Man for All Seasons*. Afterward, we went for a walk, and Irwin asked me how it felt to see my father on the screen. "Strange," I told him, not wanting to reveal that, although I no longer dissolved in tears, it still unsettled me. I particularly disliked seeing my father in the villainous roles that had become his stock in trade, including the obese, worldly, and corrupt Cardinal Wolsey.

"What do you mean, 'strange'?" Irwin persisted.

By way of an answer, I shared with him an anecdote Danny Kaye had told me about the first time his five-year-old daughter saw him perform as a comic on stage. After the show she came backstage, crying as though her heart would break, and when he asked her, "What's the matter, honey?" she sobbed, "I don't want people laughing at my daddy."

Irwin laughed. "When did you meet Danny Kaye?"

"I met him as a child when I was staying with my father in London and then years later we spent an evening together in Chicago. Danny was in town, doing a one-man show, and I was eighteen or nineteen. The strange thing was that when he was offstage and alone with you, he wasn't a bit funny. If anything, he seemed mildly depressed. He was awfully sweet, though. You would have liked him."

I was congratulating myself that I had succeeded in moving the conversation away from Orson Welles when Irwin started to tell me about the first time he saw *Citizen Kane*. He was seventeen or eighteen, he remembered, and he and a friend had wandered into the Nemo movie theater at 110th Street and Broadway in the neighborhood where Irwin had grown up. The second movie of the double feature was *Citizen Kane*. "I was so blown away by it," Irwin recalled, "that I decided I had to see it a second time even though it meant sitting through the other movie, which I've forgotten now. I'd never realized until I saw *Citizen Kane* that movies could be an art form."

We walked on together in silence. I was struck that Irwin's initial reaction to *Kane* had so closely resembled mine. It was also curious that we had both discovered this remarkable film at about the same age.

After a few moments, Irwin said, "Of course, I don't need to tell *you* about your dad, one of the greatest movie directors of all time. What's it been like for you to have such a towering figure . . . ?"

"Where are we now?" I asked, desperate to change the subject. We had walked more than a mile downtown to Greenwich Village, where Irwin lived. I had never been to this part of New York before, and strolling along the peaceful, tree-lined streets where well-kept brownstones from another century nestled shoulder to shoulder, I felt I was back in Europe, wandering down a London mews. I caught glimpses through open windows of gracious, high-ceilinged rooms with chandeliers, decorative moldings, built-in bookcases, and fireplaces. "I'd give anything to live in this part of town!" I exclaimed.

Little did I know on that balmy night as we strolled along the lamplit streets of Greenwich Village that with every step my nomadic life was retreating further into the past. I had come home.

The Final Years

THREE YEARS AFTER IRWIN had introduced me to Greenwich Village, we were married in a quiet ceremony on September 20, 1970. The only members of my family who came to our wedding were my Aunt Caryl and her son David. Horrified that I was marrying a Jew, my grandmother arranged to be visiting my mother and Jackie, who by then had moved to London. On our wedding day, my mother sent a frosty telegram of congratulations. (In another of her famous predictions, she had claimed Irwin would never divorce his first wife and marry me.)

Chris and her second husband, Irwin Feder, on their wedding day in New York, 1970.

Although my father knew from the Hills that I was getting married, he did not send a telegram or a wedding gift. However, in early November, he wrote me a seven-page letter, remarkable in itself. Postmarked from Beverly Hills, the envelope was addressed to Mrs. Christopher Feder—so he did know my married name—and the letter began with the usual protestations.

> Darling Girl,
>
> Very nearly my first frustration, upon landing again on these shores, was to find that the Feders had moved. I should have remembered that New Yorkers always do that, but what good would it have done me? The migration of birds can be charted, New Yorkers are something else again. Forgot the name of your place of business—if indeed I ever knew it—so what to do? The Hills were no use to me. That tribe has a migration of its own: every autumn they leave Florida and commence, as I suppose you know, a protracted matriarchal (and maybe, slightly patriarchal) progress among the scattered fruit of their seed . . .
>
> Why didn't I think of Becky? Well, of course I did, but not as a source of information about you. We exchanged letters and a couple of phone conversations before it occurred to me to ask if she'd had any news of you. Oh, yes, was the answer, a letter had been sent to you only three weeks before (I seem to hear the tinkle of a sisterly tin cup).
>
> So now, just before my return to the Old World, I've got your address. Next time you send for the moving van, do please slip a postcard either to [my secretary in Los Angeles] or to me [at my address in London] where I live with your youngest sister, who, by the way, ought to write you sometimes, and would be encouraged in her wavering belief that you exist if someday around yuletide she got a card to that effect.

I had read only the first two pages and I could hardly believe what he had written me. Even if he couldn't bring himself to mention Irwin—perhaps he had "forgotten" the name of my new husband as well as the "place of business" where I had worked for the last three years—at the very least he might have acknowledged our recent marriage and offered his best wishes. Instead, "the Feders" had had the audacity to move without informing him. As the post office was forwarding mail from my old address and the new one was listed in the Manhattan telephone directory, it should not have taken the deductive powers of a Sherlock Holmes to locate me.

His reference to "the tinkle of a sisterly tin cup" reminded me that I had told him Becky would write to me periodically, asking for small loans, which I would promptly send her. Then, a month or so later, she would return the money in full. "Becky gets plenty of money from me and her mother," he had responded with a hint of irritation, "and so there's no need for you to send her any." But I felt that what Becky needed from me was not the pittance I sent her but the reassurance that I was there for her and that I cared. "Nonsense, Christopher! Your sister's a born panhandler, just like my brother was. Did you know your Uncle Richard was always dunning me for money? The next time Becky rattles her tin cup, pay no attention."

Finally, it was more than annoying to be told I should send Beatrice a Christmas card to encourage her "wavering belief" in my existence when I had sent Christmas presents for the whole family and heard nothing in return. Possibly my gifts had never arrived or I had sent them to the wrong address, but in any case, why was it entirely up to me? I hadn't heard from Paola in years.

If the beginning of my father's letter had ruffled my feathers, there was worse to come. The letter continued:

> How do you feel about booze?
>
> Would you be willing to touch some money earned . . . from a likker advertisement? I assume that, like all these other young whipper-snappers, you've gone to pot. I also assume that you could use a little extra bread. So if your conscience permits (and I'll just bet it does) before the first crocus has pushed its way up out of the snow you'll be cashing a nice check from a hootch company. The hootch company is nice, too. A hundred and seventy something years old and still in the same agreeable Kentucky family. Beam is the name, and they really do make the best bourbon you can buy. To get this message to the shrinking ranks of American drinkers they have launched a campaign. "Bridging the Generation Gap" is the theme. Meaning, I suppose, "Get off the Grass." Or, "Alcohol is non-addictive and delicious"—something like that. The program calls for a series of clearly identifiable fathers

to be photographed clutching an offspring and a jar of juice, not necessarily in that order. The trouble is that the offspring of most celebrated American papas are pretty uptight about being seen in the same picture with even the smallest glass of any sort of blue ruin, booze or mountain dew. This, they seem to feel, would be betraying the Revolution. Well, in this case the price for treachery is pretty high. It has to be or there wouldn't be any quislings at all.

When I was approached about this (as the father of two mature enough to be admitted to any saloon) my choice — in response to some ancient, Anglo-Saxon call of the blood — was for my eldest. But you had vanished. This brought me to Becky who jumped at the chance to set back the march of progress for a good price. She didn't actually clutch a jar of the creature, but she clutched me, smiled widely and got photographed and paid.

Right here I'd like to mention what may well strike you as a most unlikely subject: my own conscience. For thirty odd years — quite a lot of them lean ones — I've stoutly resisted all the loot that's been offered me to pose with products, alcoholic or otherwise. But now the devils were getting at me through my children. How could I deny them the chance to get their greedy little fingers on all that easy Madison Avenue gelt?

On the other hand, why should one daughter run off with all the boodle just because her father didn't know her older sister's address? Who likes money just as much as the rest of us? Beatrice, of course . . . Well, as you know, you have a Solomon for a father, and here's the wise old man's solution. For descending into the Los Angeles smog and sweating under the photographers' lights (and for being available for these risks) Becky is to get the biggest cut — in fact, one half of the pie. The other half will be divided equally between her two sisters for staying at home and maintaining the dignity of the family. . . .

The implication behind my father's jocular tone that his "greedy" daughters had driven him to violate his conscience and prostitute his talent deeply offended me. Never in my life had I asked him for money, nor would I dream of doing so. Since the age of seventeen, as he well knew, I had been supporting

The Jim Beam bourbon ad featuring Orson Welles
and Rebecca in Beam's famous fathers and daughters
campaign.

myself with no help from anyone. When I cooled down, I tried to give him the benefit of the doubt: Perhaps this was his way of sending me a wedding present. Yet the promised check from the Jim Beam advertisement never materialized. What I did receive from Becky were copies of the full-page "likker" ad. The strong physical resemblance between Orson Welles and his middle daughter suggested why Becky had been chosen rather than Beatrice or me. For Becky's sweet sake, knowing how close she lived to the edge, I hoped she walked away from the photographers' lights carrying bagfuls of "boodle."

IRWIN AND I would often joke to our friends that two of his siblings had met my father before he ever did. It happened like this. His younger brother Jack, a psychologist then in his early forties, was traveling with his girlfriend in northern Italy and decided to stay in a luxurious resort hotel outside Vicenza, the town in which the sixteenth-century architect Andrea Palladio had lived and worked. On their first evening, they were standing on the terrace overlooking the gardens when they heard the unmistakable voice of Orson Welles. He was speaking at full volume to the lovely young woman they did not know was Oja. "You can keep all your miniskirts. Just give me this view in the moonlight." Never one to be shy, Jack walked up to my father and introduced himself as "the brother of the man who is going to marry your daughter."

"Oh really?" My father bathed him in a gracious smile. "And what are you doing in this part of Italy?"

"We're looking at Palladian mansions," Jack replied.

My father eyed him with renewed interest. "Buying?"

"No, just looking."

"Oh. Well. Give my love to Christopher." He took Oja's arm and disappeared into the night.

"As soon as he realized I wasn't a multimillionaire, he lost all interest in me," Jack told us on his return to New York. At the time, none of us realized how much of my father's life had to be spent wooing the wealthy. In one of his last interviews, he would divulge the heartbreaking fact that ninety-five per-

When I told my father in 1978 that Skipper was "at loose ends," he made him the surprise guest at the American Film Institute's seminar "Working with Welles."

cent of his time had been spent trying to raise money to make or complete his films, which had left him precious little time to function as a creative being.

The next unlikely encounter between Orson Welles and one of Irwin's siblings took place in a Hollywood restaurant early in 1975. My father was in town to accept the Life Achievement Award from the American Film Institute, a high honor in Hollywood but one that is usually given at the end of a distinguished director's career. Not yet sixty, my father had reason to feel that many productive years still lay ahead of him, and that the award was being bestowed prematurely. As Irwin and I watched the ninety-minute award ceremony on network television, I was awash in my own feelings of irony. At one point, "the family" was asked to stand up and take a bow. I stared incredulously at a "family" of two people: Paola and Beatrice.

The very next day, Irwin's sister Marlene called to tell me she had spotted my father in a restaurant where she was lunching with a friend. Being a Feder, she marched right up to him. "I have to introduce myself to you, Mr. Welles," she began, "because *my* brother is married to *your* daughter." Pause. "I understand you haven't been in touch with Chris in quite a while, and I really think you ought to be." Another long pause during which I can imagine my father's astonishment and discomfort as he surveyed the attractive blond bearing down on him. Clearly she was not going away until she got a satisfactory answer.

Finally he said, "I don't think I have the right address for her." In fact, he went on to explain, he had written me recently, but his letter had been returned.

(*Yeah, sure,* I thought when I heard this, but it turned out to be true. After my father's death, the unopened letter was found in his papers and sent on to me. It had been addressed to Ms. Chris Welles, and the name on my mailbox for the past five years had been Chris Feder.)

"Oh," cried Marlene, eager to help, "I have Chris's address at home." Elaborate arrangements were then made so that Marlene could call Orson's agent and give him my address and telephone number. Now Marlene was calling to let me know what she had accomplished so that hearing from my father wouldn't come as "a bolt out of the blue." I promised her I would not hold my breath waiting for him to call.

The phone rang early the next morning. "This is your father speaking." From the first sonorous syllable, I knew it could not be anyone else. We were polite and cautious, as we would be when talking to a stranger. I told him we had watched the Life Achievement Award ceremony on TV and how pleased I was that Hollywood had given him this honor, long overdue.

A moment of hilarity on the set of *The Other Side of the Wind* (from left to right: John Huston, Orson Welles, Peter Bogdanovich).

"No, no," he interrupted me, "the award came much too soon. It was like going to my own funeral while I'm still alive!" I said I understood how he felt, but now that Hollywood had officially recognized his extraordinary talent, I hoped the money would start pouring in so that he'd be able to finish *The Other Side of the Wind*. This feature, which he had begun soon after his return to the United States, starred John Huston, among others. "And *The Deep*. And *Don Quixote*," he added with a rueful laugh. "You have no idea how many of my children are stillborn for lack of funds."

His children. I wanted to say that Becky and I should have been sitting beside Paola and Beatrice during the ceremony, that we were also his family. I wanted to ask if he had any idea how much it hurt to be repeatedly overlooked as though I were a footnote he had lost somewhere in the voluminous pages of his life. But I knew that whenever I surfaced in his mind, his impulses toward me were kind, generous, and loving. He could never be cruel to me, as my mother so easily was, any more than he could be vulgar, even if he used vulgar words. There was a shining innocence about Orson Welles that the world could not tarnish. And that was what I loved in him and why, in the end, I was always able to push aside anger and hurt.

"I'm going to be coming to New York soon," he was saying, "so I'll be calling you again, Christopher."

"Please come to our place for dinner."

"No, no, I don't want you slaving all day over a hot stove."

"I'd love to make dinner for you, really I would."

"Well, we'll see."

"And I want you to meet Irwin."

"Irwin?"

"My husband." *We've been married for five years and you still haven't met him.*

"Oh, yes, of course. Well, you can bring him with you when you come to my hotel."

"Then you're not going to come to our home?"

"I'll call you again soon. Until then, darling girl, my dearest, dearest love."

A YEAR AND a half later, my father had neither called nor met Irwin. But he did think of me at Christmas. A tall, ungainly houseplant arrived with a gift card, not in his handwriting.

That Christmas, I wrote the Hills, "Needless to say, O.W. has not called me since Irwin's sister Marlene cornered him in a restaurant. That was over a year ago. The chances of Marlene once again finding herself sitting a table away from O.W. in a Hollywood restaurant are rather slim. Therefore, I do not expect another call for years."

"You should call Paola now and then," Skipper urged me in reply. "Orson has pretty much abandoned her."

In time I did reconnect with Paola, but during the early years of my marriage, I had a life of my own to forge. I was now in my thirties and gradually establishing myself as an educational writer for schoolchildren. After the project at Encyclopaedia Britannica ended, I had gone to work for a small publishing firm that produced elementary reading materials. When that company folded, I became a freelance writer, and soon I met Patricia Cusick, an editorial vice president at the Scott Foresman publishing company. She believed so strongly in my talent that she gave me the opportunity to write a language arts program for elementary schoolchildren.

After the success of the language arts books, there was talk of my doing a spelling series, which I happened to mention in a letter to my father. Soon afterward I received his first letter to me in eight years. "The news that a child of mine is to be given responsability [*sic*] for a text book on spelling is dizzying proof that genetic determinism is more a hurdle than a handicap. Congratulations." He signed the letter "your errant and admiring father."

"So you've finally impressed your father," Irwin observed, reading his letter, "but why should the fact that you're going to write a spelling book make him prouder of you than anything else you've done?"

"Because *he* never learned how to spell."

ALTHOUGH I COULD never persuade my father to come to our home, he did finally meet Irwin in 1980. My father was then sixty-five, and Irwin was fifty-seven. (It didn't occur to me until years later that having a son-in-law close to his own age might be a problem for Orson Welles.) On the day my father called to invite me to lunch at his hotel, I decided to take a stand. It would mean a lot to me, I said, if he would meet my husband. It didn't seem right that Irwin and I had been married almost ten years and my father had never met him. "Has it really been that long?" His voice rose in astonishment. "Then you must *both* come to my hotel and have lunch with me tomorrow."

"But couldn't you possibly come to our place instead? Just this once? It would be so wonderful to make lunch for you here."

"No, I can't do that." There was a long pause. "I didn't want to tell you, but I've been ill, and it isn't easy for me to get around."

"Oh, I'm so sorry! I didn't know."

"I know you didn't, but now that you do, I hope you understand why I want you and your husband to come to my hotel."

"But if you aren't well, perhaps we shouldn't come — "

"No, no, I'm well enough to see you, just a little weak and shaky on my pins these days. They have to push me around in a wheelchair, you know."

I had heard about the wheelchair. On our previous visit, he had joked that he always ordered one at airports and how grand it was to be wheeled in comfort and style from the cab to the plane. Then he had laughed, pretending to be delighted with himself, as though he alone had outwitted the airport gods who decree that we must all stand in a long line at the check-in counter until our knees turn to water. So I had thought what he had wanted me to think: that the wheelchair was a clever ruse. I had no idea how ill he really was or what an effort he was making to see me whenever he passed through New York.

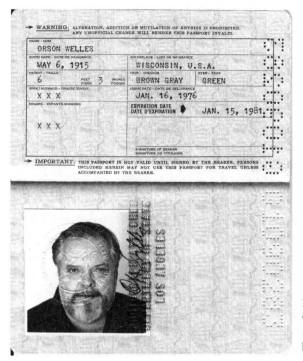

Pages from Orson's passport, which expired on January 15, 1981, less than five years before his death.

The next day Irwin and I walked down the long hallway to my father's suite of rooms in the elegant Carlyle Hotel. My palms were sweating. I kept asking Irwin how I looked and if my hair needed combing, and he kept telling me to relax. "Just be yourself, Chris, and everything will be fine."

Suddenly a door flew open at the end of the hall and my father's enormous figure stood outlined in the lighted space behind him. He was wearing a voluminous white caftan that fell to his feet. His appearance made me think of an African king, an aging Othello, but one who had spared his own life and Desdemona's and forgiven Iago his treachery. Smiling broadly, he ushered us into his domain. I made a movement to embrace him, but he warned me away. "Kiki will bite if you come too close." He stroked the head of the small black poodle nestled under his arm. "She's more jealous of me than ten mistresses." Chuckling, he sank heavily into an armchair, depositing Kiki on his lap where she crouched forward, bared her teeth, and snarled at us. "Don't pet her whatever you do. Poor little thing. She must have been horribly mistreated when she was a puppy."

How genial he was and how gracious, shaking Irwin's hand, motioning us to chairs at a good remove from Kiki, suggesting we order from room service right away as it tended to be slow, even in a hotel as grand as this one. And please, we shouldn't pay any attention to the few bread crumbs he allowed himself for lunch. We should order whatever we wanted and plenty of it. "I like to watch other people eating lunch," he told us, eyes twinkling.

I was struck once again by my father's courteous manner and what a true gentleman he was. Had he been less a gentleman, he might have introduced us to Oja, who was undoubtedly traveling with him and, for all we knew, hiding in the next room. But it was inconceivable to a man of my father's refinement that his daughter and son-in-law should meet his lover, not when we knew he was married to Paola. So on this visit and those that followed, we all pretended Oja did not exist. (Years later, when I finally stayed with Oja at her seaside home in Primosten, she told me that she had seen me more than once, arriving in the hotel lobby on my way to see Orson just as she was going out to shop or spend the afternoon in a museum. We laughed to think how easily we might have met in spite of my father's precautions.)

A knock on the door announced the arrival of lunch and my father immediately brightened as though we had come to the high point of our visit. A waiter wheeled in a table set with starched linens, silverware, and a few posies nodding in a crystal vase. He ceremoniously removed the silver domes covering our plates and then discreetly withdrew. Now my father settled down not to the business of eating — his lunch was as meager as he had said it would be — but to entertaining us with a stream of anecdotes. Often the joke was on himself. During the filming of *The Third Man* in Vienna, he told us, his old buddy Joseph Cotten made a bet with him that he would be unable to entice a certain actress into his bed. Although she was so unattractive she should have been grateful for any man's attentions, no one had managed to seduce her to date. "So I spent my entire time in Vienna chasing this woman, determined to win my bet with Jo, and all this time I was working with one of the most beautiful women in the world and ignoring her completely. Guess who it was. Alida Valli. Yes, Alida Valli." He shook his head, chuckling. "Well, I won my bet with Jo, but I lost out with the lady in question who turned out to be *terrible* in bed. The worst lay of my life, in fact. Then, after I'd left Vienna, I found out Alida Valli had been mad for me, and if I'd given her the slightest encouragement, she'd have hopped in my bed in a minute. How could I have been such an idiot?" We joined in his hearty laughter.

The hour passed pleasantly enough and then he rose, signaling that it was time for us to go. I had hardly said a word, wanting to give Irwin a chance to shine. However, Irwin also had said very little. He had simply told my father how he had been "blown away" by *Citizen Kane* when he saw it for the first time. Otherwise, he had listened politely, as I had, and laughed in the right places.

On my way to use the bathroom before we left, I passed through my father's bedroom and was shocked by the number of pill bottles on his bedside table. Even then, however, it did not fully register on me that he was a sick man pretending not to be. I was too caught up in feelings of disappointment. Did my father not see how unusually intelligent Irwin was? Irwin had his own inexhaustible supply of stories, but he had not been given the chance to tell even one of them. (Later, I would hear from Skipper the staggering notion that Orson found Irwin "too possessive" of me.)

On our way home, Irwin shared his own disappointment. "Did you notice how your father talked *at* us, not *to* us? He was like a king holding audience, deciding when we should enter his presence and when we should take our leave." Then Irwin brightened. "Well, at least I can say I've finally met my father-in-law."

I took Irwin's hand. He agreed with me that, however regal my father may have been in person, he had also been charming and cordial. Although he was not a well man, he had put himself out to entertain us, asking nothing in return. There was something sad about my father regaling us with amusing stories we had heard him tell before—and with greater aplomb—on television.

DURING THE FINAL ten years of his life, my father was earning his living, or as he put it, his "bread and butter," by making frequent appearances on television talk shows. He also found fairly steady employment as a voice-over man, narrating documentaries and doing commercials on radio and television. "I have to keep my name alive and my bills paid," he told me. While I understood that he had to take whatever work came along, it saddened me that, instead of making his own "ribbons of dreams," one of the great movie directors of the twentieth century was doing card tricks and selling "no wine before its time" on television.

Yet it was hard not to enjoy my father's guest appearances on talk shows, whether hosted by David Frost, Johnny Carson, or Merv Griffin. Orson Welles was invariably a witty, charming guest, an oversized but still handsome man sitting at his ease and ready to entertain the audience all night long, telling one anecdote after another. The exception was one Merv Griffin show. Another guest, the writer Gore Vidal, seemed hostile to my father and kept cutting him off in midsentence. After seeing that show, I wrote my father that he had handled Vidal's rudeness with admirable poise and good humor. "You came off extremely well," I told him, "whereas Vidal seemed too angry at the world to listen to anyone." My father replied that, while he was glad I thought well of him, he was not sure I was right about Gore Vidal. True, Vidal had been angry enough at him to launch a fierce attack in the *New York Review of Books* several months prior to the show. "My refusal to acknowledge any wounds may well have been rather irritating," my father conceded. Nonetheless, he felt Vidal's anger was an act. "He breaks in new versions of it every season on the lecture circuit, fine tuning the best of the one-liners for the talk shows; and if he doesn't listen to anyone it's not out of rage, just a chronic reluctance to grant his fellow 'guests' a second more airtime than he can help." What a good sport my father was about the pygmies who dogged him, piercing his shins with their poisoned arrows.

There was only one occasion I remember my father talking about me and my two half sisters on television, and that was during a ninety-minute interview with Dick Cavett. His genial, low-key host asked him how many children he had. "Like King Lear, I have three daughters," my father replied, "but unlike Lear, they have all been kind to me." He beamed like a man who has said it all and is ready to move on to the next subject, but Cavett prompted him to describe each one of us. A long pause. Then I heard myself characterized as the eldest, who was "frighteningly bright" and a writer living in New York. Rebecca was "a flower child." Beatrice was "a horse woman."

The phrase lodged in my mind: *frighteningly bright*. Did my intelligence scare my father away? Would he feel closer to me if I were not as bright? I could speculate endlessly and arrive at no satisfactory answer. I could also spend the rest of my life wondering why, when my father was alone with me, he could not be as relaxed and natural, as seemingly "himself," as he was on talk shows. Could it be that the "real" Orson Welles was not the father I met in hotel rooms but the one I saw on television?

IT WAS GRANNY Hill who had taught me to look for a loving mother outside my immediate family. From her I also learned that the children I would come to cherish in my life did not have to be biologically mine. Yet of all the pieces of wisdom she gave me, the greatest was this: "If you make those you love happy, then you will be happy, too." These were the words she lived by, this plain, stout woman whose only vanity was that she hated to be photographed—it reminded her that she did not look like Rita Hayworth. Yet on the many occasions when I poured out my troubles and found courage in her profound understanding of life and human nature, I would look at her through my tears and think I had never seen a woman with a soul as pure and beautiful as Granny Hill's.

My father shared my feelings, and the fact we had both been loved and nurtured by Granny Hill made a bond between us. He couldn't speak of her without saying he "adored" her and that she was his "ideal woman"; at the same time, he couldn't resist poking fun at the long letters she wrote him, filled with the doings of her family, friends, and burgeoning tribe of children and grandchildren. At various times, he read one of her letters aloud to me, shaking with laughter. "But I don't *know* any of these people," he protested. "Why does Hortense think I want to hear about them in such detail?" He was perplexed by her consuming interest in others and her own lack of ego. And why, in her old age, had she added the children of her cleaning woman to her already enormous brood? "I wouldn't put it past her to send them all through college," he told me, shaking his head. Then, his eyes misting, he murmured, "I was always in love with Hortense, you know. I would have married her in a minute if she hadn't married my best friend." (I assumed he meant he would have married her at least twenty years after Skipper did; at the time of the Hills' wedding, my father was still in diapers.)

I thought I had prepared myself for Granny's death. Toward the end, I had visited her several times in Rockford, Illinois, where she and Skipper had relocated to be near their family, and I had seen her ravaged face. I had listened to Skipper complain that she was becoming "ornery" and that he didn't know her anymore. Ill health was fast eroding her sweet, compliant nature. I had agreed with the relatives that "it was time for her to go," and on each of my visits to Rockford, convinced it was the last, I had parted from Granny in tears. Yet, when she died on February 5, 1982, the grief that swept over me made me know how unprepared I was to lose her.

An April memorial service was planned in Rockford. A few days before Irwin and I were to fly there, my father called from Los Angeles. "I've written some words to be read at Hortense's memorial service." he began. "I assume you're going with uh . . ."

"Yes, Irwin and I are going."

"I don't want Skipper to have to read my tribute, so I'm sending it to you by express mail. You should get it tomorrow."

"But aren't you going, Father? Shouldn't you be the one who reads—"

"No, Skipper doesn't want me there."

"I can't believe that! Skipper knows what Granny meant to you. Did he really say he didn't want you at her memorial service?"

"He didn't have to. It's the fame thing. *You* know. It'll be pandemonium the moment I appear. Reporters, TV cameras. I'll only upstage the proceedings if I show up, and Skipper wouldn't want that." He paused, waiting for me to say something, but I was stunned into silence. "Even if Skipper begged me to go, I couldn't face his children and grandchildren, that whole tribe of people who *hate* me."

"They don't hate you, Father. How could anyone hate you? They're just jealous of you."

"I've already told you, Christopher," he said quietly. "I can't go to Rockford, and you'll have to take my place."

His reasons for not going to Granny's memorial service did not sit well with me. It was hard enough to go myself without having to stand up in front of a roomful of people and deliver my father's tribute. He was the one to do it. After he hung up, I wished I had said Irwin and I would be there to fend off the reporters and blinding flashbulbs. I would push my father in a wheelchair to the podium, hand him the microphone, and stand beside him while he shared his vision of Hortense Hill with the hushed audience.

It was not to be. When the time came, I was the one at the podium to read aloud my father's words, but I did not get very far. Grief overwhelmed me. Irwin rushed to my side, took the paper from my hand, and delivered the following eulogy in his clear, strong voice.

> Children . . . and their children . . . and their children after them . . .
> Like the seed of Father Abraham, it does almost seem that the de-
> scendants of Mother Hortense are to be numbered as are the sands
> of the desert. Her *adopted* children are truly beyond counting.
>
>   For myself, I don't believe I can lay claim to more than an
> honorary membership in that community. A semi-orphan with
> something close to a surplus of foster parents before I even went
> to Todd, I was, in my childhood, determined to rid myself of

childhood, a condition I conceived to be a pestilential handicap. I counted Hortense—not as any kind of mother, but from the first as the very dearest kind of friend. What was an infantile presumption soon became, with the passing of a few brief years, a grown-up fact. And so it is that I join your voices today—not really as a member of that enormous tribe which was (and is) her family—but from a smaller and dwindling choir. Ours is the simple song of friendship. A corny old ballad sums it up: "You Are My Sunshine." That's what I share with you today, and always: She was our sunshine . . . For sixty odd years my friend, your mother, was the radiant blessing of my life.

She has gone away and left a black hole in our universe. And yet to mourn is to remember. Our grief brings memories. That shining, vivid, marvelously living presence is back with us again, and our hearts are stabbed with happiness. For just to think of her can never be anything but an occasion for joy.

Of everyone I've known she was the most truly *passionate*. Yes, passionate in every good meaning of a word I choose with care. Other great and good souls may be described as "warm," or warm-hearted. That's too tepid sounding for Hortense. Warmth is a word for comfort and consolation . . . a blanket and nice cup of soup. The word for her was *heat*. Fire. The very element itself . . . The fire in the hearth.

Given her own earthy, intensely personal preoccupations, it's a safe guess that for most of her rich and lengthy career on this planet, she had little time for the sticks and carrots of religion. But if there is a heaven after all, then it's a sure thing that she's in it . . . I like to think of her barefooted (she had such tiny ankles) wading along some celestial strand, searching for seashells . . . and waiting for her children . . .

A few days after the memorial service, my father called to find out how it had gone. I confessed that, although I had practiced reading aloud his beautiful eulogy a number of times, when the moment came to deliver it, I broke down and Irwin had to finish reading it for me.

"But I didn't want you or that husband of yours to read my eulogy!" he admonished me. "I wanted Skipper to read it!"

"But you sent it to me and you said—"

"I sent it to you because you were going to Rockford and I wasn't, and I told you to give it to Skipper the moment you got there."

You told me no such thing.

When I had said goodbye to Skipper in Rockford, he had muttered he was glad Orson hadn't come to the memorial after all; but Skipper was lying to hide his deep disappointment. When Orson Welles could spare a moment for his children or his oldest friend, he wrote words shining with love, as he did for Hortense Hill; or he created an extraordinary book of drawings, a miniature movie on paper that he called *Les Bravades* and gave to his daughter Rebecca, the one who wrote in her diary, "I will always count it as a great loss that I never got to know Father, but it is just as great a loss that he never got to know me."

TOWARD THE END of his life, my father began calling me more often. At first, we were overly polite, but with each phone call we became more relaxed and spoke at greater length. Once he called because he needed to cheer himself up, he said. A movie deal he'd been trying to negotiate for nine months had fallen through. "I'm still hoping it can be renegotiated." He gave a deep sigh. "I'm awfully good at hoping."

"I think it's terrible you're having such a hard time raising money. A great movie director like you!"

His laughter rolled across the continent, and what a life-affirming sound it was. I could imagine him at that moment: his eyes lit with the joy of laughing, his boyish face wagging an incongruous beard streaked with gray, his huge belly trembling. "Now don't you worry your pretty head about me." A soft chuckle. The tide of his laughter ebbing. "They may turn their backs on me now, but you wait and see, darling girl. They're gonna love me when I'm dead!"

It was one of the last things my father ever said to me.

After His Death

LESS THAN THREE YEARS after he failed to attend Hortense Hill's memorial service, Orson Welles was dead. Of all my losses at the time (Granny, my grandmother, and my Aunt Caryl had all died within a year of each other), none of them hit me with the cruel force of my father's death. He had died at seventy—much too young for a man still at the height of his creative powers—and I was totally unprepared.

It took me considerable time to come to terms with the sudden loss of my father and what that meant in terms of my own life, but when I was finally able to look beyond what might have been, I saw myself in relation to him with a new, hard-won clarity. I realized that for much of my life, I had been driven by hopes and expectations that were unachievable. I had wanted Orson Welles to be Dad—not Father with its echo of an age when children of well-to-do parents were shunted off to the nursery with their governess. I had seriously believed that one day I would call him Dad, and we would achieve the same cozy relationship I had observed between Irwin and his adult children. And once this miraculous transformation had taken place, we would be able to tease each other good-naturedly and discuss just about anything. I would bring him my problems and share with him my triumphs. We would have many a serious talk. Then he would have no difficulty accepting an invitation to dinner in our home and getting to know Irwin. I had heard secondhand from the Hills and even from Paola that my father was proud of me. "Dad" would tell me so himself. He would also take pride in his son-in-law, a respected professor of English who made a lasting impression on many of the minority students he taught at LaGuardia Community College, helping them to find more productive lives. Didn't Orson Welles claim to admire the teaching profession, and hadn't he always been on the side of minorities and the underprivileged? Yet when he called our home and Irwin happened to answer the phone, he treated my husband like a houseboy and demanded to speak to me. Once he was so rude to Irwin that he called back later to apologize. That would never have happened with the person I wanted to be "Dad."

Like Saul Bellow's character Henderson the Rain King, I had been lost in the jungle of my dreams, crying "I want! I want! I want!" I had been incapable of seeing Orson Welles as the phenomenon he was, even though, since childhood, I had been told he was not like other men and one had to make allowances. He had no time to be a father, they all said again and again, because he was a genius who lived for his work alone and I should not hold it against him. I should try to understand. When my mother got her divorce in Reno on February 2, 1940, she told the press that, while it was all very friendly, it was also true that Orson "doesn't have time for marriage." So I had tried hard to put Orson Welles in a special category that relieved him of having to be anyone's father, husband, or friend for more than a few incandescent hours. As Geraldine Fitzgerald once told me, "Being with Orson is like having a lovely light shine down on you . . . but then the light moves on." Yet in spite of every argument I used to defend and excuse him, my stubborn heart would not yield to reason. It kept repeating: Why can't he find more time for me? In addition to being a director, actor, magician, and one of the most spellbinding personalities of the twentieth century, why couldn't he also be Dad?

Some time after my father's death, I confided in Bonnie Nims, an old friend from Chicago, that the loss had been more "traumatic" than I had expected. "I have seen so many things about myself," I wrote Bonnie, "the choices I've made in my life, my particular struggles and dilemmas, and these insights have been painful." In particular, I recognized the strong hold my father had had on me all my life and how hard I had fought to win his attention. I was not grieving for the man who had died but for a marvelous being who lived entirely in my imagination.

At the same time, being Orson Welles's daughter had given me riches denied the children of ordinary men. I was beginning to swing my eyes away from the flawed human being who had disappeared into a box of ashes and to gaze instead at the solid treasure he had left behind. By 1988, a year overflowing with tributes to Orson Welles, I was able to write Bonnie that I was attending a retrospective of his films in a different spirit. "Even though I've seen the films before, some of them many times, I'll be seeing them in an entirely new light. All this is happening at a good time for me, when I have resolved as much as I can the pain and difficulty that my personal relationship with my father caused me; when I can now value him as a genius and take pride in being his daughter, something I couldn't fully do when he was alive."

"YOUR FATHER'S DEATH will liberate you in the long run," predicted my brother-in-law, Jack Feder, when I was still in the depths of mourning. As a psychologist, he had seen it happen with patients of his and others he knew who had been overshadowed by a famous parent. Then the parent died and the child stepped out of the shadows. "You're going to come into your own now, Chris." I was forty-seven when Jack made his prophecy.

My father's death had released me from the misery of wanting what I could never have, and the relief I felt in those first weeks was physical. It was as though an intolerable burden had been lifted from my shoulders. Returning to the comfort of work, I began to write poems in odd moments, trying to give form to the chaos swirling around in my head and heart. To my surprise and delight, I found that I was working with more freedom and confidence than I had ever felt before. Writing used to be a struggle—like trying to wrestle a fabulous winged creature to the ground—but now the process was becoming exhilarating, whether I saved the day's pages or tossed them into the wastebasket.

Of those closest to me, only Irwin and my mother truly understood what was happening to me. On March 4, 1986, almost five months after my father's death, my mother wrote me from Tisbury, England, where she and Jackie were living in a Palladian mansion converted into a retirement home. It was a rare moment of empathy on her part, one that led to our establishing a more satisfying relationship.

> I understand perfectly the upset your father's death has caused you. You feel you never got through to him and you are right. You didn't, anymore than his other daughters did, or his wives. . . . When you were a little girl in Santa Monica and Orson planned to pick you up for lunch, he'd forget and I have many memories of you standing in the hall all dressed up, waiting and crying. What could I say to you? I sent you to Todd [School] hoping that Hortense and Skipper could explain him better than I could.

They adored you and you became one of the family there. The Hills were the nearest he ever came to having parents, but when Hortense died, Orson was not at her funeral. That to me is not understandable and it must have hurt Skipper deeply. I remember how unhappy you were in South Africa—so far away from your father. I wrote so many letters to him organizing visits for you in France, Spain, Italy, etc. You went but he was busy and left you with his secretaries. He loved you when you were in front of him, but he forgot you when you were out of sight. Just like everyone else in his life.

If Orson had been Joe Dokes, you might easily have been able to handle this kind of neglect and written him off. But because he was who he was, you found it harder and harder as you grew up and his fame spread.

But now I must tell you that there was nothing you could ever have done with your life or your talents that would have got through to him. And I know how you have driven yourself all these years. And they have paid off from your point of view. You are very successful and must now write for yourself. Not for Orson's approval. Do you understand what I am saying? I have a great fear that I could hurt your feelings and that I would hate to do. I am sure Irwin is a great help to you about this. An honest, down-to-earth man who understands you perfectly and loves you. You are very lucky to have him in your life.

My mother tended to oversimplify, and she knew nothing of Oja Kodar, the one person in my father's life who most definitely "got through to him." Nonetheless, she had given me the golden key to the kingdom—"You . . . must now write for yourself. Not for Orson's approval." Feeling like a bird swept out of its cage, I began the series of poems and monologues that would grow over the next decade into a book I called *The Movie Director*.

While the central character stood in for Orson Welles in the beginning, he gradually moved into the realm of fiction. Even so, writing in the movie director's voice allowed me to slip into my father's skin. It helped me to see the world through his eyes and experience his triumphs, frustrations, and regrets. Creating a semifictional Orson Welles moved me so close to the heart and soul of the real one that I forgave him.

I MET FRANK Brady, whom I still consider one of the best and most evenhanded of my father's biographers, while visiting the Hills in their retirement home in Coral Gables, Florida. An earnest, mild-mannered man with a scholar's gray-streaked beard and heavy-rimmed glasses, he had come to interview Granny and Skipper. By a coincidence, Frank's wife was teaching at the same community college as Irwin, and it turned out the Bradys lived in Manhattan, not far from us. We all became friends.

Frank's biography, *Citizen Welles,* was eventually published in 1989. Although not the first book to tackle the vast subject of Orson Welles, it was the first comprehensive overview of the man and his work to come out in a single volume. It served me as an excellent introduction to my father's artistry, filling in many gaps in my knowledge of his achievements in radio and the theater before I was born. Frank's book also made me more aware of my father's intense involvement in American politics during the 1940s, but, most important, it deepened my understanding of Orson Welles as an independent artist and a man dedicated to liberal causes. Toward the end of the book, I came to Brady's comment about me: "And after becoming friends with Christopher . . . I found that although she had a deep love for her father, there were major gaps in the information that she had about him. 'You probably *do* know more about my father than I do,' she told me."

That was certainly true when I first met Frank. It was disconcerting to realize that someone who never got closer to Orson Welles than a long-distance phone call possessed more in-depth knowledge of his life and work than I did. I resolved that I would better inform myself by reading every book and article I could find on my father. Through Skipper, I also obtained a wealth of materials, which included my father's personal letters and his Shakespeare playbooks originally published at Todd School.

In the spring of 1988, the film school at New York University held an extensive tribute to Orson Welles that honored his work in radio, theater, and film. For me, it was an invaluable crash course in the artistry and importance of Orson Welles, and it also put me in touch with William G. Simon, the amiable chairman of the cinema studies department at NYU's Tisch School of the Arts. A sincere admirer of my father and the prime organizer of the tribute, Bill felt Orson Welles was seen as "a misunderstood genius" and that the time was ripe for a critical reappraisal. As he told the *New York Times,* "Welles is very famous for *Citizen Kane* and one or two other works, but we went on the presupposition that there was much more of interest and it was worth digging for it. We thought that to bring back into the foreground some of the lesser-known work and to deal with the relationships between the radio, theater and film work would be especially useful. I don't think there's anything like a full appreciation of his accomplishments in the public eye."

The retrospective ran from April 22 to May 15. "Orson Welles's creative output on stage, on film and on the radio was so voluminous that it's taking three weeks to cover all the bases," pointed out a reporter for *New York Newsday*. Several of the events ran concurrently: an exhibition of Welles's theater productions in the 1930s, which included rare photographs, costume and set designs, posters and playbills; the Radio Listening Room, which offered daily selections from Welles's radio broadcasts, including the famous (or infamous) *War of the Worlds;* and the rare opportunity to see *all* of Welles's films at Joseph Papp's Public Theater, not just those made in Hollywood but the six films he had completed in Europe, which were almost never shown in the United States: *Chimes at Midnight, F for Fake, Othello, The Trial, Mr. Arkadin,* and *The Immortal Story.* Finally, a three-day conference at the end of the retrospective was devoted to lectures and panel discussions, one of them led by Oja Kodar, whom the director of the Public Theater presented to the audience as "one of the most extraordinary women it has been my privilege to meet." Afterward I was tempted to walk up to Oja and introduce myself, but I felt too shy. I knew her only as the alluring young woman in *F for Fake* who moved with a dancer's grace and revealed her naked body without a trace of self-consciousness. Now in her late forties, Oja had blossomed into a fully mature, stylish, and still beautiful woman who had spoken passionately about her years with my father.

Throughout the retrospective, Bill Simon was kind and generous, sharing books, articles, and his own knowledge with me and treating me to a private showing of the filmed interview my father gave to the press the morning after *The War of The Worlds* broadcast. Tousled and exhausted from having been up all night making history, Orson Welles seemed genuinely contrite while the newsmen circled him like a pack of hungry jackals. At the same time, Bill and I agreed, it could not have upset him that he became a household word overnight.

I had told Bill that, while I wanted to participate fully in the retrospective, I also wanted to remain incognito, and he respected my wishes. I continued to stay in the background even when people attending the retrospective sought me out. Dick Wilson, who had been my father's assistant in the Mercury

Theatre and later followed him to Hollywood, seemed especially eager to establish a connection with me. He had known me as a child, he reminded me. We had been together on the set of *Macbeth,* and how "thrilled" he was to meet me again as an adult. And did I know, he exulted, that he had "copied Orson" by naming his son "Christopher"? I regret it now, but at the time I could not warm to him. Something about Dick Wilson reminded me uncomfortably of people I had known in my Hollywood childhood and wanted to avoid in my present life.

MY INCLINATION TO remain in hiding was blown away one morning in May. I received a call from the public relations firm that was organizing the opening ceremony for the new Radio Hall of Fame being established by Emerson Radio Corporation. Would I accept an award being given my father for his *Mercury Theatre on the Air* series? Orson Welles was one of eighteen "radio legends" to be inducted into Emerson's Radio Hall of Fame on May 17, 1988. The black-tie ceremony would take place in the lobby of the Empire State Building.

"I was so stunned when they called that I forgot to ask what the award was," I wrote Bonnie Nims. "Anyway it's a black-tie affair . . . which raised shrieks from me ('I've got nothing to wear!') and grumbles from Irwin ('Do I really have to wear a black tie?'), a question I relayed to the public relations person. My father never wore one, I pointed out. She said she'd get back to me. I rather hope we can go in our non-designer jeans, striking another blow for artists and mavericks."

However, by the time the evening of May 17 rolled around, we had bowed to convention. Irwin wore a borrowed black tie, and I decked myself out in a black lace formal gown, hastily purchased a few days before and never to be taken off the hanger again. A sleek limousine was dispatched to our door to convey us in style to the Empire State Building. When we got there, it was media mayhem, the lobby jammed with photographers and reporters, klieg lights blazing from all corners, and cables snaking across the floor.

Before I knew it, I was spirited away by a bevy of press photographers and was posed standing beside Arthur Marx, son of Groucho. Arthur was a pleasant, nice-looking man who bore only a slight resemblance to his famous father, made slighter by the absence of horn-rimmed glasses and a black mustache. He had flown into town to accept the posthumous award for Groucho's popular quiz show, *You Bet Your Life.*

"Well," I told him sotto voce as the klieg lights bore down on us and the flashbulbs went off in our faces like muted gunfire, "whatever problems we had with our famous fathers, this makes up for it a bit, don't you think?"

"Not really," he deadpanned back, sending me a sad smile.

I gathered that, like me, he had been fatherless for fame, but in the dazzle of the moment, what did it matter? We were there to honor our fathers and I, for one, was thoroughly enjoying myself. To my surprise, I found that I not only liked being in the limelight, I felt calm and sure of myself.

"I had no idea you were such a ham," a bemused Irwin whispered in my ear as I was led away by a documentary filmmaker from Chicago who wanted an interview.

"Neither did I!" I admitted, laughing, and yet it felt so natural, as though I had been doing this all my life.

"It must be genetic," Irwin decided.

"Are you proud of me?"

"I'm always proud of you."

The award turned out to be a handsome miniature replica of an early Emerson radio. A golden plaque read RADIO HALL OF FAME — 1988, ORSON WELLES, ANTHOLOGY SERIES — "THE MERCURY THEATER" [sic]. I was proud to take the award home and display it on the bookshelves in our living room.

A few days later, the public relations firm sent me the press releases for the induction ceremony, and I was pleased to see that I had not entirely blown my cover. Several newspapers reported that the Radio Hall of Fame award given to Orson Welles had been accepted by his daughter Rebecca.

THE NEXT TIME I came out publicly as my father's daughter was at the Museum of Broadcasting on East Fifty-third Street. In mounting its first major exhibit devoted to radio, the museum had decided to honor Orson Welles exclusively. The exhibit ran from October 27 through December 3, 1988, in the year that marked the fiftieth anniversary of *The War of the Worlds* broadcast, still one of America's most celebrated radio programs because of the national panic it caused. "Imagine a time when the world still listened," read the brochure announcing the Orson Welles exhibit, "when it was radio that entertained and informed and, in one historic instance, confused. And imagine one voice on the airwaves, ringing with a sonorous richness and laughing with a sinister knowledge of us all: that one voice belonged to Orson Welles."

To recreate the experience of listening to radio in the living rooms of the 1930s, the museum furnished one of its rooms with sets from Woody Allen's nostalgic film *Radio Days.* The result evoked a front parlor, where families once gathered after dinner to tune in their favorite radio programs. There was a stuffed sofa and armchair, a coffee table and a magazine rack holding 1930s issues of *Time* and *Life,* but the main piece of furniture was the large console radio in the corner. It made me remember that radios were once the size of small refrigerators.

In the radio exhibition room, visitors could discover the extraordinary talent of Orson Welles. If the public wanted to visit the museum every day for a month, it was possible to hear more than fifty of his radio shows. Most were adapted from literary classics and were performed by members of the Mercury Theatre. Originally called *First Person Singular,* the weekly show became known as *The Mercury Theatre on the Air* and finally the *Campbell Playhouse* after the Campbell Soup Company ("mm, mm, good!") became the show's sponsor. Visitors could sample the show that kicked off the series on July 11, 1938, a hair-raising adaptation of Bram Stoker's *Dracula,* and the show that made history on October 30, 1938, loosely based on H. G. Wells's *The War of the Worlds.* They could also hear a conversation between Orson Welles and H. G. Wells that took place at a radio station in San Antonio, Texas, two years later. There was so much to choose from: the radio drama based on Daphne du Maurier's best-selling novel *Rebecca,* which later influenced the movie directed by Alfred Hitchcock. Or several selections from *The Adventures of Harry Lime,* a popular series my father had created for BBC radio in the 1950s. It featured the unscrupulous but devilishly charming Harry Lime, arguably my father's most popular movie role. I wished I could move into the museum with a sleeping bag.

Tipped off by a friend who worked in the film department at the Museum of Modern Art, I decided to attend the seminar on Orson Welles that was held on the day the exhibition opened. The film critic Andrew Sarris would be moderating a panel discussion on the joys and woes of working with the "boy genius." The panel included my friend from childhood Geraldine Fitzgerald, whom I was anxious to see again, the Mercury Theatre veteran Arlene Francis, the ubiquitous Dick Wilson, and the writer Howard Koch, who had adapted many of the literary works my father turned into radio drama.

The moment I walked into the museum's lobby, I spotted Aunt Geraldine. She immediately recognized me, we hugged each other, and time fell away.

She greeted me warmly in her soft Irish brogue, asking for news of my mother, whom she still thought of as her close friend. It did not seem to matter that she had not seen her in years. For my part, I asked her eagerly about her son, Michael Lindsay-Hogg, once my favorite playmate and now a successful director living in England. Then, leading me by the hand, Geraldine introduced me to Arlene Francis, Howard Koch, and Andrew Sarris as "Orson's oldest." Pleasantries were exchanged. A photographer leaped forward to take a group photo. How strange it was! I felt an instant rapport with Geraldine, vividly remembering our times together on that sun-drenched beach in Santa Monica when I saw her and Michael every day, and at the same time I realized our past connection had little bearing on our present lives. Geraldine and Michael had remained in the theater, and I had moved into a world so far removed from theirs that I might as well have been living on a different planet. "Michael wanted so much to be here today," Geraldine was saying, "but he's directing a play in London and couldn't get away."

Why should Michael want to be here? I wanted to ask her. Did that mean the persistent rumors were true and Michael *was* my father's natural son? It added to the weirdness of seeing "Aunt" Geraldine again to think that Michael and I might actually be brother and sister, but we would never know one way or the other.

We filed into the auditorium where the seminar would be held. The panel members seated themselves in a row on the stage. Andrew Sarris began by saying how unfortunate it was that John Houseman, Welles's partner in "the golden age of radio," was too ill to participate. This led to a discussion of how crucial Houseman had been to Orson's early successes. Geraldine astonished me by comparing my father to a broken water pipe, his talent pouring out of him in torrents while Houseman chased after him, trying to scoop it up in cups, pitchers, and buckets. The audience laughed, but I found the analogy ludicrous. Everyone on the panel seemed to feel Welles could not function without Houseman and that once their partnership had been dissolved, "Orson was all washed up." Howard Koch put it this way: "Houseman was the base on which Orson's statue was erected, and from the time they separated, Orson lived more the life of a celebrity than that of an artist." I felt myself beginning to bridle.

The discussion moved swiftly from radio to the movies. Suddenly everyone on the panel had a negative opinion of Orson's "rise and fall" as a filmmaker. "He was a poor custodian of his talent," remarked Arlene Francis. "He just let it go." Then Andrew Sarris expounded his theory of Orson Welles as "the failed genius." *How could that be?* I wanted to point out, *Once a genius, always a genius.* My father did not wake up one morning and discover that his genius had vanished like an attack of hay fever. To the end of his life, far from being "a broken water pipe," he was a fountain overflowing with ideas that would have been realized had he found the financial backing.

Unable to sit quietly in my seat another moment, I rose to challenge Mr. Sarris and the rest of the panel. What followed was written up in the November 14, 1988, issue of *Television/Radio Age.*

> Later, when this "failed genius" part of the discussion surfaced again, there came an understandable reaction from Welles' eldest daughter, Chris Welles Feder, a writer living in New York, who just happened to be attending the seminar.
>
> "His career did not abruptly end with *Citizen Kane,*" she said, and she accused the panel, particularly Sarris, of ignoring her father's middle and late period of development, particularly his European-made films, many still unfamiliar to American audiences. Unfortunately, Sarris took it upon himself to argue rather than draw the daughter of the great producer into the discussion. But Welles-Feder persisted, and the packed theater cheered as she made her point. Welles would have been proud.

I WAS BEGINNING to find my father in the one place I had not looked for him while he was alive: his work. Starting in 1988, every tribute to Orson Welles was a source of immense satisfaction to me. I gloried in his triumphs and felt dismay when he was misunderstood or underappreciated. I was also informing myself about him at every opportunity. In the fall of 1989, I visited the Lilly Library in Bloomington, Indiana, and spent days pouring over the Orson Welles archives, but it was not enough time to do more than dip into the vast collection of correspondence, scripts, speeches, and memorabilia. I came away with some items of personal value, such as a photograph of my father's mother, Beatrice Ives Welles, when she was young and winsome. I was also touched to discover one of the stories I had written and illustrated as a child and given to my father for Christmas.

Growing bolder as time went on, I fired off a letter to the editor of the *New York Times,* challenging certain statements columnist Vincent Canby had made about my father. I was pleased that, on March 11, 1990, the *Times* reprinted my letter, which read in part:

> To the Editor:
>
> I must object to your portrayal of my father, Orson Welles, in your article "Oscar is sometimes a grouch" [Feb. 25]. As you might imagine, I have researched my father's life extensively, and, until your article, nowhere have I heard or read that, as you state, "Orson Welles first went to Hollywood with the announced intention of showing the natives how to make movies." From my personal knowledge of my father, such an announcement would have been out of character. To portray him as an arrogant "big mouth" does him a great disservice, and it saddens me to see perpetuated, five years after his death, the kind of wrong impressions that dogged him all his life. . . .
>
> Mr. Canby replies: *I erred in writing that it was Mr. Welles's "announced intention" to show Hollywood how to make movies. Rather, this was the way that the Hollywood natives perceived him as the result of all of the publicity surrounding the success of his unorthodox productions for radio and theater.* . . .

MAY 1, 1991, marked the fiftieth anniversary of *Citizen Kane*, still considered by many critics to be the greatest of all American films. To commemorate the occasion, Paramount Pictures and the Turner Entertainment Company released the picture for an unlimited run in Boston, New York, Washington, D.C., Chicago, Houston, Seattle, Los Angeles, San Francisco, and Palo Alto. The Museum of Modern Art in New York held a special showing, and thanks to our friend in the film department, Irwin and I got excellent seats. "What a thrill to see a museum quality print on a large screen!" I shared with my sister Rebecca in Tacoma, Washington, urging her to drive into Seattle and see it herself. "It was a very moving experience."

I was also overjoyed that Ted Turner had failed in his attempt to colorize *Citizen Kane*. A group of film directors led by Woody Allen had protested that it was sacrilege to even think of colorizing *Kane,* but in the end what stopped Turner was my father's powerful contract with RKO. Turner may have acquired *Kane* when he bought RKO's film library in 1987, but he could not undo the contract that had contributed to making it such a unique work of art. In the words of a spokesman for Turner Entertainment, "Orson Welles's contract with RKO provided sufficient creative control that we felt our right to colorize this picture was questionable and therefore we decided not to do it."

Not to be undone, Turner himself told the crowd at a celebrity screening in Hollywood that he still thought *Citizen Kane* should have been made in color. "If they had known how good it was going to turn out, they would have made it in color," proclaimed Mr. Turner, determined to have the last word.

But the last laugh belonged to Orson Welles.

1 3

Meeting Oja Kodar

In March of 2004, a fascinating Orson Welles retrospective was held at the Film Forum in lower Manhattan. It was a rare opportunity to view footage from his incomplete films, such as *Don Quixote, The Other Side of the Wind,* and *The Deep,* which I had never seen before. I imagine it would have distressed my father, the most meticulous of film editors, who preferred to work in secrecy, had he known people were jamming the Film Forum every day to view films he had set aside, waiting for finishing money that never materialized, or that had still been evolving in his mind.

What artist wants the world looking over his shoulder before he is ready to unveil his creation? But once he is dead, what can he do to stop the endless scrutiny? Every scrap of film Orson Welles had produced during his lifetime was of intense interest to film scholars and sophisticated moviegoers. In the nineteen years since his death, he had changed from a celebrity into a legend, finally attaining the status of an icon. This was brought home to me when a friend sent me an advertisement for Apple computers. It shows a black-and-white photograph of Orson Welles in his beguiling youth, reading a movie script, cigar in hand. Under the Apple logo, the text reads, "Think different." These words stand for the independent spirit of the true artist that my father has come to symbolize.

I had been attending the screenings at the Film Forum every day but remaining incognito. Then one evening, on an impulse, I decided to introduce myself to the tall, handsome German who had been presenting the films and providing us day after day with enlightening background information. He was Stefan Drössler, director of the Munich Film Museum, distinguished film scholar, and the man who had organized the Welles retrospectives here in New York as well as in Los Angeles. When I stepped out of the shadows and introduced myself as Orson Welles's eldest daughter, Stefan seemed delighted to meet me. He readily accepted my invitation to come to our home the following afternoon and bring along his attractive companion, the French actress and director Anne Le Ny.

Comfortably settled in our living room with Anne sitting quietly beside him, Stefan made himself at home. For all his knowledge and air of authority, there was a shy reserve and sensitivity about him that I liked at once. As the afternoon wore on, he told Irwin and me a great deal about the work of the Munich Film Museum, which had acquired from Oja Kodar most of the footage my father had left to her in his will. This included not only his incomplete films but programs he had made for BBC television, pilots he had made for American television, and other glittering fragments from the mosaic of his life's work. Oja had given the footage to the museum in Munich with the proviso that it had to be shown at a film festival or other noncommercial venue every two or three years. So the enormous and ongoing task of restoring, assembling, and, in some cases, editing the work had fallen into the capable hands of Stefan and his staff. Their plan was to show at each successive Orson Welles retrospective footage that had not been seen before.

Stefan told me that a major retrospective of my father's work, in fact the largest to date, was going to take place the following summer in Locarno, Switzerland, during its international film festival. While he was still working out the details with the festival directors, what he had in mind was a combination of daily screenings and workshops so that certain aspects of my father's work could be examined in greater depth. He turned to me expectantly: Would I be interested in coming to Locarno? I could come for a few days or the whole time. I could remain incognito and my privacy would be respected, or I could take an active, public role. It was entirely up to me, but he hoped I would take advantage of this opportunity to see a far wider range of my father's work than could be shown at the Film Forum. I would also have the chance to meet the Welles scholars and former associates who would be participating in the workshops.

"Will Oja Kodar be there?" I asked him. Her image was fresh in my mind from having seen *F for Fake* once again, especially the segment where a captivating Oja passes Picasso's window at different times of the day and drives the artist into a frenzy.

Chris with Oja Kodar at Oja's home in Primosten, Croatia, September 2005.

"She will probably come for a few days." Stefan explained that Oja rented out her house in the summer, which made it difficult for her to be away from home for any length of time.

Stefan was sure I would enjoy staying in Locarno, a lovely small town nestled on a lake and encircled by snow-capped mountains, one of the most scenic spots in Switzerland. Surprised and flattered, I was not sure how to respond. Half of me wanted to say yes at once, while the other half held back. I told Stefan I would like to think about it and let him know closer to the time. Yet already I knew. The old Christopher might be tempted to hide in the familiarity of her private cave, but the new Chris was not going to let her. The time had come for me to step out of obscurity and joyously celebrate my father with the rest of the world. The time had also come to reconnect with Oja Kodar.

I FIRST MET Oja Kodar in 1994 when she came to New York to show *Don Quixote* at the Museum of Modern Art. Inspired by the tragicomic adventures of Miguel de Cervantes' eccentric knight errant and his more earthbound retainer, Sancho Panza, this was a film my father began in the 1950s and shot intermittently over several decades, whenever he could cobble together the funds, but it was left unfinished at his death in 1985. Meanwhile, the film-in-progress had aroused such speculation and assumed such legendary proportions that my father joked he was going to retitle it "When Are You Going to Finish *Don Quixote*?" Barely a year after his death, when Oja showed some of the footage in her possession at the 1986 Cannes Film Festival, she described it in these words: "*Don Quixote* is a dream which Orson never finished, a dream from which he was never able to rouse himself."

Although I had seen Oja from afar at the 1988 tribute to my father at New York University, I had not been able to step forward then. In some ways I was still "the old Christopher," shy and private. Nonetheless, I had taken away from that occasion a lasting image of an intelligent, articulate, and passionate woman who lived close to her emotions and was not ashamed to show them. Tall, slender, and blessed with a body a goddess would envy, Oja was, as they used to say in Hollywood, "drop-dead gorgeous." It was all in her eyes — dark, wide-spaced, and aglow with her playful wit and nimble mind. I did not need too many glimpses of Oja to understand what a bright, engaging companion she had made for my father during the last twenty-odd years of his life, nor was it in the least surprising that of all the women he had known and loved, Oja had been the most important to him.

Now that I had laid to rest the painful feelings that rose up in me after my father died, I was eager to meet Oja. As it happened, our encounter at MOMA on October 13, 1994, was not only brief but took place under troubled circumstances. Looking strained and exhausted, Oja seemed privately distressed, which I put down to the fact that Yugoslavia, where she had returned to live after my father's death, was then at war. She had also struggled under near impossible conditions to make a film about children affected by the war, which she was going to show at a film festival in Canada. This seemed reason enough for her wan appearance that evening, but it turned out that she was upset about something else entirely: the English-language version of *Don Quixote* edited by Jess Franco, which she had just seen for the first time. "I went to New York to introduce the film to the audience," she would tell me years later, "but when I saw the film myself, I was appalled." Taking the footage that Oja had given him, Franco "just threw it together," and he and his underlings "also changed things" in the footage Orson had already edited himself. "Who are they to change Orson's material?" demanded the outraged Oja. She had believed in Franco, who had worked as assistant director on *Chimes at Midnight* and claimed to be Orson's admiring friend, never imagining he would prove himself so unworthy of the precious footage that had been entrusted to him.

Stunned by my own disappointment in *Don Quixote,* I did not know what to say. In any case, Oja and I had no more than a few minutes together before the photographers descended. Yet, years later when we recalled that sorry night at MOMA, we had both known in an instant that we liked each other.

"I had the feeling we could become great friends," Oja told me. I had felt the same way and had given her my address, but I did not hear from her in the years that followed. The time was not yet right.

I believe things happen in one's life when they are meant to, not before. When I invited Stefan Drössler to my home in early March of 2004 and it became apparent that he was in frequent contact with Oja, I decided to ask him for her address, which he gave me. Then, when I mentioned that I did not feel I could write Oja "out of the blue," almost a decade having passed since our last meeting, Stefan gallantly offered to call her on my behalf and let me know how she felt. A few weeks later, he relayed the message that Oja would welcome hearing from me, and I should feel free to write or call. Here is most of the letter I sent her on March 21, 2004, a week before my sixty-sixth birthday:

> Dear Oja,
>
> I often think of you and how important you were to my father during the last twenty years of his life. Then, a few weeks ago, I met with Stefan Drössler. . . . Here was an opportunity to get in touch with you, which I have been wanting to do since we first met. . . . Although we have been living in different cities and on different continents ever since, I have continued to hope our paths will cross again.
>
> I wish very much that you and I had met while my father was alive, although I understand why we did not. I want you to know, though, that I see you in the most positive light, and that I am extremely grateful to you for having gladdened the last years of his life to the extent that you did. It was you who continued to give him hope and courage, who worked by his side, who became the most important woman in his life. . . .

I concluded with the hope that my letter would open a dialogue between us:

> I knew Orson Welles best in his vibrant twenties and thirties. . . . And you knew him in his later decades. . . . So I feel we each have much to tell the other.

Weeks passed, and then, one morning, the telephone rang and I heard an effervescent voice with the hint of a foreign accent on the other end. "Hello, Christopher? This is Oja." She began by saying how much my letter had meant to her. "A family member" had finally recognized what she had done for Orson. We talked at some length, and then she invited me to come and stay with her in Croatia, an invitation she was to extend again and again in the months ahead.

Meanwhile, at Irwin's suggestion, I sent Oja a copy of my book, *The Movie Director.* I was a little nervous about what her reaction might be. Several weeks later Oja called to say how much the book had meant to her and how profoundly it had moved her. There was a tremor in her voice, and she paused as if to clear her throat. Then she said, "I heard Orson speaking through your words, and I felt you gave him back to me."

The writer in me rejoiced. If my book had given Orson back to Oja, that was reason enough to have written it.

OVER THE YEARS and from various sources, including my father's tribute to her in the December 1983 issue of Paris *Vogue,* I pieced together the early life of Olga Palinkas before she evolved into Oja Kodar. Half Hungarian, half Croatian, she came from a close-knit family, the middle daughter of three. Her father was an architectural engineer and her mother a teacher. Oja was especially close to her younger sister, Nina—"We are like two peas in a pod," Nina assured me when we finally met. A tall, striking blond, Nina's shapely legs had once so distracted pianist Artur Rubinstein during a recital that he had asked her to move from her seat in the front row—a story Oja loved to tell with her merry laugh.

Oja began studying sculpture at the Academy of Fine Arts in Zagreb. "I'm proud to say that I was the first woman ever accepted by the sculpture department," she once said in an interview. In *Vogue,* my father pointed out that Oja was also the *only* female student in her sculpture class. After quoting her—"Women are allowed to paint . . . but most men are still convinced that sculpture is a man's work, like driving a bulldozer"—my father laments that beautiful women are rarely taken seriously. Then he shows a full-page color photograph of one of Oja's sculptures, a rounded, sensuous form carved out of a magnificent piece of wood with a grain that melts from cream into golden brown. Clearly it is the work of a sculptor to be taken seriously.

It was while Oja was studying in Zagreb that she reconnected with the cameraman Edmond Richard. They had met the year before in Belgrade, where she had taken time off from school to work in television and earn money to help support her family. Although both her parents were professionals, they were poorly paid in communist Yugoslavia, and money was tight for the three girls. As it happened, Edmond was working in Zagreb for Orson Welles, shooting scenes for *The Trial*.

One evening Edmond invited Oja to go with him to a nightclub, which she found very exciting, having never been to one before. It was there that she first saw Orson Welles. Edmond pointed him out: "Don't look now, but there's Orson Welles!" Orson was wearing a dark

Oja Kodar's statue of Orson Welles in Split, Croatia, 2007.

suit, and in the blinking light of the nightclub, all Oja could see were his eyes, but as she later remembered, "His eyes were his most important feature." He must have seen her remarkable eyes as well, because he came over to her table a few minutes later.

After that first encounter, the two of them met several times in Zagreb. Oja visited Orson on location in a cavernous hall where hundreds of people were sitting like robots behind hundreds of desks, pounding away on typewriters. One of the more chilling scenes in *The Trial*, it captured the facelessness of bureaucracy and its lumbering, unstoppable momentum. She remembered that Anthony Perkins, the American actor who plays the antihero Joseph K., was running around and around the building. When she asked Orson why he was doing this, he replied that he wanted Tony "totally out of breath" in the scene he was about to shoot.

On another day, over lunch, Oja showed Orson some of her stories. One of them, entitled "F for Fake," was about a painter inspired by a beautiful young girl he had been observing from afar. "Orson said he liked it and found it very amusing," Oja recalled, "but I didn't really believe him, because it was obvious that he liked me and found me attractive. You know, you can be young, but you don't have to be a fool." It was not until many years later, when Orson incorporated Oja's story in his film, *F for Fake,* using her title as well, that she realized he really *had* liked her story and found it amusing.

After Orson left Zagreb, Oja wrote to him a number of times and was upset when she never got a reply. Then, in 1963, the talented sculptor of twenty-three was accepted as a student at the Ecole des Beaux-Arts in Paris. In those days, many young Yugoslav women were marrying Italians to escape the communist regime, but Oja made it out of the country on her own. To support herself in Paris, she worked in a department store, modeling bathing suits and lingerie. The work was so well paid that she was able to send money home to her parents who set it aside for her. (Later Oja used the money she had earned from modeling to buy land on the Dalmatian coast and build a home near Primosten.)

Meanwhile, my father was in Paris, editing *The Immortal Story,* his first movie in color, which he had made for French television. Starring Jeanne Moreau, the film was based on a short story by the Danish writer Karen Blixen, who wrote her Gothic tales in English under the pen name of Isak Dinesen. My father professed a wild passion for the Baroness Blixen, which I have never fully understood. He told me his own Gothic tale of traveling to Denmark to meet her in person, only to discover at the last moment that he could not go through with it. It would be too brazen an invasion of her privacy, he felt, to knock on her door and lay his intense admiration at her feet.

Somehow my father found out that Oja was living in Paris. She is still not sure who told him—she had been going to great lengths to avoid him—but it may have been his cameraman, Edmond Richard, with whom Oja had stayed in touch. In any event, my father immediately hired a private detective to track her down, which struck Oja as "a very American thing to do, but to me, coming from a communist country, it seemed so extravagant and unbelievable." When he showed up at her apartment one day, she refused to let him in. She was still mad at him for not having answered her letters, but her extravagant, unbelievable suitor banged on her door until he actually broke it down. He then took her to the Hotel Raffael, where he was staying, and showed her an aluminum briefcase in which he had saved all her letters to him as well as his unmailed letters to her.

"Why didn't you send me these letters?" Oja demanded.

"I thought you're so young and I'd interfere with your life," he replied.

"And now you break down my door and don't worry about interfering in my life?"

"My bad nature got the better of me . . . and I desperately wanted to see you again."

It was the beginning of a love affair and creative collaboration that did not end until my father died twenty years later. Sadly, of the many projects they worked on together, the only one that came to fruition was the brilliant essay film, *F for Fake*. In addition to being a guided tour through the maze of truth and fakery, art and illusion, it is also my father's tender love poem to Oja Kodar.

"I AM SO touched that you would like me to come and stay with you at Villa Welles, and that is something I would very much like to do," I wrote Oja in April of 2004, suggesting that Irwin and I might come the following summer. Our initial plan was to go to the Locarno festival in early August of 2005, join up with Oja there, and travel back with her to Croatia, but this turned out to be impossible. We could not stay with Oja in August because she had already rented all the apartments in her house until the end of the month. She proposed that we come instead in early September, when the renters would be gone along with most of the tourists who were flocking to Croatia in unprecedented numbers. The weather would still be lovely then, she told me. "But come early in September, before the rain starts."

So we decided to make two separate transatlantic trips, an exhausting proposition for my husband of eighty-two, but knowing how important both these trips were to me, he bore up valiantly. Because of the difficulty of booking our flight to Split, we could not arrive at Oja's before September 13, 2005, but we were in luck. The gods smiled on us and gave us glorious weather for the entire week of our stay.

Oja lived within walking distance of Primosten, a small fishing village that had once been an island. From the moment the taxi dropped us off at her front gate in a private cul-de-sac and she rushed out to embrace us, leading us merrily inside, we knew we had come to a special place. The villas in that part of the world are built into rocky cliffs that drop precipitously to the sea below, and Villa Welles is no different. We had actually arrived at the top of the house, where the driveway was situated. We would be staying in the roof-level apartment, which had its own entrance, a walkway thickly covered with hanging vines. Everywhere I looked I saw a jungle of greenery, trellises, and plants in profusion, which increased my feeling that we had entered a secret world hidden from prying eyes. When I exclaimed at the beauty of "the jungle," Oja told us she had done the planting with her mother years before, when both her parents were living here.

"Did my father ever live here?" I asked her.

"No, he was planning to, but . . ." Tears welled up in her eyes. On another day, she would show me the small swimming pool she had built especially for Orson. It was finished a few days before he died. Now the pool stood empty and unused.

Yet the spirit of Orson was everywhere in Oja's house. The first thing I noticed in our glamorous quarters were Oja's pen-and-ink drawings that recorded her life with him. They hung in a row in the entrance hall, revealing the artist's saucy love of life and mischievous eye for detail. Here was Orson directing a naked Oja in the erotic scene that erupts in the front seat of a car in *The Other Side of the Wind*. Oja's drawing shows the tricks Orson used to get this incredible shot and to make the viewer believe it was taking

Oja Kodar's drawing of Orson holding a pet bird on his hand.

place on a Los Angeles highway rather than in the garden of Orson and Oja's home in Orvilliers near Paris. A number of other drawings capture the joy and mayhem of their movie life together, but I was especially moved by Oja's tender glimpses of the private Orson. In one, he stands at the picture window of their home in Los Angeles in his voluminous white caftan, puffing on his cigar, a bear of a man, who looks gentle and pensive, holding a tamed bird on his raised hand. In another, conquering insomnia for a few hours, he sleeps in a tousled bed, the eye of calm in a hurricane of mess: clothes, newspapers, empty mineral water bottles strewn on the floor, several pairs of eyeglasses scattered about and one pair dropped in the precise spot where they will be crushed underfoot when Orson gets out of bed.

Our rooftop apartment was spacious, charming, and flooded with light from two walls of sliding glass doors, one leading to a private terrace and the other to a walkway on the roof. One of Oja's bold oil paintings hung over a round, king-size bed. We even had our own kitchenette. "I wanted you to have this apartment," Oja was telling us, "because it has the best view." She slid open the glass doors and the wind swept in from the Adriatic, a dry, exhilarating wind that woke up my senses and made me feel good to be alive. We walked onto the terrace, partly shaded with hanging vines. Two huge oval lounge chairs, padded with blue and white striped cushions, invited us to sink into their depths and never get up again. Irwin and I would spend many hours here, gazing at the sea before us, mesmerized by the blue siren glinting in the sun and showing off her jewels. There were islands off shore — wild, green, mysterious places where no human seemed to live — and hills all around, covered with villas and vineyards. But what animated the scene were the boats — yachts, sailboats, motor launches, an endless flotilla that drifted in and out of view. How my father would have loved this view, this house, this enchanted place!

EARLY EVERY MORNING, the man who worked for Oja brought our breakfast on a tray. Then, a leisurely hour later, while we were still sitting around in our bathrobes, Oja would appear at our door, fresh-faced and beaming. She did not bother with makeup and wore her dark hair pulled back in a casual twist. In spite of her exposure to Hollywood, I was glad to find that she had remained herself. "Can I come in?" she would ask, as though we could possibly say no.

These were precious hours, when she and I could talk in private and share our "Orsons." Yet, inevitably, the moment came when tears swam into her eyes and her voice began to tremble. I could see that this reminiscing was hard for her. Her love was still fresh—and passionate—for a man who had been dead twenty years. After half a week of seeing Oja's lovely eyes awash in tears, I suggested that perhaps we should stop talking about my father. The last thing I wanted to do was upset her.

"Oh, but you are his daughter," she cried, wiping her eyes, "you have the right to know!"

"Yes, but I don't have to know everything at once. We'll have other visits, won't we?"

"Oh yes, I want you to come and stay with me every year."

"Then we'll have years to talk about him. So let's put the subject aside for now."

"That would be better," she agreed, her face lighting up with a smile of relief.

Yet in the days that followed, Oja brought my father up in every other sentence. Orson had said this. Orson had done that. Her thoughts, her memories were welded to him. Something one of us said would remind her of the time she and Orson had been in Paris. In Rome. In Split. The more she shared with us, the more clearly we saw the nomadic life she had led with him: moving from country to country, hotel to hotel, with several dogs and battered suitcases in tow, then settling for a time in houses Oja bought and sold. How willingly she had left her country, her former life, and thrown herself into the tempestuous adventure of sharing Orson's days and nights, his triumphs and joys, frustrations and disappointments. In spite of the age difference—she had been twenty-one when they met and he forty-seven—they proved to be entirely compatible in habit and temperament. And he had never seemed old to her. "There was such youth in him," she recalled, "such vitality."

During my father's last and most difficult years, Oja was at his side, keeping illness and despair at bay, doing whatever needed to be done to keep him going, including staying up most of the night to massage his bloated legs so that he would be able to walk the next day. "His doctor told me I added ten years to his life," she told us with pride, "and I know it was true." She sighed. "Orson was a good man, a kind man. So few people know what a big heart he had . . ."

But you and I know, I thought, putting my hand over hers. The bighearted man Oja was describing closely resembled the Daddy I had known at sixteen.

And then I realized the beautiful thing that had happened: Oja had given him back to me.

"I WISH WE could have met while my father was alive," I told Oja while she was visiting with us in our apartment one morning. She was wearing a purple beach dress that fell to her ankles, not a trace of makeup, her raven black hair swept off her face and held in a hair clip.

"It's obvious why we didn't," she replied.

"I know, but I can't help wishing it. And you know what I wish even more, Oja? That you'd married him."

She giggled, her dark eyes dancing. "Orson asked me when we were in Spain if we shouldn't get married, but I told him everything was fine the way it was." In any case, she went on, she had always been a little against marriage and more than a little mistrustful of men, especially after her own sister's ugly divorce. As soon as a woman signed a marriage contract, Oja believed, the relationship changed, and in a way, the woman became her husband's property. "Much as I loved and trusted Orson, I preferred to keep my independence so I could always say, 'I'm Oja Kodar, not Mrs. Orson Welles, and I'll go my own way.'"

We sat a while in silence, each of us contemplating what might have been. Then Oja said, "I can be with people, go out at night and enjoy myself, but by nature I am a loner. That's another reason why Orson and I were so well suited to each other."

During his last years in Hollywood, when ill health kept him close to home, Oja didn't miss the parties or any part of Hollywood's social whirl. In fact, she preferred staying quietly at home with Orson. She had her sculpture, her writing, and the many projects they worked on together.

"Perhaps you're not really a loner but a person who needs time alone, which is not the same thing," I suggested. "Most creative people need periods of solitude."

"No, Chrissie, I am happiest when most people leave Primosten, not just the tourists but the many Croatians who have summer homes here, and then I have the place all to myself!"

"But don't you ever get lonely, Oja?"

"No, I have my memories. Not a day goes by that I don't think of Orson . . . and I still miss him very much."

Her eyes were brimming with tears again, but by now I realized there was no way to avoid this. My father had enfolded her into his life while she was still very young. He had put his mark on her. Forever.

EVERY MORNING AFTER our visit with Oja, Irwin relaxed on our terrace while I went swimming in the clear waters of the Adriatic. Then, at lunchtime, we convened in Oja's apartment, one flight down from ours. We saw at once that we were in the home of a cultivated woman, the walls lined with books and art, the comfortable leather sofas and chairs inviting us to stay a while. Several of Oja's handsome wooden sculptures stood on tabletops, and, when I admired them, she said that although she no longer worked in wood—it had become too difficult to find good materials and she no longer had a proper studio—she kept a few of her pieces on display "to prove that I really was a serious sculptor." That anyone would doubt it or mistake Oja for a dilettante struck me as sad, but I remembered my father's remark: "Beautiful women are not taken seriously."

Of the many reminders of Orson Welles in Oja's living room, I was most drawn to an intimate portrait taken by his cameraman, Gary Graver. Gary had caught my father in a moment of serene contemplation when he was most himself. This was the face of Orson Welles that few were privileged to see, and I remembered Gary's remark to an interviewer: "Oja and I were his real family." Once, such a remark would have hurt me, but now I understood how crucial Oja and Gary were to my father during his last years. Without them, my father would have been hard-pressed to make *F for Fake, The Other Side of the Wind, The Dreamers,* and all the other works, complete or incomplete, that filled his days and nights from 1970 until his death fifteen years later.

Oja had a bookcase dedicated to books about Orson Welles, and I had brought her a copy of *Les Bravades* to add to her collection. This was the "portfolio of pictures," as he called it, that my father had made for Rebecca when she was eleven years old and given to her for Christmas in 1956. His delightful drawings in watercolor, crayon, ink, and gouache were sketched on whatever paper came to hand and accompanied by his equally delightful text—sometimes typed, sometimes handwritten—which told the story of the festival held each year on the feast day of Saint Tropez "in the pretty little fishing village which proudly bears his name."

During one of our lunches, I told Oja how *Les Bravades* had been transformed from "a portfolio of pictures" made for Rebecca alone into a published book available to everyone. In 1990, desperately in need of money, Rebecca decided to part with our father's gift, and while it was upsetting to think of this treasure leaving the family, I understood her predicament. So when Becky asked if Irwin and I would help her sell *Les Bravades,* we agreed. We offered it first to the head of the well-endowed Lilly Library in Bloomington, Indiana, but he pleaded poverty, claiming he could not compete "with wealthy private collectors." Then Irwin and I helped Becky auction off the work at Swann Galleries in New York. Although we advised her against it, Becky was persuaded to sell her publication rights as well. In the end, *Les Bravades* sold for thirty thousand dollars, which I felt was the bargain of the century, but Becky was thrilled. Living as simply as she did, thirty thousand was a lot of money.

"You won't believe what happened next," I told Oja. In 1995, Workman Publishing agreed to publish *Les Bravades* and the editor assigned to the project, Sally Kovalchick, was the same editor who had worked closely with me on Brain Quest, a series of children's games I did for Workman. One day I got a phone call from Sally. She had found some spelling and punctuation errors in my father's text, and she wondered what she should do about them. "Leave them," I told her. "Print the text exactly as my father wrote it, errors and all."

"But this is not possible," Oja objected. "Orson had a superb command of the English language. He would never make a spelling mistake." She seemed deeply offended.

"They were typographical errors," put in Irwin, the diplomat.

"Oh, well, that's different."

Irwin and I exchanged looks while Oja began clearing the table. It was not the first time she had bridled at the suggestion that her Orson was capable of error. On another occasion, I had mentioned that, when my mother was Mrs. Orson Welles, my father would arrange to meet her for lunch at Sardi's or for dinner at 21, and then arrive hours late—if he arrived at all.

"With me, Orson was never late," Oja retorted.

Alas, dear Oja, he was not as perfect with others as he was with you.

ON SEVERAL EVENINGS during our weeklong stay, we took Oja to dinner in Primosten. From her house, it was a twenty-minute walk over a rocky path that hugged the shoreline and was shaded by pines with twisted limbs leaning toward the sea. Jasmine and oleander grew by the wayside, their perfume mingling with the tang of salt in the air.

"Look!" exclaimed Oja as we rounded a corner, and there, before our eyes, was Primosten aflame in the setting sun. The village rose in layers of stone houses topped with salmon-colored tiled roofs. We lingered to enjoy the view, the feeling that we had stepped back in time and were seeing Primosten as it must have looked centuries ago. Then we continued on our way.

Soon we were settled at an outdoor table in Oja's favorite restaurant. The specialty of the house was grilled fish fresh from the Adriatic. To dine outside on a balmy night added to the pleasure of the meal.

"Did you ever live with Orson?" Oja asked me during dinner.

"Only when I was a toddler." I explained that before my father went to Hollywood in the summer of 1939, he and my mother had agreed to a trial separation. My mother had gone to stay with Geraldine Fitzgerald in Ireland, and I had been left with my nanny in New York. However, as soon as my father was settled in a rented house in Brentwood, he sent for me. "It turned out we were living next door to Shirley Temple," I went on, referring to the child movie star who was a national idol. "I was about sixteen months old and just beginning to walk. One day, while I was playing on the lawn with my father, Shirley Temple's mother wandered over with Shirley by her side. 'When are you going to put Christopher in pictures?' Shirley's mother asked my father. 'Oh, I'm going to wait until she's two years old,' he answered. 'I want her to have a normal childhood.'"

Oja laughed. "Orson was such fun, always making jokes. People don't realize what a wonderful sense of humor he had . . ."

Before tears could fill her eyes, we asked her to tell us about Primosten. It used to be a remote island, she began, but in the sixteenth century, it was settled by farmers and fishermen who were fleeing from the Turks. Eventually they built a bridge to the mainland and Primosten ceased to be an island. "Today, everyone who lives here depends on tourism, especially during the summer months." She sighed, remembering the still undiscovered village she had known as a child.

Yet Irwin and I found Primosten relatively unspoiled. One day, we went exploring on our own, and once we had distanced ourselves from the souvenir shops with their outdoor racks of postcards, we found the part of the village that retains its authentic flavor. Here were narrow, winding streets paved with cobblestones worn smooth from centuries of fishermen in heavy boots, tramping home with the day's catch. One street led us to a sleepy square lined with restaurants and outdoor cafés, a place to linger over a cup of Turkish coffee and listen to the rustling leaves of the shade trees. It was past noon and we decided to stop and rest.

All of a sudden, a group of Croatian men sitting at a nearby table burst into song. It was so spontaneous and so lovely. In four-part harmony, their pure and mellow voices filled the little square with the folk songs of their fathers and grandfathers. They were singing for themselves, not for us. Some traditions not even the invasion of tourists could touch.

JAKOV SEDLAR, A Croatian filmmaker, was directing a documentary about Orson Welles, and I had agreed to be interviewed for it while I was staying with Oja. While Jakov and his crew were setting up the lights and camera in Oja's living room, I wandered around, as I had before, enjoying the art on the walls and especially the oil my father painted of himself and dedicated to Oja and her family. In this unusual self-portrait, the face of the large man seated in an armchair with a watchful dog on his lap has been left vague, as though covered in white veils, whereas every other detail in the painting is clear and exact. There were photographs everywhere of Oja's parents and her sisters, who loved Orson and adopted him as one of their own. Oja had given him not only the gift of herself but a home and a family in Croatia.

During my interview with Jakov, he asked me how I felt about the fact that my father had taken up with Oja Kodar. I smiled. Here was my opportunity to tell the world that Oja had been the most important woman in my father's life. "Why was she so important?" Jakov persisted. I was glad to elaborate. Oja was far more intelligent and evolved than the other women in his life; so my father could never grow bored with her. As an artist herself, a talented sculptor and writer, she was capable of understanding a man like Orson Welles at a profound level, and of empathizing with his struggles as an independent filmmaker. But one reason above all others made Oja a unique figure in my father's life. I paused while Jakov leaned forward expectantly. "My father's life was his work," I continued, "and of all the women who attempted to live with him, only Oja was capable of entering fully into his creative life. She worked by his side, day after day, acting in his films, collaborating on his screenplays, doing whatever needed to be done at any hour of the day or night."

When I had finished the interview, Oja, who had been listening in the next room, came out and hugged me. "It was a poem, what you said. A beautiful poem." Her eyes were moist with emotion. Then she took me by the hand. "Now we are going down to the sea, and I am going to tell you a story about Orson, and Jakov is going to get it on film."

It was late afternoon when we walked down the steps to the garden at the bottom of Oja's house, then passed through the iron gate that led to the sea. In place of a sandy beach, rock formations jutted over the water. Some formed natural platforms for sunbathing, but most were jagged outcrops. Easy as it was to dive off the rocks into the inviting sea, it was almost impossible to clamber out again without the aid of the ladders that hung down into the water.

Today, though, we were not dressed for swimming. Oja and I were wearing white pants, sandals, and summery tops. Jakov told us to walk slowly down the stone steps carved out of rock and sit together on the bottom step, looking out to sea. Oja and I did this several times while Jakov shouted at the crew rearranging their equipment on the perilous rocks. Soon the sun would set, but now it blazed down on the water. A few sailboats did their stately dance around the islands. "When you and I are dead," Oja murmured, "we will still be here on film. This is forever."

The camera started rolling and Oja told me the story she had been saving for this moment. When Orson was living in Italy and she was in Primosten, he would hire a boat and cross the sea to visit her, a trip that took seven or eight hours. Hoping to come and go unnoticed, he usually arrived at dawn and left in the middle of the night. On the days she expected him, Oja would come down to the sea and sit on the rocks, as we were doing now, and watch the horizon for Orson's boat to appear. One day, which happened to be her birthday, he arrived with a huge red ribbon tied around his chest. "What do you think I am bringing you for your birthday?" he asked her.

"Your heart," she answered correctly. He also brought her a recording he had made especially for her. "Now every year on my birthday," Oja continued, "I play Orson's recording, and I come and sit here on the rocks and look out to sea, and sometimes I imagine that if I look long enough, I will see Orson's boat coming toward me."

"Do you mind telling me what was in the recording? If it's not too personal, that is."

She paused half a breath before answering, "A declaration of his love for me." She had decided to tell this story because, just as Orson had often said how proud he was to be seen with her, she was proud that he had loved her so much. "I wanted people to know this," she concluded.

"I always knew how much he loved you, even before I met you."

"You knew about me, Chrissie, didn't you?"

I loved it when she called me by my childhood name. "Yes, I knew . . ."

The cameras were still rolling, but Oja and I were no longer conscious of being in a documentary. I squeezed her hand. "My father is here with us. Right now. I can feel it." The strong connection I felt with Oja, and she with me, had brought him back.

With Oja's hand in mine, I thought, *No one has loved him more generously or understood him more profoundly than the two of us.* We saw, without malice or envy, what a towering figure he was and will remain. We are the ones who trace his silhouette against the sky.

14

"Darling girl, they're gonna love me when I'm dead!"

EARLY IN 2005, STEFAN Drössler and I began discussing my participation in the Orson Welles retrospective to be held at the Locarno International Film Festival for eleven days beginning on August 3rd. Even though Stefan had given me the option of attending incognito, I had decided to represent my father publicly. So I told him I would be glad to introduce my father's films to festival audiences, participate in the daily workshops, and do whatever I could to add a personal touch to the occasion. Delighted, he replied that he had several ideas in mind. Most of all, he wanted me to introduce *Macbeth* on the evening it would be projected on a gigantic movie screen in the Piazza Grande, the huge square in the old part of town. During the festival, the Piazza Grande was converted into an outdoor movie theater with a seating capacity of nearly eight thousand. Was I prepared to get up in front of such a crowd and say a few words about being in *Macbeth* at the age of nine? "Of course," I told him.

Although I had agreed to do whatever was asked of me, the reality did not sink in until a blustery day in March when I met the festival directors, Irene Bignardi and Teresa Cavina, who were passing through New York. They came to our home for a glass of pinot grigio before the three of us went out to lunch in a nearby Italian restaurant. "You realize that every journalist in Locarno will want to interview you," Irene began soon after we were seated. She was a tall woman with a strong, handsome face, dark hair, and arresting blue eyes. "I hope you're prepared for all the media attention you're going to get." Teresa, a blond, mild-mannered woman with a soft voice and dreamy look, added that they would do their best to coordinate the interviews so as to leave me free to spend most of my time at the Welles retrospective.

"I know I can handle it," I assured them. "But please tell me about your film festival. I've heard of the ones at Cannes and Venice, but I'm sorry I don't know anything about the one in Locarno." Irene laughed, admitting that their festival was not as famous or as star-studded as the others I had mentioned, but that Locarno had found its own prestigious niche. "We are known for being avant-garde and showing innovative films," Teresa added. (*What a perfect venue for an Orson Welles retrospective,* I thought.) Unlike the other festivals, theirs was dedicated to showing films from third-world or developing countries. One of the main events was a juried competition of films from around the world. Finally, there would be the tribute to my father, which was to be called "The Magnificent Welles."

Toward the end of our lunch, I asked if Irwin might accompany me to Locarno. The two women exchanged a look and a smile. "We don't usually pay for spouses and companions," Irene finally said, "but in this case, I think we can make an exception and find the money for Irwin." It was agreed that Irwin and I would come for the entire festival.

In the months leading up to our departure, I could think of little else. The prospect of being interviewed on television and speaking in public inspired me to slim down and shop for "movie star" clothes, but it did not make me nervous. I confided to my good friend Patricia Cusick, "Put me in the spotlight and the Wellesian genes take over. Fortunately, this is happening at the right time in my life, when I can take satisfaction in representing my father, which I couldn't have done when I was younger. It should be a wonderful experience from start to finish."

FROM THE MOMENT our small plane from Zurich set down in the tiny airport of Lugano, Irwin and I stepped into a dream. In Zurich, it had been cold and dismal—we had dashed to the plane through pelting rain— but here it was sunny, dry, perfect. We were met by a festival car that took us the forty miles to Locarno and gave us our first spectacular views of the Alps topped with snow and tidy Swiss towns hugging the slopes. We had come to the land of majestic lakes and mountains known as the Ticino, the Swiss canton that borders Italy and retains a distinctly Italian character. In fact, Italian was the primary language spoken here, followed by French and German. So here I was back in Switzerland where, as a student in Lausanne fifty years ago, I had first learned French, little realizing how useful it would prove.

We were put up at the best hotel Locarno had to offer, the Reber au Lac, the kind of gracious hotel that my father would have loved. Located on the lakefront with its own dock for swimming or sunbathing, the hotel was far enough out of town to be peaceful, yet not so far from the festival grounds that we couldn't walk to the Piazza Grande in a leisurely twenty-minute stroll. However, when our driver deposited us at the hotel, he gave us the telephone number to call whenever we needed a car and—pronto!—one would be dispatched to pick us up wherever we happened to be.

It was clear I was getting the celebrity treatment. Our hotel room was spacious, elegantly furnished, with French doors opening onto a balcony that overlooked Lake Maggiore. A table held a welcoming bouquet of flowers, a basket of fruit, our festival programs, and passes that would allow us free admission to whatever we wanted to see. Rifling through the program, Irwin announced that we could be up day and night, rushing from "The Magnificent Welles" offerings in the Cinema Rex to the films screened until dawn in the Piazza Grande.

But first things first: the view from our balcony. Before even hanging up our coats, we threw open the doors and sank into the lounge chairs. It was tempting to sit here all day, letting our eyes sweep across the shining water to the opposite shore where the Alps climbed the sky.

Directly below our balcony was the hotel's terrace restaurant where breakfast was served every morning in full view of the lake. This became an occasion to strike up conversations with our fellow guests. We soon learned that the jury for the video competition was staying at our hotel and that one of its members was the attractive Canadian actress Alexandra Stewart, who had been married to French director Louis Malle. It turned out she had known my father in Spain. When people who had known or worked with my father were introduced to me, it was clear that it meant a great deal to them. I had anticipated that they would be pleased to meet me, but it hadn't occurred to me that they would be thrilled.

It was not until months after the festival that I realized the degree to which I had been standing in for my father. As Pat Cusick put it, "A festival about a deceased director can be a little barren without the presence of someone to represent the figure being celebrated. You filled the bill for them and made the event come alive. People could reach out to you and feel they were connecting to Orson Welles himself."

This was certainly true of the people who came up to me in the Cinema Rex and elsewhere, asking for my autograph. At the time, though, I found this bewildering. "But I'm not famous," I would protest. "My autograph isn't worth anything." The autograph hunters just smiled at my foolishness, thrust their pens and festival programs under my nose, and pleaded, "Please sign here, Miss Welles." And while I was signing away, photographers appeared out of nowhere, flashbulbs popping.

So this was what my father's life was like, I told myself. *Always in the public eye, having to smile for the camera, be nice to strangers, field impertinent questions, and hand out one's signature as though it were candy.* I could see that being the center of attention was a turn-on for a while, but wouldn't it get tiresome in the end?

Before one of the screenings in the darkened theater, while I was resting my head on Irwin's shoulder, an unknown photographer rushed up to record our private moment. I remembered that my father had never seemed to mind the continual invasion of his privacy. But I did. While it was a lark to be here for eleven days, nothing was more wonderful than the life awaiting me back in Greenwich Village. There my public appearances would be confined to the supermarket, post office, gym, or dry cleaner's, and it would no longer matter what I was wearing or if I was having "a bad hair day." No one would dream of coming up to me in the checkout line to ask for my autograph.

"You know," I told Irwin at dinner one evening, "I could have easily become an actress and gone the celebrity route, and now that I'm getting a taste of what it's really like, I'm so glad I didn't! And yet it feels so natural to be in the limelight, it's almost scary. I guess I must get that from my father."

"But you're not your father. You're you." Irwin took my hand across the table and held it fast. He told me how proud he was of the way I was handling myself at the festival, and then he teased that if I kept on "busting his buttons," I was going to have an awful lot of sewing to do when we got home.

We laughed at this as we wandered down to Locarno's lakefront and sat on a bench bathed in moonlight. It was a balmy night. Ferryboats glided by and the sound of dance music drifted across the water. On the opposite shore, the lights of faraway villages blinked like fallen stars.

No MATTER HOW many times I have seen my father's films, I welcome the opportunity to see them again, especially my four favorites of the six he made in Europe: *Chimes at Midnight, F for Fake, The Trial,* and *Othello.* My father would have been gratified to see the enormous crowd that turned out for *Chimes.* "If I wanted to get into heaven on the basis of one movie, that's the one I would offer up," he once said to me of this picture, in which he plays lovable Jack Falstaff, then breaks our hearts when Falstaff is spurned—"I know thee not, old man"—by the young king he had served so well. Perhaps his most poignant moment on the screen, it never fails to bring tears to my eyes, for it reminds me of the personal betrayals Orson Welles had to endure in his final years.

The retrospective offered an overwhelming bounty of features, shorts, documentaries, and assembled footage from the Welles archives at the Munich Film Museum. To take it all in, I would have had to arrive at the Cinema Rex at nine a.m. and camp out there until one a.m. Happily, I could be selective, having seen many of the offerings the year before at the Film Forum in New York. Even so, there was too much to absorb, and here and there I had to give up a workshop or screening at the Rex, no matter how interesting, for a siesta or revitalizing swim.

In planning the most comprehensive Orson Welles retrospective held to date, in a year that marked the ninetieth anniversary of his birth and the twentieth anniversary of his death, it was Stefan's intention to show the full scope of my father's achievement. He felt that Citizen Kane and The Third Man hovered "like shadows" over Welles's career, while the rest of his work was often neglected. So, as Stefan wrote in the festival program, the Magnificent Welles retrospective would reveal that, in addition to his twelve completed films, Welles had already shot material for at least that many more, as well as television productions, commercials, appearances in films by other directors, his work narrating, commentating, dubbing, and other creations. Orson Welles "was incredibly prolific," the program said, "and it will be a long time before any complete listing of his work is possible." Yet to spend even a few days viewing the offerings in the Cinema Rex was to understand why director Martin Scorsese once said, "Welles has inspired more people to become filmmakers than anybody else in the history of cinema."

Throughout the retrospective, it was Stefan's idea to run a workshop every morning. "If the retrospective had comprised nothing but workshops, Wellesians would have gotten their money's worth," wrote Leslie Weisman, reporting for the Washington, D.C. Film Society newsletter. "In addition to hearing, observing, and taking part in live discussions with renowned scholars and legendary performers . . . participants found their experience incalculably enriched by films, videotapes, home movies, slides, and radio programs illustrating the often first-person testimony. An added bonus was the presence and invaluable contributions of Welles's eldest daughter, Chris, both onstage and occasionally from the audience."

The first workshop was led by Jeff Wilson, webmaster of Wellesnet: The Orson Welles Web Resource (wellesnet.com). He gave a fine presentation on my father's years in radio, playing excerpts from a wide sampling of his radio shows — over a thousand in all, Jeff told us. By the time my father went to Hollywood to try his hand at making movies, he had become one of the best-known stars in radio. In fact, it was the national furor he had caused with *The War of the Worlds* that had interested Hollywood moguls in hiring him.

What I found of particular interest in reviewing my father's radio career was that it reflected his political growth at a crucial stage in his life. By the time he launched his radio show *Orson Welles' Almanac* in 1944, he had become strongly opposed to fascism and racism. Although he never joined the Communist Party, the FBI had a file on him and was following his every move. It was typical of my father's appreciation of African-American life and culture that he used the *Almanac* to promote jazz. At the time, he was among the few who considered it an art form and major contribution to world culture.

In the summer of 1946 he made fervent political broadcasts on a new weekly series, *Orson Welles Commentary*. His purpose was to make the American public aware of the injustice done to a black war veteran, Isaac Woodard, who, shortly after his honorable discharge, was brutally beaten and blinded by a policeman in South Carolina. Woodard's "crime" was wanting to use the restroom at a bus stop. My father's eloquent appeals on his behalf helped identify his attacker, Sheriff Lynwood Shull, and bring him to trial. (The sheriff was eventually acquitted.) Because my father refused to stop championing Woodard's cause on his show, the sponsor withdrew, and the American Broadcasting Company took the show off the air. I had not known this before coming to Locarno. That my father had put his principles above his career made me feel especially proud of him.

Also of great meaning to me was a filmed interview with Norman Corwin, the well-known writer, producer, and director. On the day my father was scaring the nation with *The War of the Worlds* broadcast at CBS, Corwin was working on the floor above. He knew my father well and had no scores to settle with him. Speaking in the measured tones of a man in his ninth decade, he recalled my father in the full vigor of his youth, much as I myself remember him, and declared without hesitation that Orson Welles was one of the major talents of his time . . . or any time.

At the end of each workshop, I would join Stefan and whoever had been on the panel that day. We would troop up the hill into town and gather for lunch at the Manora, a buffet-style restaurant. Here most of us settled in for the rest of the afternoon, continuing the lively discussions that had begun in the workshops. As Roger Ryan, an admirer of my father, would write to me later, "The highlight of each day was the chance to share lunch with those who share a love of your father's work." (Roger had brought to Locarno his fascinating reconstruction of my father's film *The Magnificent Ambersons*.)

It was a great pleasure for me to meet Welles aficionados who had devoted years of their lives to my father's work, such as the distinguished French film scholar François Thomas and his colleague Jean-Pierre Berthomé. As co-authors, they have published extensively on the oeuvre of Orson Welles. I took an instant liking to the shy, modest François, who joined our daily lunches at the Manora, where he hardly said a word. However, on the day we saw a short film that captured Orson Welles's appearance at the Cinémathèque Française in Paris, François told me he had been a film student in the audience. It had been the same day—February 24, 1982—that my father received France's highest award, the Légion d'Honneur, and then proceeded in the best of humor to address the students at the Cinémathèque. Seated on stage, at his most relaxed and charming, he answered the students' questions, gave sound advice, and shared his experiences as a filmmaker. It was one of those moments in life when time collapses like an accordion: We had just seen my father on film in 1982, and now François, who had been in that audience, was reliving the experience with me twenty-three years later in Locarno.

Some of the people I met at the retrospective had known my father personally. One was the writer and film scholar Joseph McBride, who confided one night over dinner that he had not been well received by the movie director he had so admired from afar. It seems that my father had been as cool and dismissive with Joe as he had been with Irwin. We speculated that perhaps Orson Welles felt uneasy or defensive with men who were extremely bright, well-educated, and opinionated about his work. Yet Joe was able to put aside lingering hurt and come to my father's defense, when needed. In the workshop on *It's All True,* Joe presented solid evidence that, contrary to the reports of Welles's unbridled extravagance—a myth that haunted him to the end of his career—he was actually under budget when RKO killed the project.

Another associate of my father was the lively and perceptive French producer Dominique Antoine, who had been welcomed into his inner circle.

"Orson always treated me as his intellectual equal and his friend," she told me. "He loved to discuss politics with me, especially American politics."

Dominique began working with my father in 1971, becoming the producer for *F for Fake* and the incomplete feature *The Other Side of the Wind*. "But when you worked for Orson," she told me, "you did a little bit of everything." Laughing, she remembered her "bit" during the shooting of the erotic car scene in *Wind*. To create the effect of passing headlights reflected on the car, Dominique was enlisted to shake pieces of tinfoil in front of the floodlights while my father urged her, "Dominique! Your wrists. Be more supple, please."

Dominique had come to Locarno for the express purpose of attending the workshop on *The Other Side of the Wind,* hoping she would hear that some progress was being made toward its final completion and release. This particular workshop drew the largest crowd of all—it snaked down the steep, uphill street all the way to the Piazza Grande. With the excited buzz of the crowd and flashbulbs going off like firecrackers, it felt like a Hollywood premiere. I had previously seen at the Film Forum the footage that was shown again in Locarno, and it was hard to tell from these episodic fragments what my father would have done with the film in his final edit. Only here and there did I feel the unmistakable rhythm, tension, and pacing of an Orson Welles masterpiece.

At the conclusion of the workshop discussion, the ultimate fate of *The Other Side of the Wind* remained as uncertain as ever. A substantial amount of finishing money still had to be raised and, equally if not more important, a distributor for the film needed to be found. "It will never be finished," declared Dominique, adding that it was "obscene" that Orson's last chef d'oeuvre could not be shown to the world. We trudged out of the theater, feeling dispirited, and I could see that revisiting *The Other Side of the Wind* had taken an emotional toll on Dominique. When we said our goodbyes a few days later, she told me the only positive thing that had happened to her in Locarno was meeting me.

The final workshop was devoted to Orson Welles the magician. Stefan asked me to be on the panel because at the age of five I had seen my father's magic show for the troops. Although I knew the art of magic had fascinated him all his life, and I had vivid memories of his entertaining me as a child with magic tricks, I had always assumed he was an amateur. I had no idea that he was, in fact, a serious professional, or that he was esteemed by world-class magicians who saw him as a major figure in their secret society.

Attending the Orson Welles retrospective in Locarno, Switzerland, 2005 (from left to right: Abb Dickson, Stefan Drössler, Oja Kodar, Oja's sister Nina, Gary Graver, Alexander Welles).

"If your father had done nothing else with his life, he would go down in the history books as one of the most important magicians of all time," according to Abb Dickson, a jolly, rotund little man with a mischievous smile, who has been aptly described as "a three-hundred-pound pixie." As one of the top magicians performing today, Abb was in a position to know what he was talking about. "Your father invented his own tricks," he added.

"He did? How many?" I expected to hear a total of five or six.

"Hundreds. They're written up in a secret bible of magic that's circulated among professional magicians." Of all the things I was learning about my father, this was the most astonishing.

Abb was another Locarno participant who had established his own unique relationship with Orson Welles. A frequent visitor to the house in Los Angeles where Orson lived his last years with Oja, Abb had spent hours closeted with Orson, trying out the latest magic tricks, which Orson would then radically change to make his own. Abb believed that the hours they spent together, practicing magic like mischievous schoolboys, released Orson from the frustration and disappointment that clouded his return to Hollywood.

Sometimes Orson invited Abb to accompany him to a meeting with studio executives. On these occasions Abb donned a suit and pretended to be Orson's lawyer. At a certain point in the meeting Orson would announce that he had to consult in private with his lawyer. The "suits" would withdraw from the

Chris in Locarno, Switzerland, for the Orson Welles retrospective, 2005.

room and Orson and Abb would spend the next half hour or so practicing magic, until Orson's good humor was restored.

It seems fitting that on the day of my father's death, he was found slumped over his typewriter, where he had been at work on a script for his next essay film, to be called *The Magic Show.* "To me, magic begins and ends with the figure of the magician who asks the audience, for a moment, to believe that the lady is floating in the air," he once said. "In other words, be eight years old for a moment."

IT WAS MY *big* night in the Piazza Grande, yet I had no idea of what was about to happen. While I waited to be called to the stage, Irwin stood next to me, holding my hand.

"Are you nervous?" he asked.

I shook my head. "It's funny, but I've never felt so sure of myself."

"Do you know there are seven and a half thousand people out there? Irene told me every seat's been taken. And you don't feel even a little nervous?"

"No. I can't wait to walk out on the stage . . ."

"You're your father's daughter all right." Irwin stared at me in amazement. Then, after telling me "to break a leg," he went to join the festival directors, who were sitting in the front row.

When a few moments later I came on stage and was introduced as Orson Welles's daughter, I was greeted by thunderous applause. I was standing under the mammoth movie screen, facing the huge crowd but unable to see beyond the first rows. Darkness swallowed up the rest of the audience. Yet I could feel the faint hum of its presence, its suppressed energy, like a crouched animal waiting to roar. How calm I felt, how at home on that stage in Locarno under a clear, starlit sky. A pretty young woman stood beside me, waiting to translate my remarks into Italian. Directly below the stage, a video crew was projecting our image in one corner of the screen so that even those in the back row could see us in close-up.

I was there to say a few words about Orson Welles's *Macbeth,* which would be shown later in the evening. After thanking the festival directors in Italian for their generous hospitality, I continued in English. "I am so happy to be here with you tonight, celebrating my father and his great achievement in the world of cinema. Once I told my father how distressed I was that he couldn't raise the money he needed to complete his films. My father replied, 'Christopher, don't you worry your pretty little head about me. They're going to love me when I'm dead.' And in Locarno, we do!" When this was translated, the crowd went berserk.

It was quite a while before I was able to continue. "The other night I was invited to a banquet and the president of our festival, Marco Solari, got up to speak. He said, 'Orson Welles was one of the greatest creative forces of the twentieth century.' And I agree!" The crowd replied with a prolonged standing ovation.

This is my father's legacy, I thought, *to me and to the world. And through his work, I am connected to him forever.*

From then on it didn't matter what I said. The crowed roared and stamped and clapped and cheered. I could feel waves of love rolling toward me, and it felt as though my whole life had been an arduous journey to this moment—but now I was here. I had arrived. Of course, I knew that the ovation was for my father, but it was partly for me as well. And somewhere in the darkness my father was looking down on me with a tender smile, saying, "You're my darling girl."

THE END

ACKNOWLEDGMENTS

MY HUSBAND IRWIN likes to say I was "born under a lucky star." I think he might be right when I consider the exceptional people who assisted in the birth of my book, beginning with my agent, Joan Raines. Joan stood by me during the early struggles and false starts, never losing her faith that in the end I would get it right. Yet much as I relied on her warm support during the six years it took to produce a final manuscript, I came to appreciate even more her counsel, sharp editorial eye, and skill with a red pencil.

My next stroke of good fortune was to have Chuck Adams as my editor at Algonquin Books of Chapel Hill. No author could ask for a more intelligent, perceptive, and sensitive editor. I was similarly blessed to have my manuscript copyedited by the late Bob Jones, who completed his excellent work on my book shortly before his untimely death.

My thanks go to Peter Workman of Workman Publishing, who read my book in manuscript and approved its publication by Algonquin Books. I also thank my publisher, Elisabeth Scharlatt, for responding so positively to my book. I am grateful to everyone at Algonquin who has helped transform my manuscript into a book of quality.

My good friend Gregory Downer did a fine job of restoring the vintage photographs in my private collection so that they sparkle on these pages. I am indebted to Welles scholar Catherine Benamou, who introduced me to the treasure trove of photographs in the Orson Welles Collections, which she helped establish at the University of Michigan at Ann Arbor. Both Catherine and Peggy Daub, director of the Special Collections Library, were most helpful throughout my stay in Ann Arbor. I wish to thank Sally Vermaaten, who assisted me at the library, and Sarah Rentz, who scanned over fifty photos so that I could take them home on compact disks.

In addition to contributing photos and artwork from her own collection, Oja Kodar vetted the last chapters of my manuscript. During his final decades, no one knew more about my father and his entourage than Oja, his beloved companion, and I deeply appreciate her corrections and constructive comments.

My close friends Meredith Rose, Denis Forster, and George Dickerson read the manuscript in its early stages and offered important feedback. The one person I have yet to mention is my husband, Irwin, my most valuable reader and critic. His steadfast love and support make clear that I *was* born under a lucky star.